Old Land New Waters

Freelands Foundation

Freelands Artist Programme

Contents

Foreword
Elisabeth Murdoch

The launch of the Freelands Artist Programme remains the most ambitious undertaking by the Foundation to date.

We committed to supporting 80 emerging artists, working with four arts organisations across all four British nations, all selected via open call, for an innovative £1.5m five-year programme.

I am delighted therefore – and proud – to be able to present this beautiful publication as the first tangible record of that endeavour, as we conclude two years of work with our first cohort of artists.

One of my driving motivations for setting up Freelands Foundation five years ago was a desire to address the discrepancy in both funding and opportunity in the visual arts between London and the rest of the UK. It seemed clear that promoting vibrant arts communities throughout the country was an essential precursor to breaking down barriers to the creation and enjoyment of art for all.

The many strong partnerships we have developed with arts organisations across the UK since 2015 have gone some way to tackling this challenge. However, in areas we believe demand particular support, we have also initiated practical action to create impact through our own flagship programmes. The first of these, the Freelands Award, was targeted at promoting mid-career female artists in collaboration with arts organisations outside of London. The Freelands Artist Programme was conceived in the same vein but to support emerging artists, outside of London, at scale.

Our objectives were clear: to support early-career artists in their creative and professional development and in doing so, to support progressive arts organisations across the country in their work with those artists, both strengthening their engagement with local communities and building new relationships across the sector.

The decision to launch an open call was a bold statement of intent and it led us to four very different organisations: Talbot Rice Gallery, part of the University of Edinburgh; PS², an artist-led organisation and studio provider based in Belfast; Site Gallery, a Sheffield contemporary art space specialising in new media and performance; and g39, an artist-run space in Cardiff. Very different and yet united by the vital work they were all doing in support of early-career artists in their localities.

Our aim was to provide each one with the financial firepower and curatorial support to expand these activities within their own area, while also making introductions and facilitating collaboration between the organisations – and their artists.

Right from the start, we were clear that each institution should set their own bespoke approach within the programme. This independence of perspective is immediately apparent in the work presented in this publication. The breadth of media and range is a testament to the strength of emerging artistic practice across the UK.

I had the great pleasure of meeting many of our first cohort at our June 2019 Symposium in Sheffield. I was impressed by everyone's energy and commitment and delighted to see the new connections brought to life between the artists and the organisations.

Indeed, the real success of this programme will be when we have fostered a true sense of community and collaboration across the four institutions and their artists, building a network of support which sustains well beyond the end of the programme.

The fact that the artists have succeeded in producing such incredible work is all the more remarkable given the backdrop of the COVID-19 pandemic and the profound challenges it has presented for all the artists and organisations in the programme. This resulted in our decision to extend the programme by three months with additional funding. But it also underlined the importance of community to successful artistic practice.

I'd like to congratulate all the artists in this first cohort, and the teams at the four organisations for their creativity and commitment throughout the programme. Our ambition is rewarded by the results of your work, just a sample of which is set out over the following pages. I feel incredibly excited for your futures.

Elisabeth Murdoch is Founder and Chair, Freelands Foundation

Introduction
Edward Ball

It felt like a deep breath. The chance to slow down a little, at least at the beginning. Two years stretched ahead somewhat shapelessly, alive with a sense of possibility. All that space and all that time.

Let us rewind to autumn 2018, as the first cohort of artists on the Freelands Artist Programme are about to begin a two-year schedule of activity. There is no prescribed outcome, no targets to be met. What there is, however, is potential. There is the chance to think longer-term, not necessarily more slowly, but certainly differently. Two years in which to form a close peer group, to strengthen the bonds of a local artistic community. Perhaps most temptingly of all, the programme offers a new temporal relation to practice, and a more sustained engagement between art institution and artist. Four organisations across the UK – g39, Cardiff; PS², Belfast; Talbot Rice Gallery, Edinburgh; and Site Gallery, Sheffield – each begin a close collaboration with a group of five artists. The programme fosters possibilities for artist and institution alike: to step aside from previous patterns of working and perhaps changing course; to develop a new, longer-term body of research; or to create an alternative way of being to the more frequently pressured cycle of artistic production.

But let's take another breath first – I don't want to let this sensation slip away, not yet. Although two years have passed, *Old Land New Waters* is a deceleration, a moment of repose. This volume borrows its title from a work by the Vietnamese filmmaker and postcolonial theorist Trinh T. Minh-ha,[1] and draws a deep influence from her wider, remarkable body of work. The work's title, which separates land from water, old from new, also connects them in soft juxtaposition. So, too, it unfolds an image of the horizon – where land or where water meet the sky – in the mind's eye. Minh-ha's films foreground a sensual, slippery experience of time, and in so doing, reveal the impossibility of ever truly seeing. Could we think of artistic practice in this way? As a sensory and poetic terrain not to be traversed, mapped or known, but rather glimpsed at, and experienced from a sited perspective at a specific moment in time? I think of Minh-ha's 2001 film *The Fourth Dimension*, which centres on the artist's perception of time via a visual journey of Japan. In one shot, the artist's camera lingers on a waterfall in free flow, before later returning to the same image, now seen in slow motion.

Minh-ha's filmic time is elastic and expansive, and this temporal quality has been sensitively and materially captured on the page by the book's designers, Claire Lyon and Wayne Daly of Daly & Lyon.

What follows ahead is a journey through two years of artistic practice, without claiming an all-encompassing vision. As the American artist, writer and activist Julie Ault has written, 'Chronicles record rather than historicize',[2] and the rather humble editorial gesture of marking the date of each artist essay was an instinctive way to site each contribution in its own present moment, while also disrupting any kind of linear telling across the book in its entirety. Instead, what we encounter is a series of states of enquiry – an idea unfolding, a recontextualisation of something considered long before, a proposition for the future. This new critical writing on each artist asks what is at stake at this moment, and often we are encountering artworks that are still in progress or at points of departure. I am hugely thankful to each artist for their trust and generosity in presenting images, works and ideas that are ongoing. The artist sections offer an engagingly diverse range of expression: whether artist writing by Janie Doherty; dynamic interplay of text and image in the work of Fern Thomas and Stephanie Mann; collaborative writing by Siân Williams and Kelly Best; images of work in progress by Zoyander Street; or the source materials which inform the work of Aideen Doran. Each is a privileged insight into practice. This sense of motion continues through new commissions by Andrew McMillan, Jan Carson, Natalie Ann Holborow and Adrien Hester – each chosen for their connections to the landscapes and surrounding ecosystems of our four partner organisations. Each writer unfolds a psychic terrain of place, conjuring a vivid geography on the page.

Almost the entirety of *Old Land New Waters* has been realised against the backdrop of the COVID-19 pandemic, and such a context cannot be ignored. I have been amazed at the resilience of the artists in this cohort, willingly adapting practice – granted, often out of necessity – to an abruptly altered reality. How strange the first annual Freelands Artist Programme Symposium in summer 2019 now seems – all of us, some 50 people thrown together for three days, meeting for the first time, hosted by Site Gallery in Sheffield. This year, we will meet virtually. Thank you to Helena Reckitt, Grace Ndiritu, George Clark, Luís Silva and João Mourão who each contributed to this first Symposium and to this publication. Despite all of our encounters being mediated through a screen throughout this book's realisation, the often remarkably open and wide-ranging conversations that followed have shaped the course of this book. I am hugely grateful to the editor and writer Eileen Daly for her incisive copy editing, which deftly retains a plurality of voice yet intimacy of tone throughout.

> The time now is small, mobile, portable I, light blue.[3]

One last breath. How rare, how special, to follow the unfolding of 20 practices across two years, and doubtless onwards still. Although this first cohort of artists are concluding their time on the programme, new cohorts of artists are soon to join, and the Freelands Artist Programme continues on, growing a wider community of artists and organisations. I hope that this volume lets some light in on the remarkable process and context of this time. As is so often the case, the writer Janet Malcolm says it best: 'The goal is to make a space where a few ideas and images and feelings may be so arranged that a reader will want to linger awhile among them.'[4] This programme has been its own opportunity to do just that. And while this book cannot but mark the passage of time, it also articulates a number of departures – as 'endings pass into beginnings'.[5]

Edward Ball is Artist Programme Curator, Freelands Foundation

1 Recently Trinh T. Minh-ha's work has been the subject of a year-long season of public events and conversation, 'Trinh T. Minh-ha is on our mind', 24 September 2019 – 4 September 2020, at The Wattis Institute for Contemporary Arts in San Francisco, California, and she is profiled by Patrick J Reed in *Art Review* Asia's autumn 2020 edition.
2 Julie Ault, *In Part: Writings by Julie Ault*, Julie Ault and Nicolas Linnert (eds.), Dancing Foxes Press and Galerie Buchholz, 2017, p.211.
3 Trinh T. Minh-ha, *Elsewhere, Within Here: Immigration, Refugeeism and the Boundary Event*, Routledge, 2010, p.1.
4 Janet Malcolm, *The Silent Woman: Sylvia Plath and Ted Hughes*, Vintage, 1995, p.205.
5 Trinh T. Minh-ha, *op.cit.*

g39

Cardiff, Wales

Kelly Best

Jennifer Taylor

Neasa Terry

Fern Thomas

Ian Watson

g39: An Introduction

g39 began as a temporary artist project in July 1998 from a gallery base in a small townhouse on the fringes of Cardiff city centre. Our project connected the region's numerous networks, alliances and groupings of artists in one exhibition programme which gradually built a committed audience and developed the critical discourse surrounding contemporary visual art in Wales.

Now based in a large open-plan warehouse, g39 is one of a number of artist-facilitated spaces in the UK that pioneers innovative and alternative structures to those of larger institutions. A major strand of our activity centres on developing alternative models for artist training and professional development. g39's Warp scheme (Wales Artist Resource Programme) is an open-access resource space and training programme for artists – particularly focused on early- and mid-career artists – who live and work in Wales.

g39 has worked with a vast number and range of artists since 1998. The professional support of the organisation has contributed to the career development of many contemporary visual artists who now have significant reputations both nationally and internationally, including James Richards, Heather Phillipson, Megan Broadmeadow, Sean Edwards and Bedwyr Williams.

The g39 Fellowship scheme, as part of the Freelands Artist Programme, fosters, develops and facilitates a peer group of artists over a five-year period. Each year g39 invites five selected artists to take part in a two-year structured programme of studio practice and self-directed research. The artists receive a six-month intensive period of support, followed by six months to reflect and act on the support they have received. The Fellowship offers workshops, training, mentoring and contact time with visiting artists, curators and g39 staff, as well as a programme of guest speakers and lectures, group peer-critique sessions, away days, research visits, remote networking and social activities.

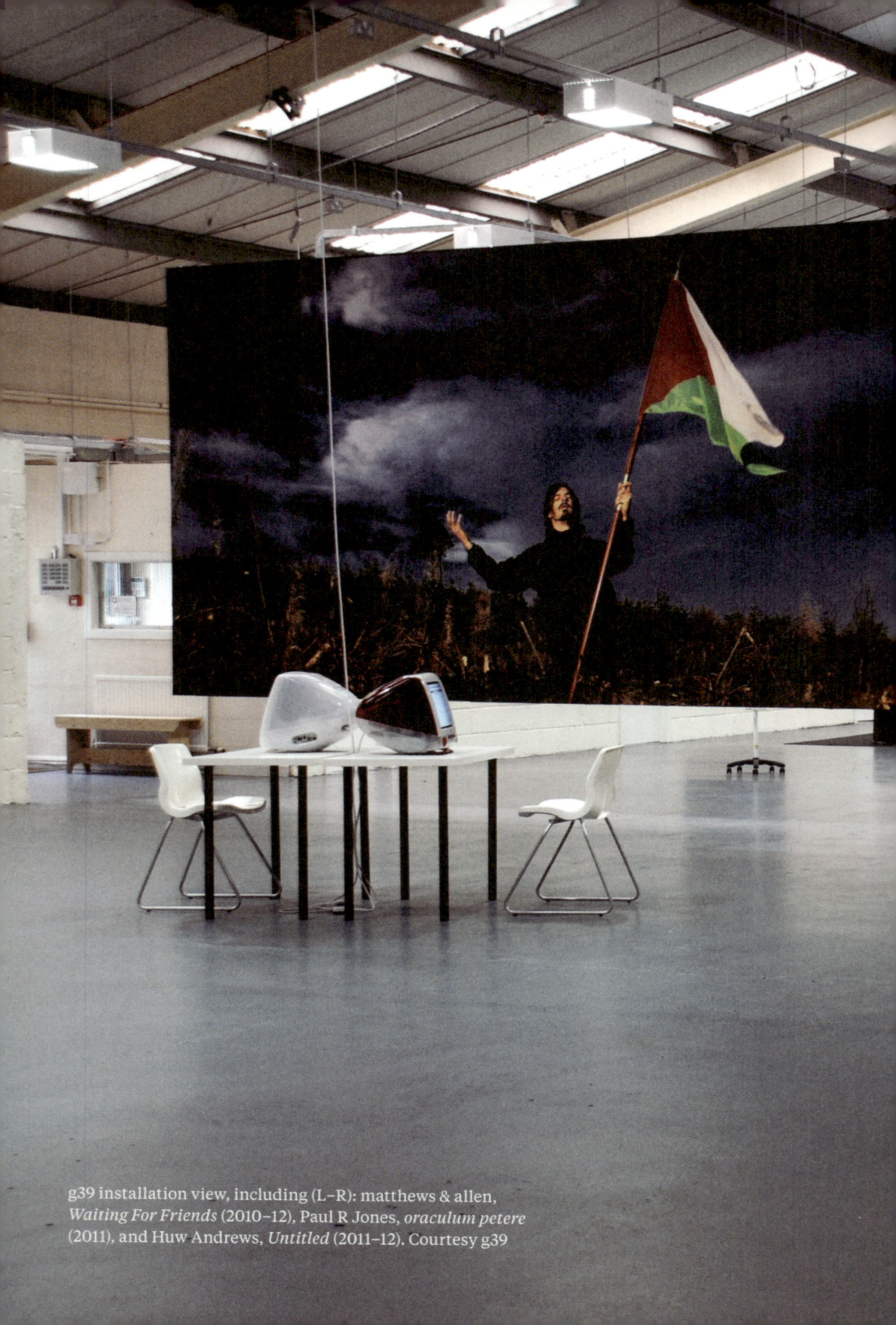

g39 installation view, including (L–R): matthews & allen, *Waiting For Friends* (2010–12), Paul R Jones, *oraculum petere* (2011), and Huw Andrews, *Untitled* (2011–12). Courtesy g39

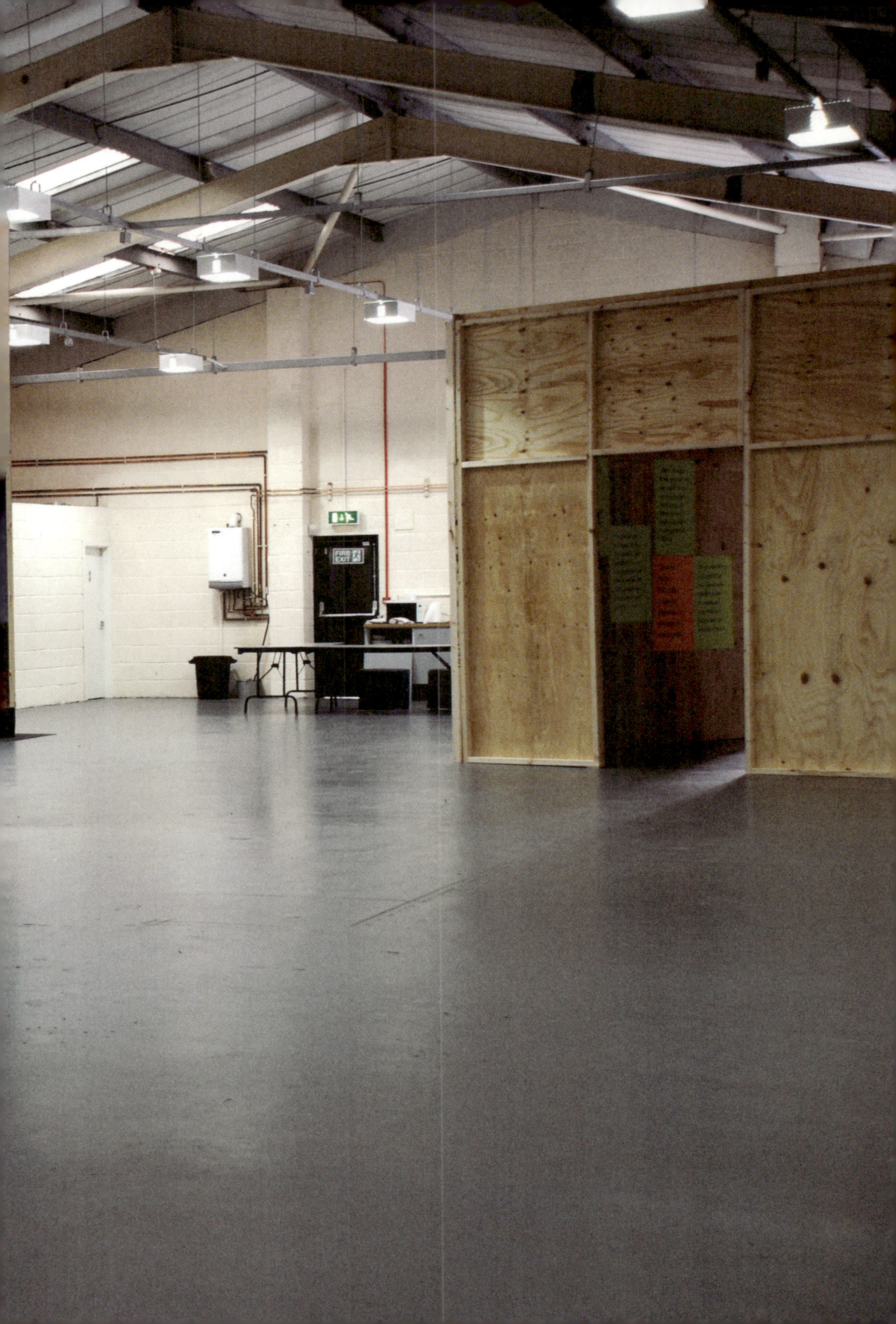
FIRE
EXIT

Anthony Shapland, Creative Director

Our approach was casual. Meticulously thought through, but casual. We thought we knew how things worked, because for some years much of our programme has been spent advocating for artists through peer support and mentoring.

That support was in shorter chunks. Problems that people brought with them could be unpacked and reassembled. All solutions were possibilities and the focus was on trial and failure, and learning and finishing, with a lot of open paths to follow.

The Fellowship grew differently. There was more time, but people felt more pressure. If too many things are unpacked it can be hard to pack them away when there is no deadline: there can be too many possibilities, too many questions: what is the difference between a studio practice and career success? How do I know if something is good? How do I deal with uncertainty? How do I exist in a complex family of peers and also allow room for my own complex family? How do I get seen but not looked at? How do I network without feeling like an idiot? Why have they got that and I've got this? Can I do this? What about this?

The open structure now seemed intimidating. Like a cartoon character attempting to stay ahead by hurriedly laying down track for the train as it hurtles along.

We had to ask ourselves questions. How do we level things out so that true peer learning happens? How do we modulate a range of voices to ensure everyone is heard? How do we dismantle deeply embedded ideas of what success is and is not when artists have been told that any gap, pause, change of direction, is dropping out or failing? We share the space with each other, and the hierarchies that exist during, before and after need to be acknowledged and questioned if they are to be negotiated.

By this point it was less casual and more complex. We know this is a group, but the group is made up of individuals. There are relationships, commitments, different needs. On some days it felt like I was amongst siblings – middle child – reading situations, trying to make sure everyone was okay. I understood that there needed to be more of a framework, more stability, more structure, because once that was put in place there would, paradoxically, be more freedom to stray, to evolve. To grow.

The artists have shown me that there is no fixed direction of travel with a programme like this. If it is going to be peer-led, then it can, and does, react to individual concerns and to external influences. The studio (private) and the gallery (public) balance vulnerability and confidence. The rawness of making combined with showing. Sometimes just showing, sometimes 'Showing Off'. It is a complex place – between the two – and we all operate at points along the line.

So, we started off casual, thinking it was the best approach to peer learning, and we've come back there. Casual structures. Professional but informal.

Kelly Best

Dear Georgie. Are you happy

Hopscotch

This was never going to be a standard artist text, but Kelly likes things this way. I'm going to try and be specific without any specifics. A hop, a skip and a jump. Here goes:

Kelly's practice is like catching water between your fingers.

Kelly's practice is about control.

Kelly's practice is an open work.

Kelly's practice makes you part of the game.

Kelly's practice likes informality.

Kelly's practice is quite quick. (Do I mean this?)

Kelly's practice wants you to enjoy the process.

Kelly's practice is a sideways step.

Kelly's practice edits itself in real time.

Kelly's practice isn't as abstract as this all sounds.

You could probably stop reading here. Or jump to another paragraph and circle back if you like. This is just one direction of travel. Kelly has told me that she hates arriving, always wanting the journey to go on a little longer. Writing about Kelly's work is about contours rather than a methodical meticulous mechanical trudge through individual works. It's fine to jump about a bit, I think.

Julio Cortázar's 1963 counter-novel[1] *Rayuela* (Hopscotch) jumps about too. You can either read it from the beginning, ending on chapter 56, or you can hopscotch your way through, according to his precisely defined instructions in the table of contents, beginning with chapter 73. The second half of the book becomes expendable if you choose the straightforward option. But if you take the non-linear path, darting from chapter to chapter, those superfluous moments you might otherwise have missed fill in some gaps from before. Kelly's work doesn't suit a linear telling either. Thinking and making are elastic experiences, so why not s t r e t c h our reading a little too?

Kelly likes the less trodden path

the edges

the

s
i
d
e
s

the
underneath.

Presenting things as they are isn't to aestheticise the point, she's just more interested in the game. Kelly likes the feeling of 'now', and enjoys the diversions and digressions:

> 'Life's too short to be constantly tidying up everything and I enjoy the simplicity and demystification in presenting something as is. There's a reality and pureness in that and I think that's part of the interest in improvisation too.'[2]

Kelly understands that the context keeps changing, both for us and for her. If a work's reception is always anchored to a specific time and place, how do you keep alive the possibility for continued renegotiations of its meanings? I think Kelly is hopeful about this, that her work isn't a full stop. An ellipsis, perhaps... Kelly just wants to explore the full potential of her work, to keep learning. I don't know if there's really a wrong answer with Kelly. The odd misstep, of course.

for me to put all our work online?[1]

1 YES!

If you've skipped ahead, by the way, that's fine. I think Kelly would like it if you had – taking some agency as a reader, making two and two into your own kind of four.

Kelly's work is a direct address.

An iceberg's critical mass is 90% beneath the horizon line. I think Kelly's practice wants you to see that part – all the ideas and the things and the processes below the surface. It's about switching up our vantage point. Maybe we need an underwater perspective?

But the work is grounded, not floating listlessly in the current. It's political, if we think about representation. Writer and philosopher Susan Sontag cautioned against fixed interpretations, but maybe it needs repeating: 'To understand is to interpret [...] It is to turn the world into this world.'[3] Kelly's world can't be distilled. It won't stay still.

Be agile.

I've managed to get all the way to the end and not mention a single work. It's not really the end though. I've asked Kelly about failure, but that seems less important now. If there is such a thing as failure, for her it's getting too comfortable. The practice is change.

Kelly collaborates. She's good at encouraging different ways of working and seeing. This text is a bit of a collaboration, all told. Kelly's practice is about meeting each other halfway, in the moment, and going somewhere together. The second this lands on the page it will be out of date too. Hello to the next person.

23 June 2020

1 Julio Cortázar's own term used to describe the novel's style. *Rayuela* was published in Spanish in 1963 by Editorial Sudamericana and first published in English in 1966.
2 Email correspondence with the artist, Thursday 21 May 2020.
3 Susan Sontag, *Against Interpretation and Other Essays*, Penguin, 2009, p.7.

Hopscotch. Between the gaps. 28/08/2020.

This was supposed to be a work about memory. Can we remember the content of the text we just read? Edward begins by saying this was never going to be your standard artist text. Perhaps it will turn out to be a more standard text than this one. So it goes:

Kelly's typing furiously. I can hear her typing, but I can't see her. Maybe she isn't typing but trying to catch water as it falls through her fingers.

Kelly's practice often involves Georgie. And excessive amounts of control.

Kelly's practice is enjoying this process. It never feels like work.

Kelly's always trying to make Georgie part of the art but Georgie hates art. I don't hate art, I'm just playing a different game.

Kelly's practice makes my head hurt. Are you sure that it's not too much screen time? Maybe it's the new glasses you got. I love your informality.

Kelly's wondering why Edward is questioning his own thinking. Don't we all do that?

Kelly's playing games with everything. It's all about the game and sometimes about process.

Kelly's doing some kind of unusual movements with her body. Hop, skip, stretch, and one giant side step.

Kelly's playing games with me. And time.

Kelly's trying really hard to remember how this short sentence went. I'm listening but there is no sound.

You can skip ahead if you like because Edward thinks that Kelly thinks that you as the reader would like to do that. Or you can linger longer.

Writing is really fun with other people. It's more surprising than you'd think.

Julio wrote a book about hopscotch. Sometime in the 1900s. Have you read it because we want to know if it is as easy to jump around and skip the parts that bore you as Edward says it is? Do you want to know too?

Kelly likes the less trodden and more unpredictable path.

The sides and the edges and the layout is all over the place. What's underneath?

Presenting things as they are is just fine, 2 + 2 is 4 but it can also be 5. Or 6 puppies were born on Sunday night at Dan's mum's house. Furry digressions.

"Life's too short to be tidying up and I think that's why I like improvisation. And changing the rules too."

Kelly doesn't remember saying that but it's in quotation marks so she must have. It could be a misquote, of sorts but it's really hard to misquote people these days because everything is recorded. Unless it's written from memory, of course.

If you digress in your writing you'll have to add another footnote to help make your point clearer. 4.

Kelly's enjoying the journey and hates the fact that this is nearly the end. Something about a direct address ?

An iceberg is really huge and mostly invisible because it's critical mass is 90% below the horizon line. I like this perspective.

But I'm really struggling to fill in this gap. Memory feels fragile.

I've got to the end (wrote Edward) and haven't written about a single work. What a refreshing change.

Kelly thinks Georgie's memory is pretty good. Georgie thinks Kelly is a great big iceberg and that the next person that this is handed over to will have to fully take the plunge to join the game. Are you that person?

George	→	Best
↓		↑
Grace	→	Kelly

p.28 and p.31: Kelly Best, 'Do Without', an ongoing collaborative project between Kelly Best and Georgie Grace, (2015–)
above: Kelly Best, *Kelly and Georgie type Edward's text from Memory*, 'Do Without' (2015–)

*aboutaboutaboutaboutaboutaboutaboutaboutabout*about*aboutaboutabout*

Siân Williams

Kelly Best

I've been thinking about weaving for a while now, how each individual thread wraps itself under and over another to make one large piece of fabric; something solid made of many parts. I've been thinking about the fullness and the strength of that and how Anni Albers described weaving as 'many-sided', and how she thought of it as nomadic architecture. July 2019

↓

When you think about it, it always comes back to weaving. Everything in life is woven together. Life, a network of support, absolute interdependence, one giant piece of fabric. August 2019

It's not a particularly well-woven textile. Frayed threads expelled to the margins, and patterns that should lead them back to unity and solidarity are purposefully misaligned to arrive at dead ends, at isolation. Is wear and tear an aesthetic choice? Or a frank reflection on reality? July 2020

aboutaboutaboutaboutaboutaboutaboutaboutaboutaboutaboutaboutabout

I've been thinking about movement, and the movement of a hanging object as a reaction to something or someone passing it; how that could be a moment when you realise that your presence in a space changes things. I've been thinking about proximity and the relationship between things, and maybe I've been thinking about intimacy too. I've been thinking about watching a performer at a Trajal Harrell show, of how closely I was standing next to them, how intently I watched them, and how strange it seemed for that to feel normal. July 2019

↓

It was about the end of March, early April. Impossibly I find myself back there. I'm here too. Here being now and there being then. It's August and I'm in the same place, just different times. I'm moving between the two which is strange because I'm lying on my bed. Back then I was standing. Standing was my choice. I remember how normal it felt to choose to stand and how strange it was that everyone else was sitting down. Perhaps they already understood the intimacy potential of standing and realised the chairs would act as protectors. But I did not need protection. And certainly not from a chair! August 2019

aboutaboutaboutaboutaboutaboutaboutaboutaboutaboutaboutaboutabout

I've been thinking about six people in a park in Cardiff playing a game in which they could go anywhere, but they always had to know where the others were. I've been thinking about the shapes as we spread out, the rhythms of movement that happened in waves; first quickly, then slowing down as we paused to check on each other. I've been thinking about secret collective acts and about how no one else in the park knew what we were doing. I've been thinking about how our awareness connected us, like an invisible elastic band keeping us together, and about how I could almost feel the tension and resistance as we moved. July 2019

↓

The game was about to begin. Everyone was in position. Even the 'non-players' were in position, though they did not yet understand how their bodies formed part of *this* game. These 'non-players' claimed variable mobile boundaries, areas of void that could not be accessed by the players. The players could not yet understand this, their collective secret demanding absolute attention for the entirety of the game and long after the players thought it had ended. The ending. Where was that exactly? It was pretty hard to locate, but not as complex as tracing the beginning. August 2019

aboutaboutaboutaboutaboutaboutaboutaboutaboutaboutaboutaboutabout

I've been thinking about being led to that park with my eyes shut and how the sounds around me became much more voluminous when I had no sight to ground them. I've been thinking about the tiny gestures my companion gave as she guided me; her fingers pressing into my waist when we started or stopped, the funny shuffling steps we took to warn of an approaching curb, the settling of her body against mine as we waited to cross the road. July 2019

 Continued on page 212

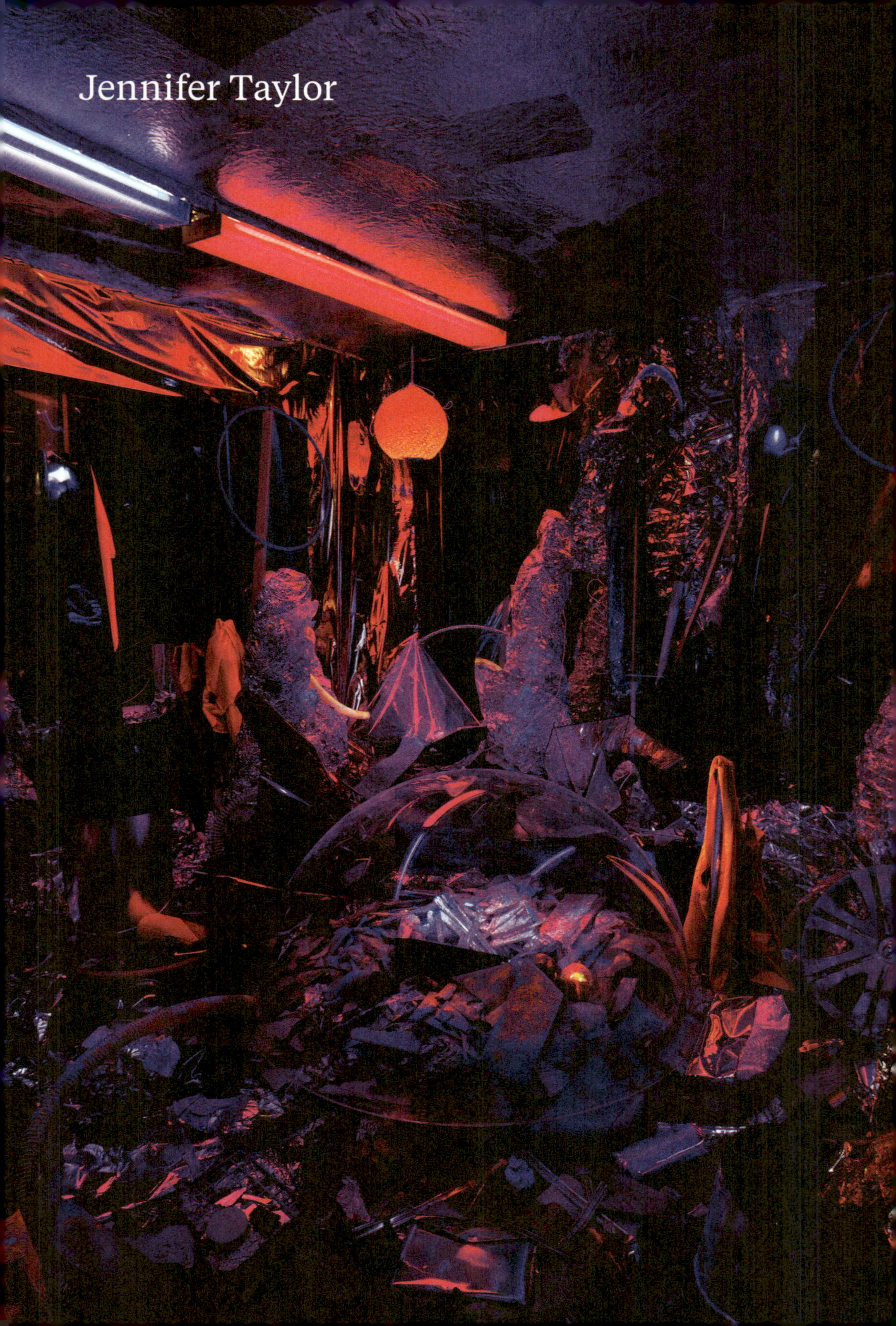
Jennifer Taylor

In This Mirror

There's a strange calm to this junkyard sci-fi scene, amid the iridescent bric-a-brac and mechanical hooting and howling. *Lunar Dawn* (2020) looks to be a ritual of sorts. A cast of human-ish characters in garish garb circle around a gold-painted figure, prone on a makeshift surface. The group busies itself in the process of tinkering, gathering, and moving debris and scraps of wire from one spot to another. No one seems to be in charge. A ripple of absurdity runs through the whole scene. What is the point? Later, this central figure curls into a foetal position, before a clear plastic dome covers over them. The clustered figures perform a bizarre kind of cosmic ultrasound. Whether a rebirth or an un-birth, it's a ceremony out of place and out of time, where language is stripped away.

Jennifer Taylor leaves a trail of happenings, gatherings and communitarian rites in her wake. Fleeting, spectacular visions with lo-fi means become living things, burning bright before fading to rubble and dust. Performances are cobbled together, revelling in their own DIY spirit. There is a touch of the twisted school pantomime about their saturated, luminous illogic, which allows you entry to the scene with the wide-eyed spirit of a child. Making artifice apparent is just one of Taylor's devices, and elsewhere, an almost bawdy humour stops things from getting too sophisticated, or from being taken too seriously.

Happenings get out of hand. There are no instructions, no rehearsals, barely a blueprint. Performers bring their own things. Taylor storyboards where the work might go, and leads everyone in the process, but it's makeshift – piecing it together as you go along. Taylor is interested in the potential of this defined framework of chaos. Not knowing what to do and having to improvise means those involved often end up helping each other out. The work's horizontal command structure delights in its brief rupture from order and systems of control. Stepping on set is to relinquish things you held tightly before.

The Brazilian conceptual artist Hélio Oiticica created a series of wearable textiles, or *Parangolés,* in the 1960s that were intended to be worn and danced in. The material flutters, moves and shimmers to create a visual spectacle, transforming spectator into performer. They are 'alive' only for the duration of time in which they are worn. The word *parangolé* itself is a slang term for an 'animated situation and sudden confusion and / or agitation between people'.[1] Like Oiticica, Taylor creates communitarian, involved and performative spectacles to highlight the absence of authority. This ultimately controlled situation relies on a collective abandonment of control. Oiticica noted of his work: 'The experience of dance (of samba) therefore gave me the exact idea of what creation through the corporeal act may be, a continuous transformability.'[2] Taylor, like Oiticica, finds generative potential in the unfolding spaces between idea and event, in the creative heat of subjectivities rubbing up alongside one another.

Taylor's temporary, provisional spectacles hold a subversive mirror to the arcane rituals of life. But what happens at their close, once the happening has taken place? Does life return to what it was before? The Russian philosopher Mikhail Bakhtin proposed the carnival, or 'carnivalesque', as an emancipatory literary mode, one which 'belongs to the borderline between art and life [...] during carnival time life is subject only to its laws, that is, the laws of its own freedom'.[3] Humour and chaos open up new possibilities on an individual and collective level, windows into how life might be otherwise. But Taylor's performances don't stop there – they have a half-life. Once the *Lunar Dawn* is risen, and the ritual has concluded, all the performers return to the real world, trailing the detritus of the happening along with them – carnivalesque seeds scattered to the wind. This small gesture also laughs at the conventions of performance. The stage is set, the lights are down, the audience awaits. The performers arrive, perform, finish. Hold for applause and depart. Taylor is dubious as to beginning, middle and end, preferring a delirious continuum. A technicolour drip-feed.

Taylor's work collapses time by elasticating it to epic proportions: distilling sweeping histories of humanity into vignette and momentary spectacle. Aesthetically too, we hover in a kind of mythic time, in ambiguous limbos between the Neolithic and distant cosmic futures. The future requires imagination, but so does the past. Taylor's ritualistic performances mine seemingly ancient traditions, so removed from our present that we can only speculate as to their reality. In so doing, Taylor reminds us the past is just as unbridgeable, as fictitious, as the future. Her short-form video series 'The Lastborn' (2017) is a window on to prehistoric-looking landscapes, in which a human figure in a full body suit – thus occluding their human features other than the contours of the body – tries to birth themselves from a giant balloon. An impossible mix of farce and poignancy, in their quicksilver lifespan, the works are a complete life cycle: a whole history told in a moment, suggesting the futility of their telling in the first place.

Taylor's early installations and tightly framed performances-on-camera operate almost like film sets: cinematic apertures into spaces and situations. But windows are all they can be. Right now, her work uses the medium of liveness. We're in carnival time now, and anything can happen. Curious rituals descend further into farce and further out of time, revealing the thin line we tread between reality and absurdity. We emerge, blinking, into the sunlight. Suddenly things look rather different.

8 July 2020

1 Hélio Oiticica, 'Dance in My Experience', in Claire Bishop (ed.), *Participation: Documents of Contemporary Art*, Whitechapel and MIT Press, 2006, p.75.
2 *Ibid.*
3 Pam Morris (ed.), *The Bakhtin Reader: Selected Writings of Bakhtin, Medvedev, Voloshinov*, Arnold, 2003, p.198.

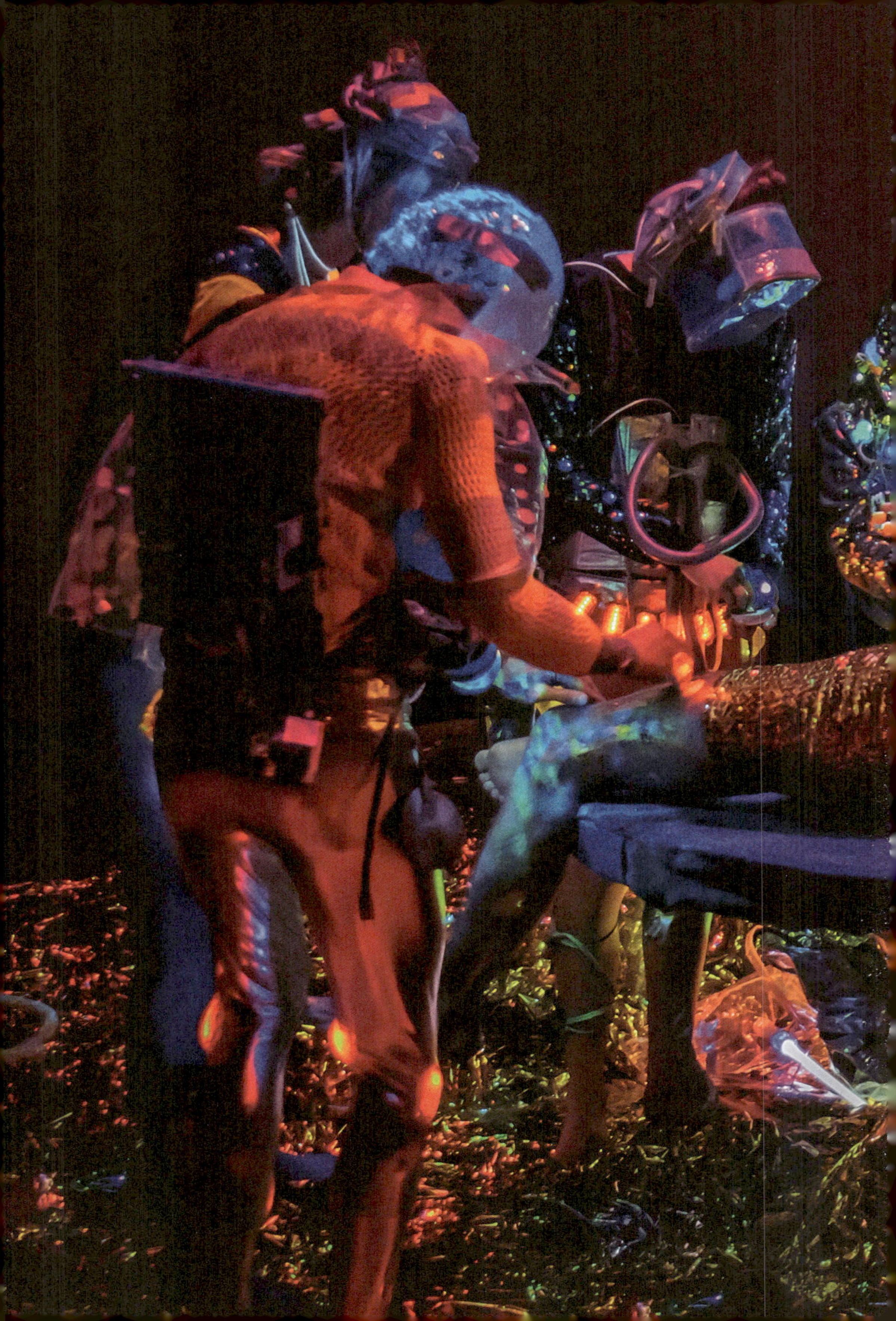

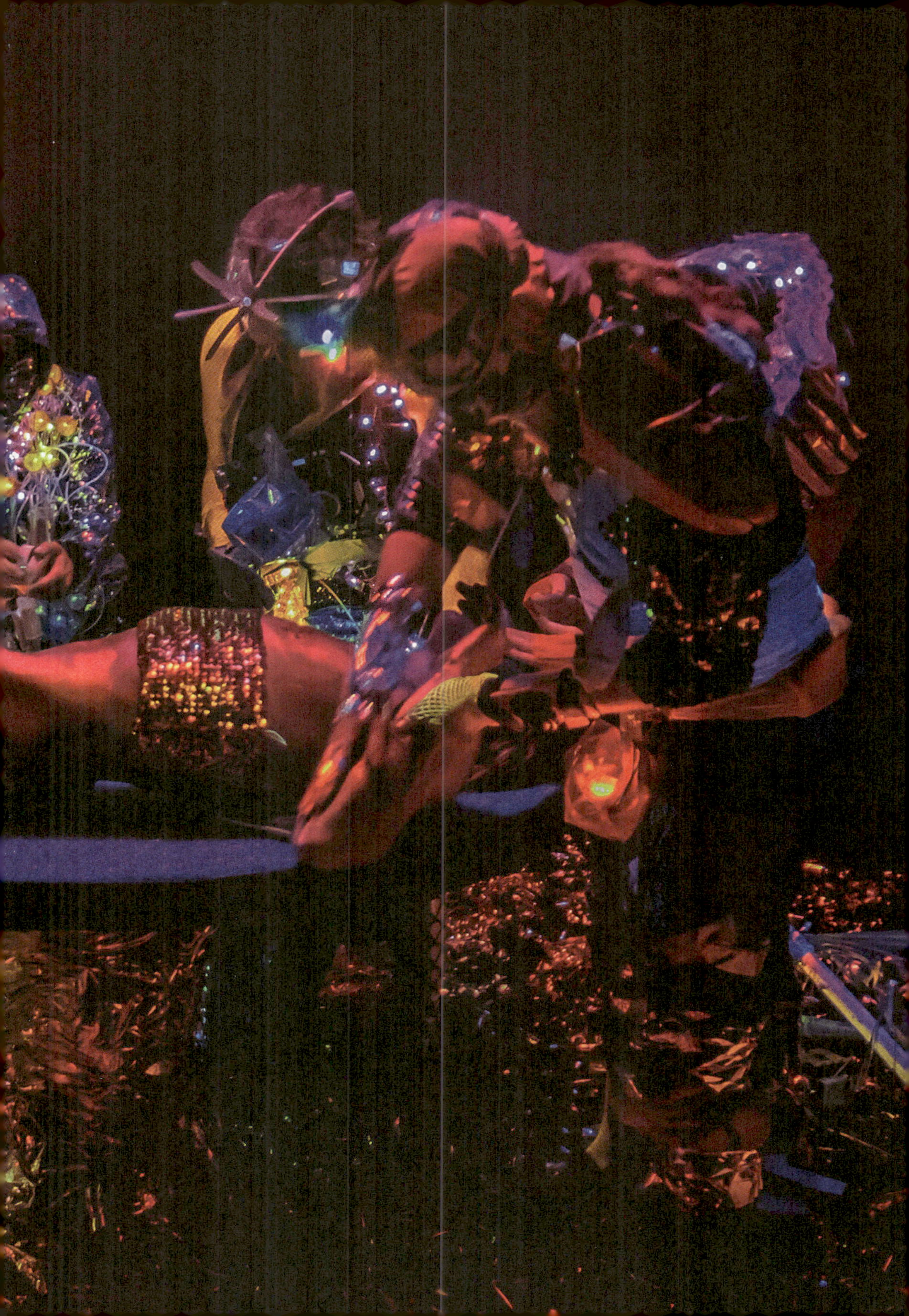

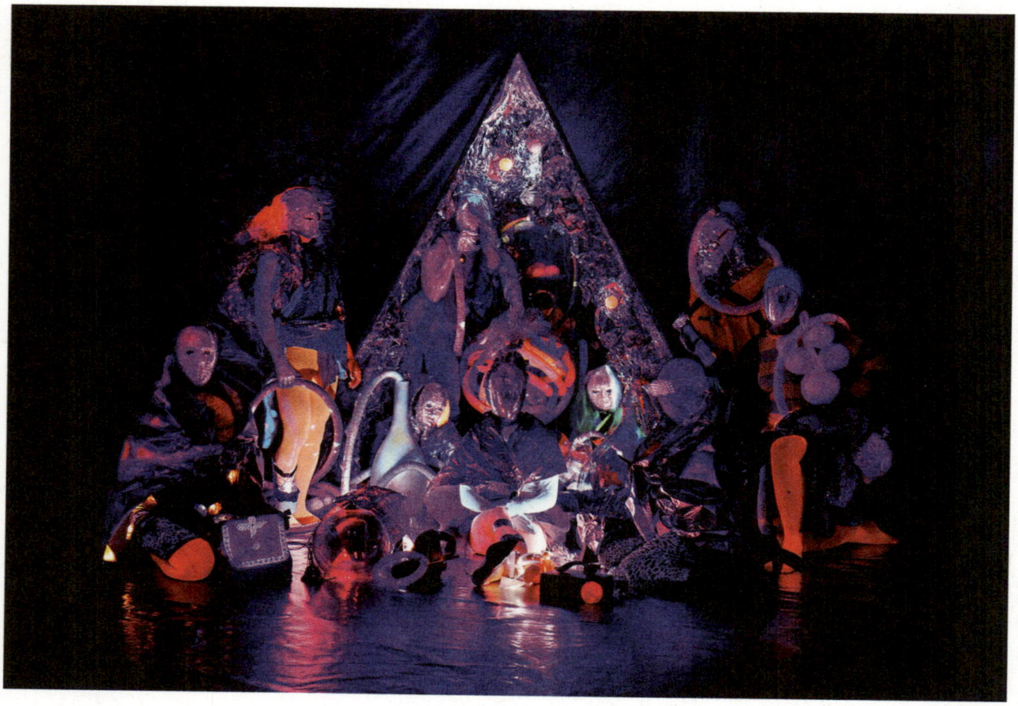

p.36: Jennifer Taylor, *Empire*, immersive installation, *UnderTheCounterCulture*, Cardiff, 2020
pp.40–41: Jennifer Taylor, *Lunar Dawn*, live performance, g39, Cardiff, 2020. Photo: Dave Daggers
above: Jennifer Taylor, *Vigil*, live performance, Culture Colony Intervention, Machynlleth, 2019

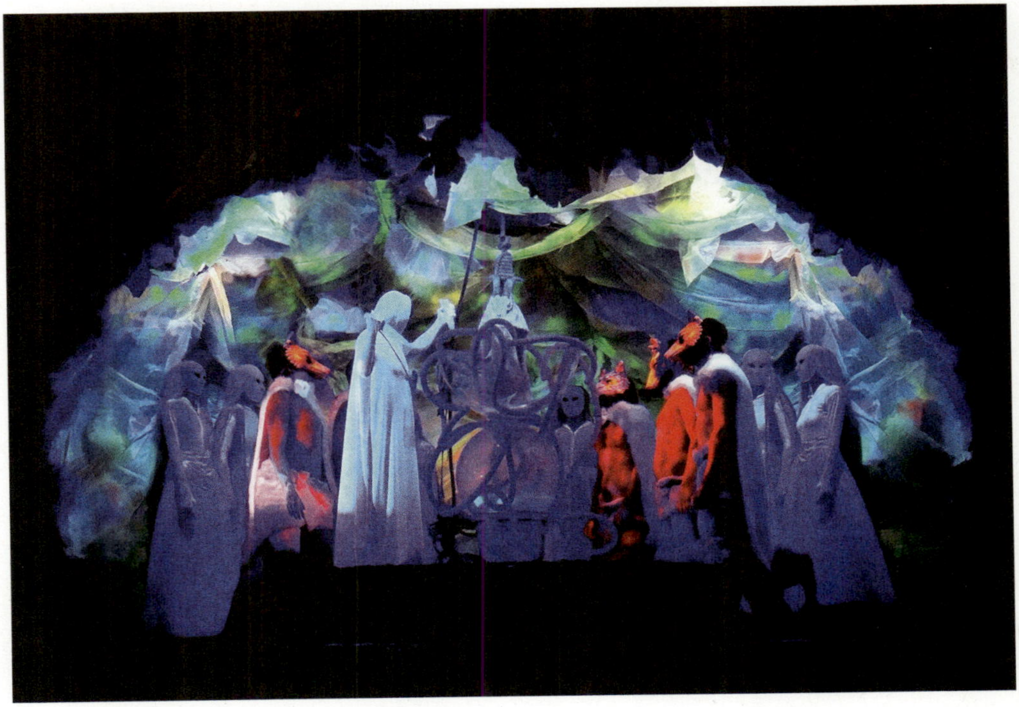

Jennifer Taylor, *Lupercalia*, live performance,
The British School at Rome, 2017

Neasa Terry

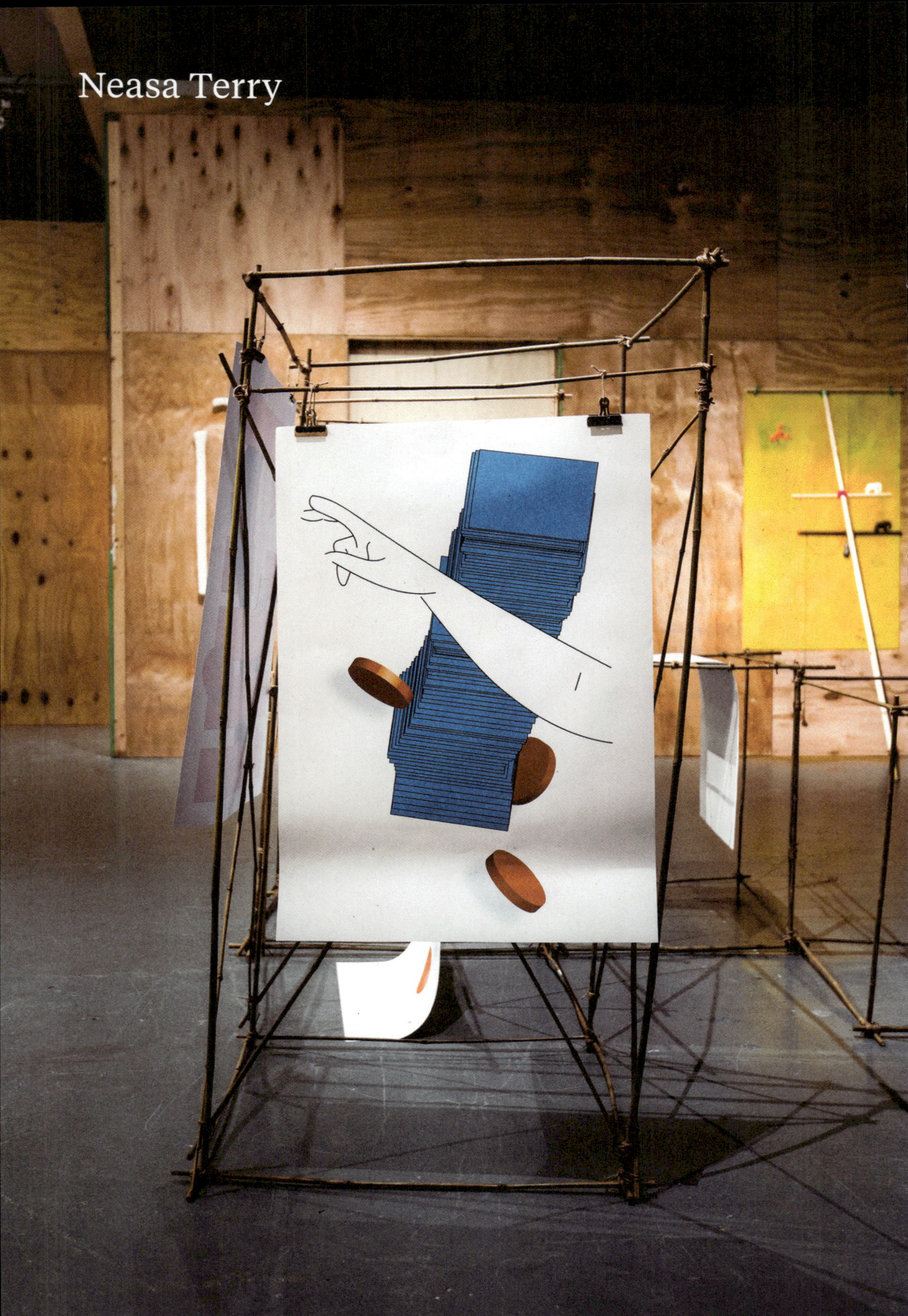

Keeping Score

An expanded metaphor of notation runs throughout Neasa Terry's work, whether the simple act of 'noting down', or something more melodic and musical. Terry notates as gesture – a series of markings and mark-makings to track and organise thoughts. Over time they stratify and accumulate, these scraps of thought forming a kind of archive.

For Terry, notation is a way of bringing disparate elements together – research into brass bands, space travel and mining are among her recent subjects of inquiry. This process of gathering and arranging is a way for Terry to corral her instinctive interests into shapes of thought. These gestures, as composition, build into idiosyncratic visual scores. If we try to visualise this process, it might appear as a spiral: broad at first, moving inwards through ever smaller concentric circles towards a central core. Terry's process sees her create 'research posters',[1] an ongoing companion to her practice. These works, frequently digitally produced, incorporate a range of discrete objects and motifs onto a plain or otherwise spatially ambiguous background, as if these objects were thoughts swirling through the ether. These items – geometric shapes, scraps of language – circulate in an economy of their own, connected by loose threads of research and intuition.

Neasa Terry trained as a printmaker, and her practice sits across art and design. This cross-disciplinary interest led to Terry's participation in The Rejoinders, a network of artists and creatives between India and Wales, established to explore the collaborative process, the visual arts and 'in between' spaces.[2] Following a residency in Mumbai, India, Terry produced *Flatlands*, an installation comprising nine A1 posters, for her participation in a group exhibition at g39 in 2018.[3] The posters were draped from and hung off of makeshift bamboo support structures. The installation pivoted musically between movement and repose, flatness and three dimensionality. Terry named her title from the satirical novel *Flatland: A Romance of Many Dimensions* by the English schoolmaster Edwin Abbott Abbott, which was first published in 1884. The novel explored Victorian social conventions, but its most enduring influence concerns the book's reflections on dimensions and perception. Terry's installation explored hierarchies of composition, toying with architecture, foreground and background, in so doing introducing a fluid sculptural dimension to the display of two-dimensional prints. With a nod to the mechanical means of the work's production, the installation had a rhythmic quality, like paper rolling off a printer. The slickness of each composition coolly suggests the absence of the human hand, as if programmed solely by algorithm. Within each composition, however, objects are occasionally bridged by softening curvilinear lines, suggesting musical notation – abstract forms to be decoded, perhaps even played.

Terry's interest in mechanical reproduction moves between printmaking and sound-making. In an interview as part of a residency with Oriel Davies gallery, Newtown, Wales in 2017, Terry stated:

> As part of my research, I've been looking at a variety of ways of making and translating sound. These translations have led me to start experimenting with various programmes and technologies, including Max / MSP, machine learning and Arduino in order to create, manipulate and translate sound.[4]

This body of research led to a number of works exploring the programmatic implications of Arduino technology, and the elisions between human and machine. In Terry's *As Above, So Below* at g39,[5] a system of lights controlled the score as performers enacted instructions given via a screen. Each performer interacted with a 'vacuum-formed mountain'[6] according to instructions such as Hold, Clockwise, Rise, Fall. There are minor yet perceptible variations across each of the four performer's movements, despite all acting in unison. The work reflects on the divergences that occur during translation from technological to human – that is, analogue – action. Terry's interest in this variance manifests across her printmaking practice too. Her work asks: is fidelity of reproduction possible, even desirable? Whether making sound or image, a notation only ever provides the blueprint for producing likeness.

A visual score amounts to a process in and of itself, yet its resultant form must also be read, interpreted, even performed. This necessarily requires an imaginative process of translation – to turn a series of signs into another form, whether sound, image or effect. Jazz musician Miles Davis famously instructed to 'play what's not there'. Terry's work resides in the imperceptible spaces between intention, reception and intuition. It's all connected; you might just not hear the melody at first.

24 July 2020

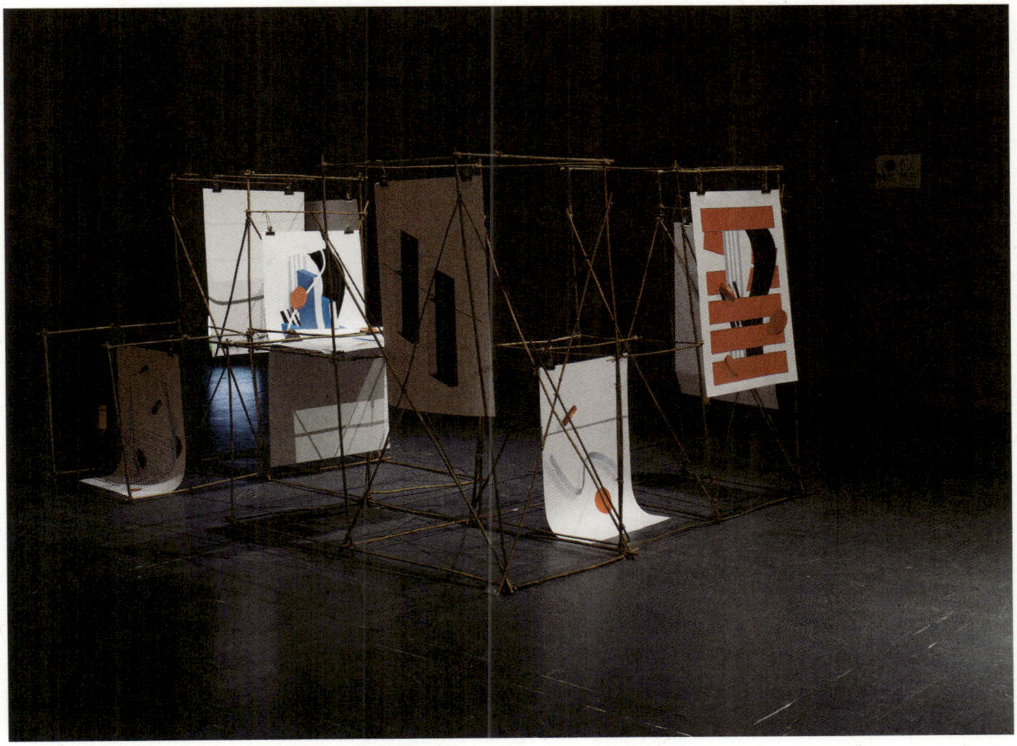

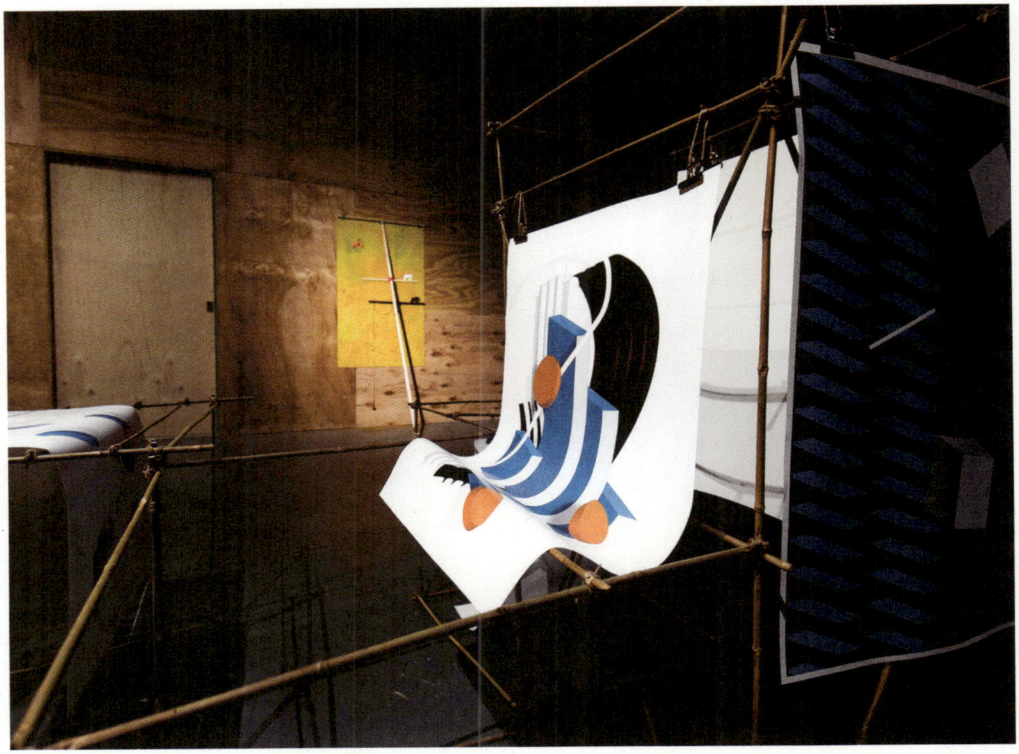

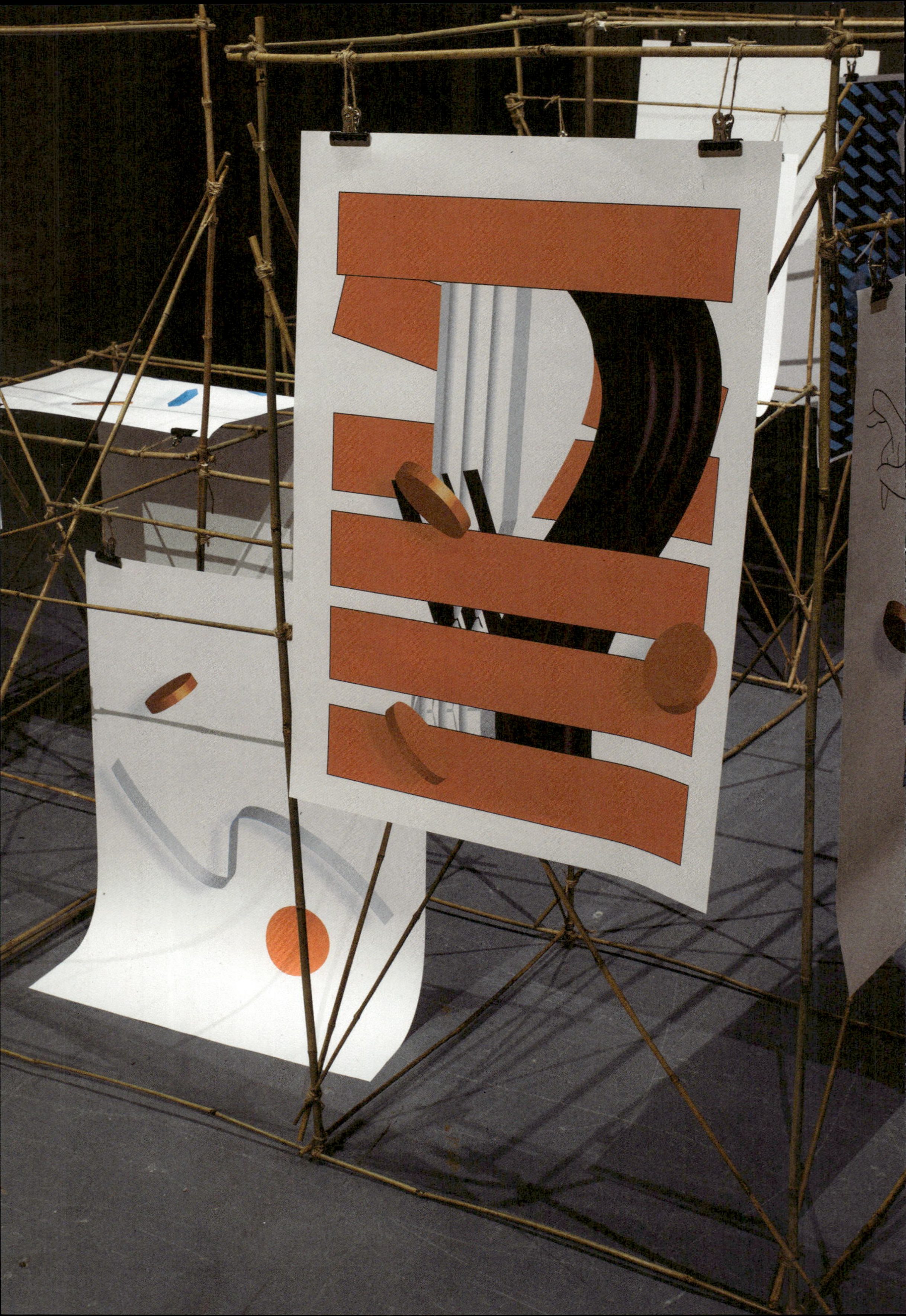

1 In conversation with the author, studio visit Tuesday 6 November 2018.
2 Part of the UK/India Year of Culture 2017, https://wales.britishcouncil.org/en/arts/india-wales-building-relationships-through-art/rejoinders.
3 *The Rejoinders*, g39, Cardiff, 2018.
4 Interview as part of Neasa Terry's Litmus residency with Oriel Davies, 2017, http://www.orieldavies.org/en/exhibition/litmus-residency-part-3.
5 *Unit(e) Summer School*, g39, Cardiff, 2017.
6 The artist's term; each performer interacts with a small cast object on a plinth.

all works: Neasa Terry, *Flatlands*, nine digitally printed A1 posters on bamboo scaffold, installation views g39, Cardiff, *The Rejoinders*, 2018. Photo: Polly Thomas. Courtesy: g39

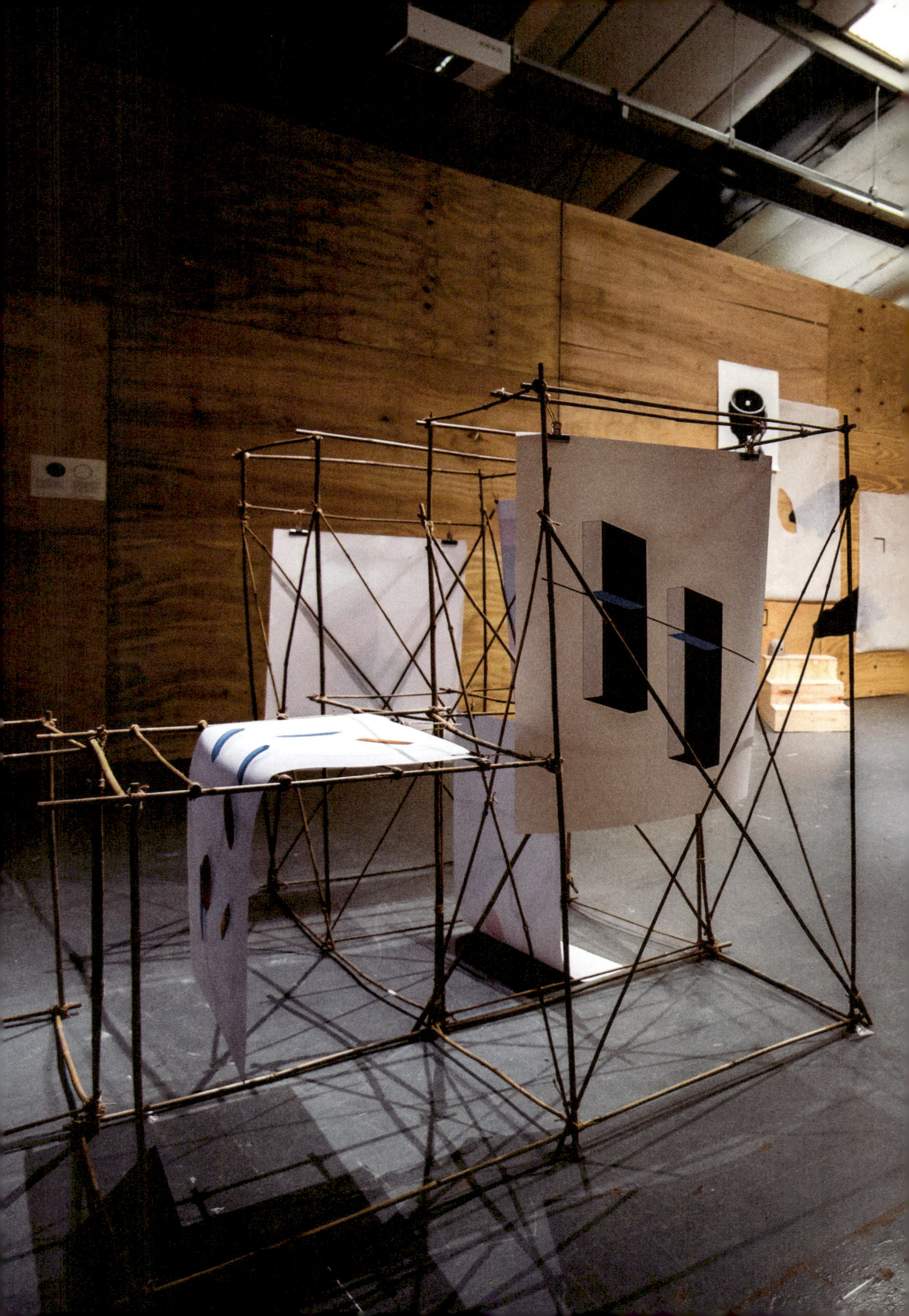

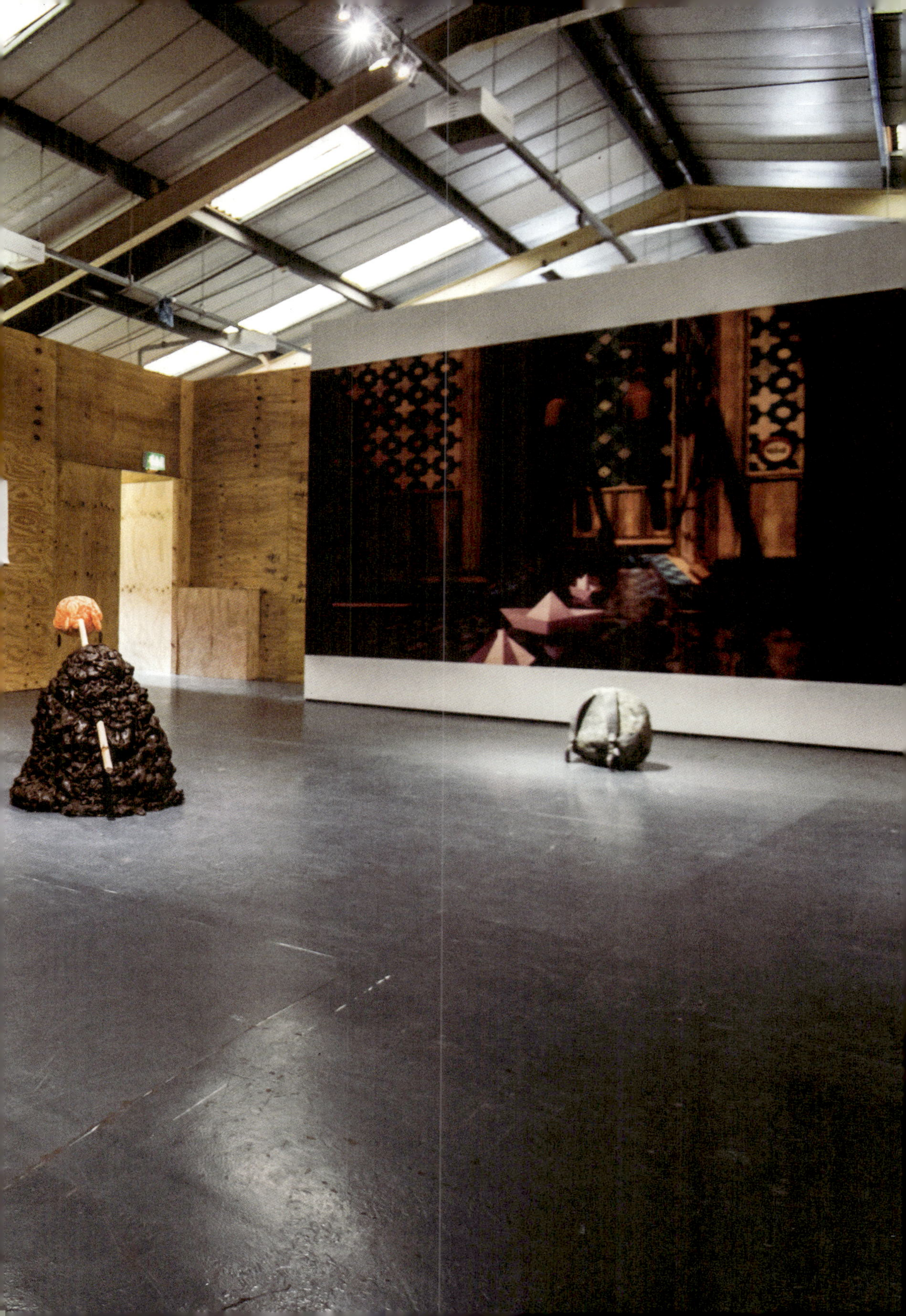

Fern Thomas

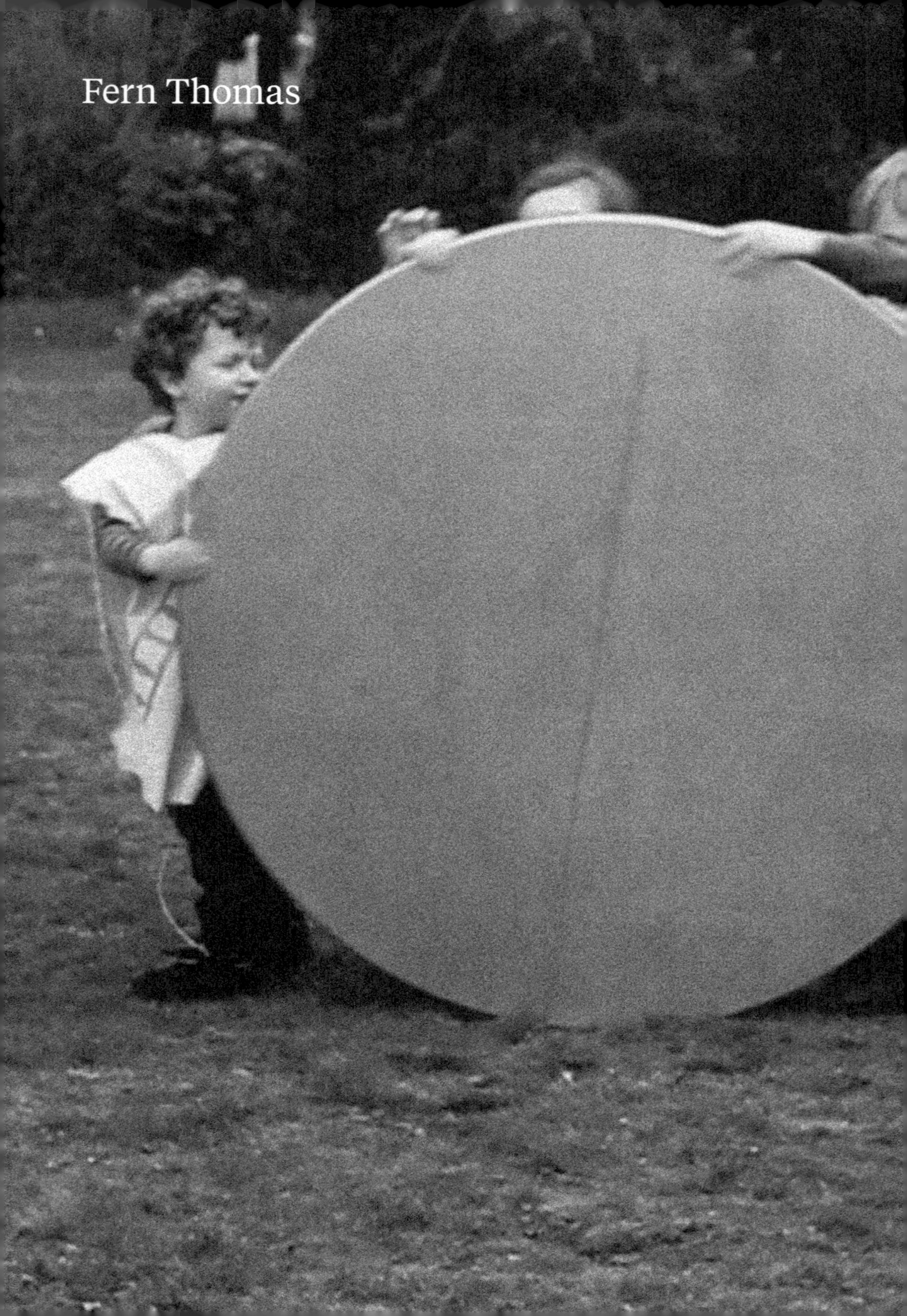

An Idea, an Action, a Becoming

To talk of practice is – often – to talk of a body of work. Of themes interrelated. Of artistic development, across time. Can we imagine a landscape? ... artist, the work, the world – ecosystem.

To talk of Fern Thomas's practice is to talk of a practice of connection; practice as potential. Her way of living and being is rooted in social sculpture – a theory developed by artist Joseph Beuys in the 1970s, which posits everything as art, and suggests that, in turn, all aspects of life can be approached creatively. Everyone can be an artist. Everyone can, and does, shape the world. Art-making is just one of the modes in which a citizen 'is' and 'does', in relation to others and to the world. 'Work' begins with thinking, ethics and values, with one's immediate environment being the point of departure. Work is imagining new ways of being, with the intention of moving towards a vision of a humane and ecologically viable society.

Thomas's everyday life is shaped by her local community in Swansea, Wales and her experience of being a mother to two young children. She imagines a better world not just for her immediate community, but also for her children and their future on this planet. Her practice of motherhood is to build resilience and empathy in her children, and to create a place for this to flourish. This expansive goal departs from a more immediate question: how to create a space for the children in her community to come together? A recent video work, *for a spell* (2020) convened her children, their friends and the local community. Thomas sought to create a space for the children – to encourage them as their own community – through the collective enactment of folkloric ritual. The work drew from Thomas's residency at the Glamorgan Archives (2018–19), where her research focused on the supernatural and mystical aspects of the collection.[1] Filmed at an old bowling green in Swansea, the work rethinks and reframes the tradition of the 'Ceffyl Pren', or wooden horse. This Welsh custom functioned as a tool for self-governing in local communities. In a kind of public ritual humiliation, the adjudged offending person in the community would be paraded around the village tied to a wooden frame. In rethinking this problematic tradition, Thomas also drew on the more celebratory folk custom of 'Mari Lwyd',[2] a communal activity based around the use of the hobby horse. In bringing aspects of both folk cultures to bear in the present: children parading around the green together on hobby horses to live folk music, their actions creating their own new form of ritual. In this sense, folkloric customs that once took place on the same lands are lived out in a new way, for a new context. Thomas's work is alive to the generative potential of the imagination, yet regardful, too, of what the past can teach us.

for a spell is a kind of collective role play, with echoes of Brechtian theatre tropes designed to mobilise people internally through participation. Where Brecht worked with distancing and disruption, Thomas employs strategies of inclusion and connection to the same ends, arranged in the style of a Brechtian learning-play.[3] Bertolt Brecht's experimental works explored the possibilities of learning through acting, playing roles, adopting different postures and attitudes. Crucially, primacy was not placed on the end result – the process was as, if not more, important. Thomas, too, trusts in the process. External manifestation of ideas into material, into process, are employed as ways to encourage people to become more internally active – to 'scratch on people's imagination', to borrow the language of Beuys.[4] The function of acting out is to be open to new possibilities within a framework of play. This process questions whether in briefly becoming Other, might you become different when stepping out of that role, back into your citizenship?

Thomas's way of introducing the children to structures of community can even be thought of as a form of consciousness-raising. The term arose in relation to the Women's Liberation Movement as it developed in the 1960s, in which small groups of women came together initially with the goal of raising awareness of issues among themselves, and then to much larger groups in society. Meetings were structured so that all women were able to speak, a coming together forming a change-making democracy. This dynamic sought to build both individual and collective resilience – sisterhood. Group processes such as these were geared towards transformational individual experience, in order to go on and, hopefully, transform the consciousness of others. While these groups arose to tackle specific forms of oppression, Thomas's folkloric learning-play raises the children's consciousness in relation to each other as a way of building kinship, ensuring they meet as equals, together.

Perhaps envisioning change must always come from one's immediate environment, which then allows further steps out into the world, Thomas's practice is hopeful: believing that positive action can and does change the world, however small each action might be. Yet it is a practice grounded in reality – one recognising that we must radically reconfigure our relationship to the earth and to each other. But what can be imagined, and how can the acting out of the imagination allow for different transformative processes? It seems to me that this practice is a 'putting-into-practice'. It is also an approach to art-making that takes place out in the world, in the landscape, unconfined to a gallery. A seed in the ground is just an idea of a flower. It takes an idea, belief, and time to bloom.

19 June 2020

1 The Glamorgan Archives, based in Cardiff, is a public collection of the history and people of Glamorgan, Wales.
2 The Mari Lwyd tradition entails the use of a hobby horse which is made from a horse's skull mounted on a pole and carried by an individual. It is typically celebrated in Wales between Christmas and New Year's Eve through communal procession and song.
3 Learning-play is playwright and poet Bertolt Brecht's own translation of the term, from the original German *Lehrstücke*.
4 See in particular Shelley Sacks and Wolfgang Zumdick, *Atlas of the Poetic Continent: Pathways in Ecological Citizenship*, Temple Lodge Publishing, 2013.

In that moment when a whale would float across the screen,
slow, ethereal, spectral.
It felt like a real encounter.

The belugas move through the water in a way I would hope to move through my dreams.

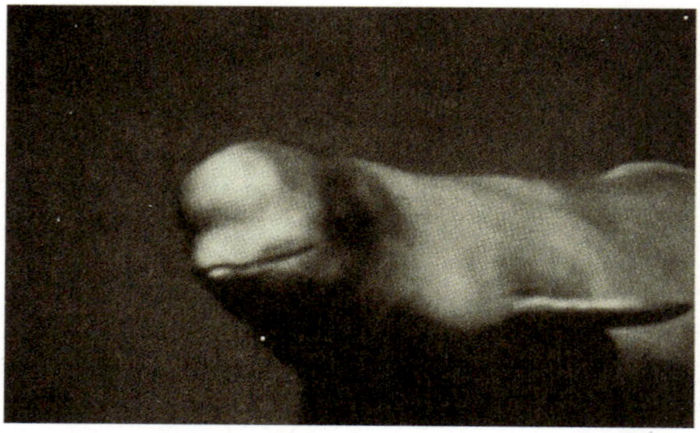

Floating in and out of the frame.

When in shadow their bodies dissolve into the blue of their surroundings.
They are shape-shifters, fluid, ancient.
They offer an invitation to be submerged in something.
To go deep.

There was one beluga who made me think about my own body, a softness in the belly that seemed to move to its own rhythm.
It felt like a maternal body.

I later watch that body birth a calf. For a time there is an extra tail swimming along with the mother, as part of the mother, as the rest of the baby is waiting to be birthed.

A double swim, a phenomenon. And then out in a gush of blood, born in a twist like the spinning of our bones, the calf arrives.

I tell them stories of rising waters and how
it was okay because there was still hope.

I make things familiar, snowstorms and floods.

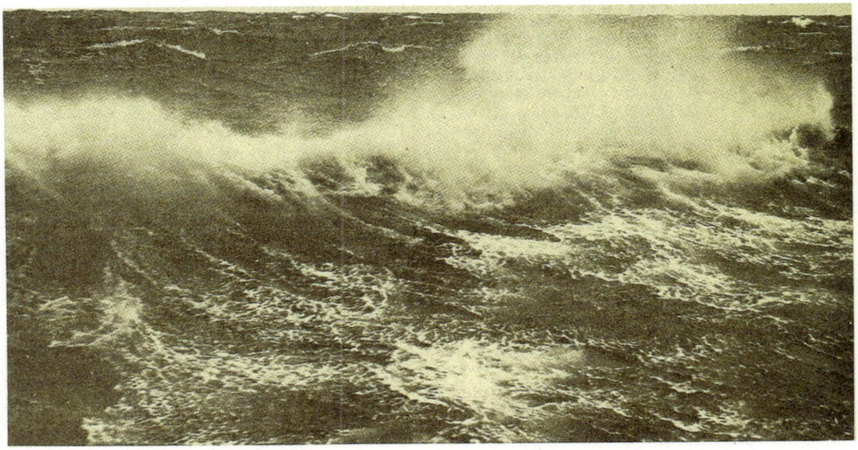

We enact them, try to embody them.

Playing out a snowstorm in case one day extreme
weather conditions become their reality.

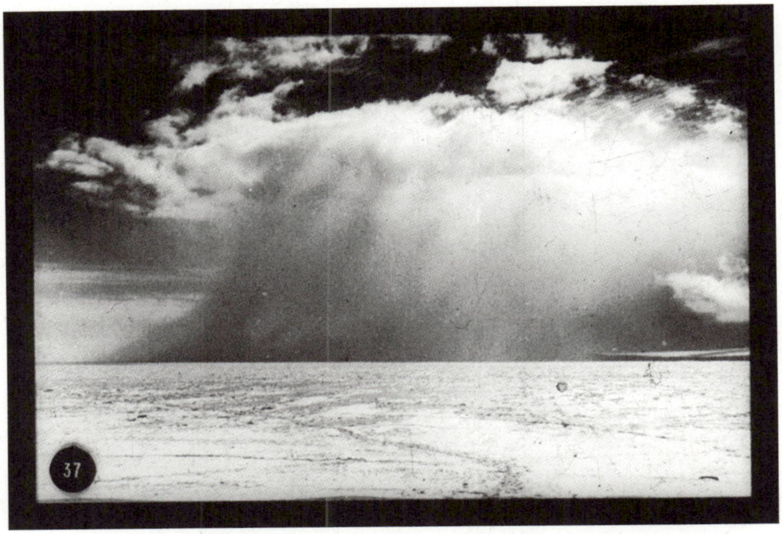

NOW MAKE YOUR BODY LIKE A GIANT WAVE

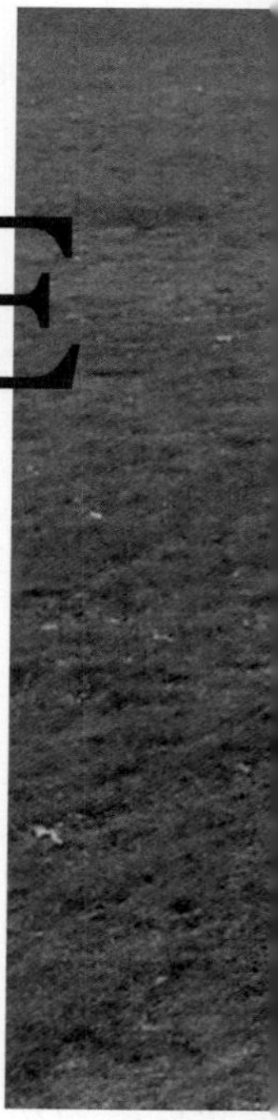

p.52 and opposite: Fern Thomas, *for a spell*, video (still), 2020
p.56 both images: Photograph by Veronique Lesage, from *The Canadian field-naturalist*, Ottawa Field Naturalists Club, 1919
p.57 top: Photograph from the *Commercial Fisheries Review*, c.1946
p.57 bottom: *An Antarctic Wind Storm* by Herbert George Ponting. Part of a collection of photographs taken on the Terra Nova expedition 1910–11
pp.56 and 57: images licensed under Creative Commons

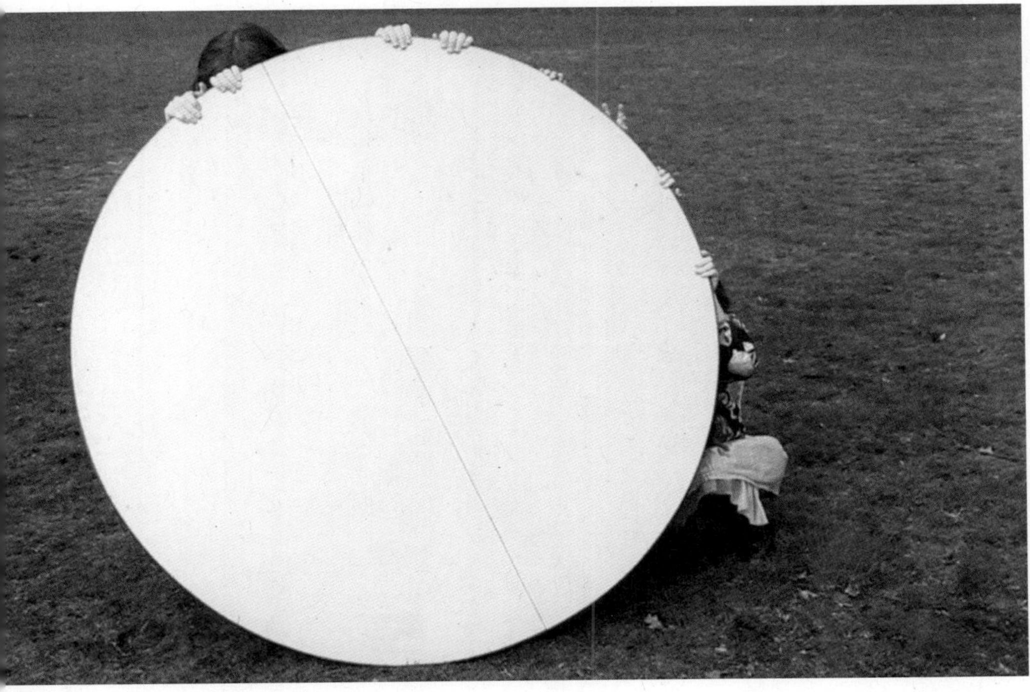

Ian Watson

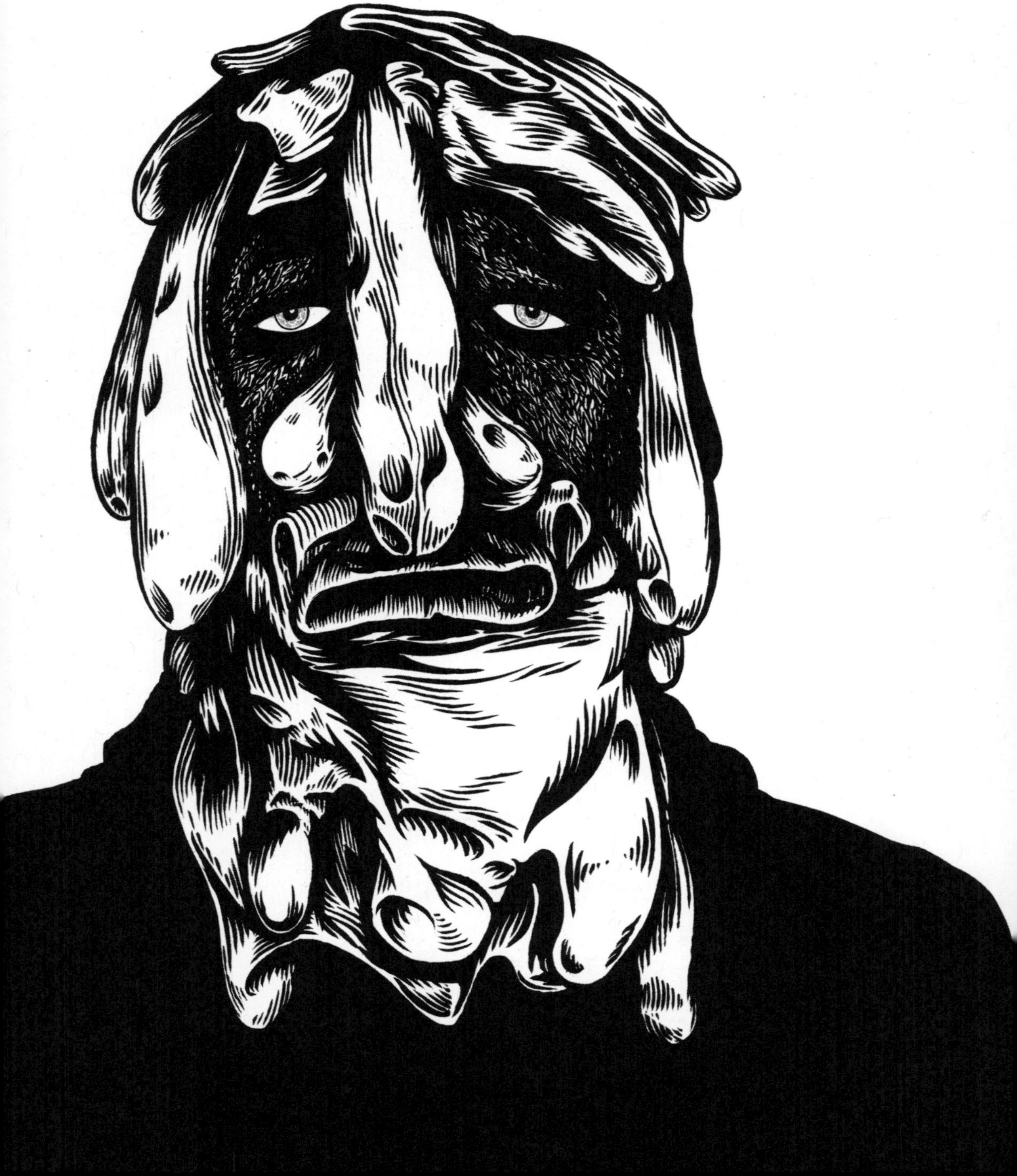

Music for Chameleons[1]

'The path seemed as if it only led in one direction.'

So opens *The Path* (2020) – a somnambulant stagger across a dystopian terrain of not-quite-and-non-places. Ian Watson's echoing, vibrational animated film upends us, taking us out of earthly and human perspectives. Not only does the path lead in all manner of directions and tangents at once, I'm not actually sure of the existence of the path at all, nor quite of its whereabouts. It's a journey without beginning, middle or end.

A ghoulish narrator fills in some blanks, but in so doing creates other, larger ones. The narrator appears and disappears, slipping through folds of fiction and perception. They stop, start, stutter, as ambient ripples of soundtrack strain at their vocal cords. Among things uttered, speculated and inferred, there is a promise of a future, but one which carries no possibility of return. Words are delivered in an uncanny monotone, like the sound of the same piano key tapped over and over.

Rocks turn to landfill. Birds appear, and circle. A momentary clearing in the woods. Uncertain geographies make us doubt our sense of place. Does imagination or perception create a place? We move through a series of nowheres: impossible capitals, edge lands and interstitial zones, while hearing of heralded sites, such as 'The Pile' or 'The Spot', which are as real as they are mythologised. We appear to have taken a nightmarish turn in Italo Calvino's *Invisible Cities*. Calvino's novel, written in 1972, is one without storyline – the only characters are an aging emperor Kublai Khan and a young explorer Marco Polo, as Polo regales Khan with tales of the cities he has seen journeying to the far reaches of the ruler's vast empire. Each short chapter describes a different city – fantastical, beguiling places, where things are never as they seem. *The Path* takes us too on a Polo-esque journey, guided by our unknowable interlocutor. Literary critic Wayne C Booth introduced the theory of the 'unreliable narrator' in fiction,[2] and our narrator here is certainly unreliable, for they don't seem to have all the facts. That isn't to say they aren't trying to help. Perhaps their knowledge doesn't translate.

We are recounted with a tale of folk who take rest at 'The Pile', and of how it became 'a communal sculpture and record of sorts'.[3] Each traveller left a stone there as a memento, and consequently, over time, 'each stone's importance lessened as the pile grew'.[4] This posits 'The Pile' as an idea of monument, something that's real because it is imagined by those who journey there. A monument-as-idea. Yet as it becomes physicalised, its constituent parts become lesser, and its mythological size diminishes. This fable-like narrative of a hill of stones is its own metaphor for Watson's work: seemingly wandering or digressive ruminations circle back to lend an oblique perspective of life on earth. This vignette recalls the roundabout closing of writer Samuel Beckett's *Molloy,* and the tale of the sucking stones. A man becomes obsessed with transferring 16 stones 'turn and turn about' – from pocket to pocket. He glumly ponders: 'But deep down it was all the same to me whether I sucked a different stone each time or always the same stone, until the end of time.'[5] Watson allows us to imagine our interlocutor trying to make sense of some of the very possibly pointless things we do on earth, our own monuments and records, of sorts.

These stones recur from a previous work: Watson's ongoing 'Pylons & Spires' series (2019–). At ArcadeCampfa gallery and project space in Cardiff, a TV monitor was held aloft atop a pile of stones.[6] Watson whittled these stones from blocks of polystyrene, concealing speakers within. The rocks are a shaky pedestal, emitting an unsettling, jangling audio. This form, and its attendant metaphors, resound into *The Path*. The two video works call out to one another, as if hearing a remote broadcast from another part of the solar system. Though related, the works are Watson's first forays into narrative video. Sound work is a significant strand of Watson's practice, which increasingly concerns itself with soundtracking his own works. Source material for these sounds is often sought from the by-products of daily life. Watson uses VLF (very low frequency) radio to expose the electromagnetic behaviour of cell phones, laptops and other domestic electronics. The artist also uses wind-up music boxes, allowing them to run over and interrupt one another, 'in order to produce chaotic soundscapes that when recorded and slowed dramatically become a sort of macro study of generative melody in the style of Brian Eno's *Music for Airports* [...] the results are usually mistaken for analogue synthesis.'[7] Watson's interest is in things taking on lives of their own, with this unknown generative pathway leading us to hitherto unfamiliar perspectives. His recent works recall the American artist Ian Cheng's living digital ecosystem, *BOB (Bag of Beliefs)* (2018), in which an algorithm mutates and develops 'organically', and a cast of flora and fauna interact, intermix and reformulate.

Watson's own melding of unearthly perspectives with an interest in the generative follows a post-humanist path. 'Be as human as you can

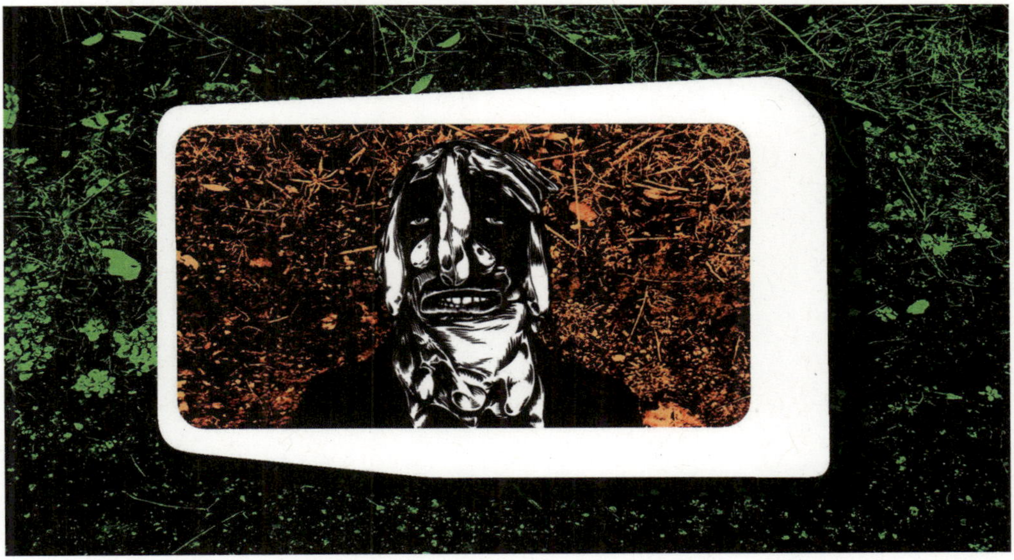

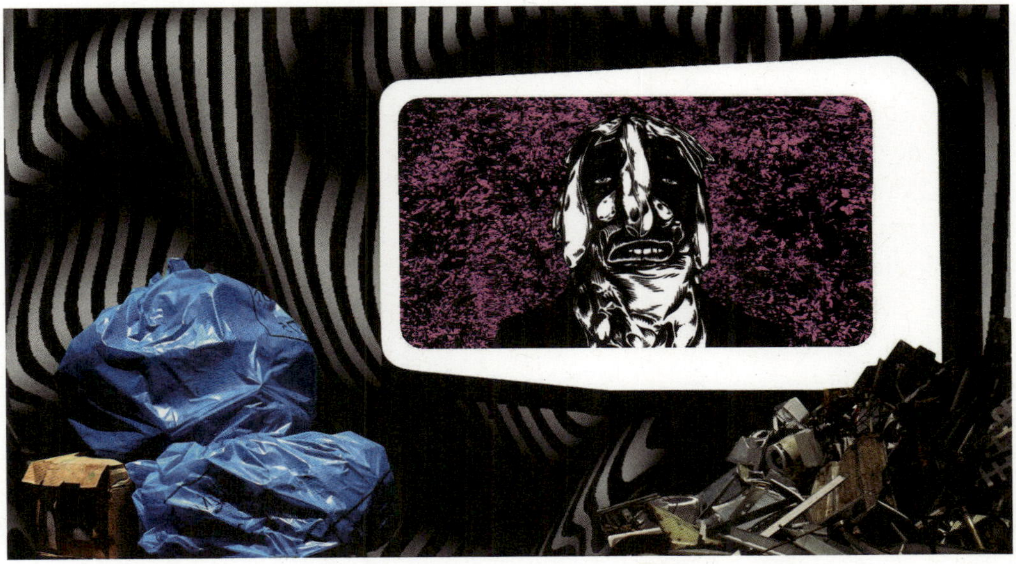

p.60: Ian Watson, *Narrator – The Path*, ink on paper, 2020
above: Ian Watson, *The Path*, digital video (stills), 2020

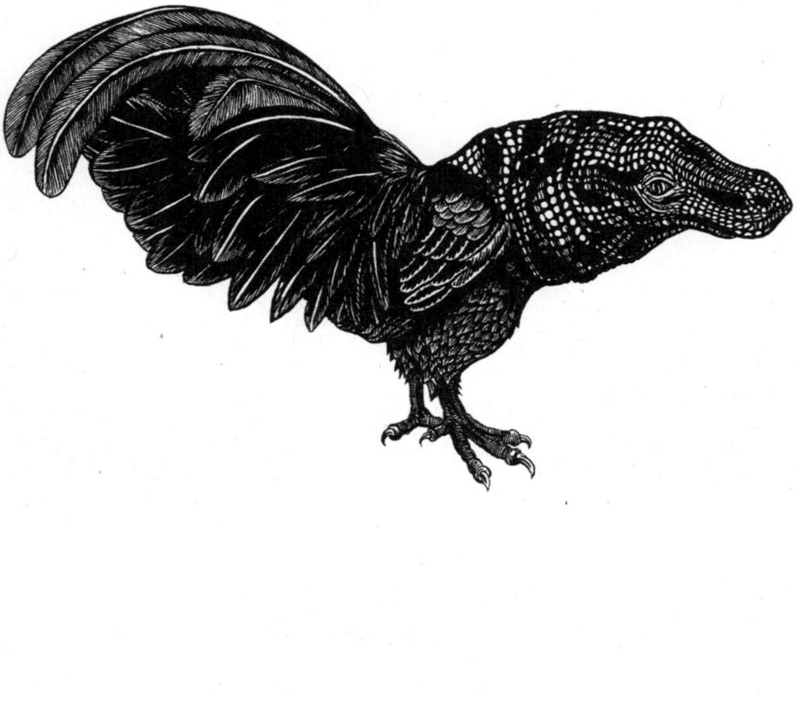

Ian Watson, *Chimera – from Pylons & Spires*, ink on paper, 2019

muster',[8] *The Path*'s narrator enjoins – acknowledging the artifice of performing humanity. The work seems to reject the transhumanist philosophy of seeing technology as a tool to extend and improve human life and functionality. The implications of technology in Watson's work only move us away from the human subject, undermining distinctions between human, animal and technological in the process. Watson's characters are non-human, inhabiting worlds not purely biological. These mutant narrators draw us out of an egocentric Western humanism, which is to understand the world around us from our own vantage point alone. Cultural theorist Donna Haraway proposed the cyborg as an ambivalent metaphor for contemporary human life, where our porous bodies are open to all manner of technological modification and interference.[9] Watson takes us further down the same path, beyond a body that is readily human at all. These non-human ciphers allude to signs of life going on around us, beyond our knowledge and perception. *The Path* is a woozy site in which to find new relations. Does *The Path* bring clarity? No, that's a human concept.

7 July 2020

1 You could listen along to Gary Numan's 1982 track of the same name while reading, if you like.
2 Wayne C Booth, *The Rhetoric of Fiction*, University of Chicago Press, 1983.
3 Ian Watson, *The Path*, 2020.
4 *Ibid.*
5 Samuel Beckett, extract from *Molloy* (1951), *Paris Review*, issue 5, spring 1954, https://www.theparisreview.org/fiction/5116/from-molloy-samuel-beckett.
6 *Superfreight*, ArcadeCampfa, 2020.
7 Email correspondence with the artist, Tuesday 9 June 2020.
8 Ian Watson, *The Path*, 2020.
9 Donna Haraway, *Simians, Cyborgs and Women: The Reinvention of Nature*, Routledge, 1991.

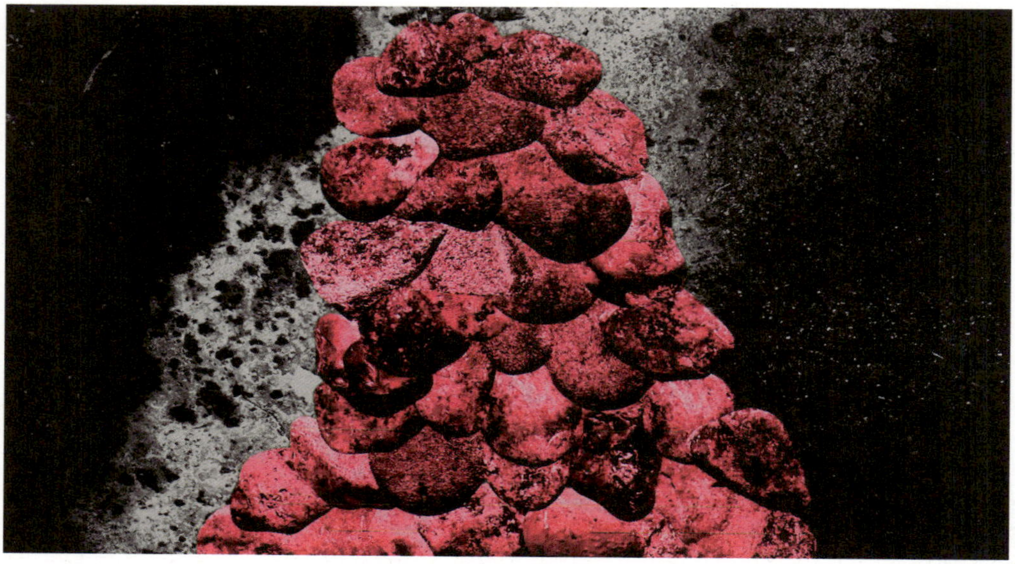

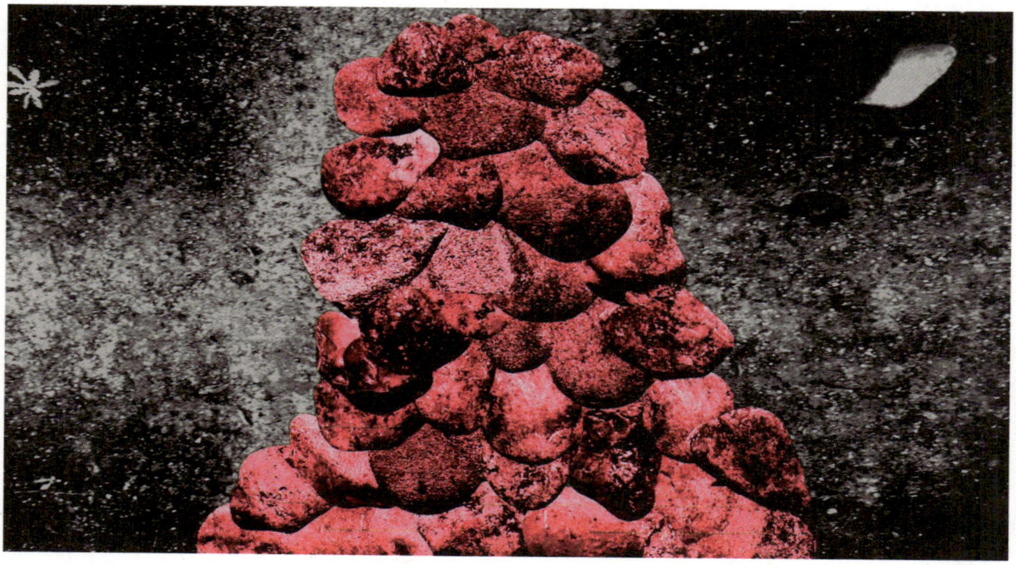

above: Ian Watson, *The Path*, digital video (stills), 2020
opposite: Ian Watson, *Narrator – from Pylons & Spires*, ink on paper, 2019

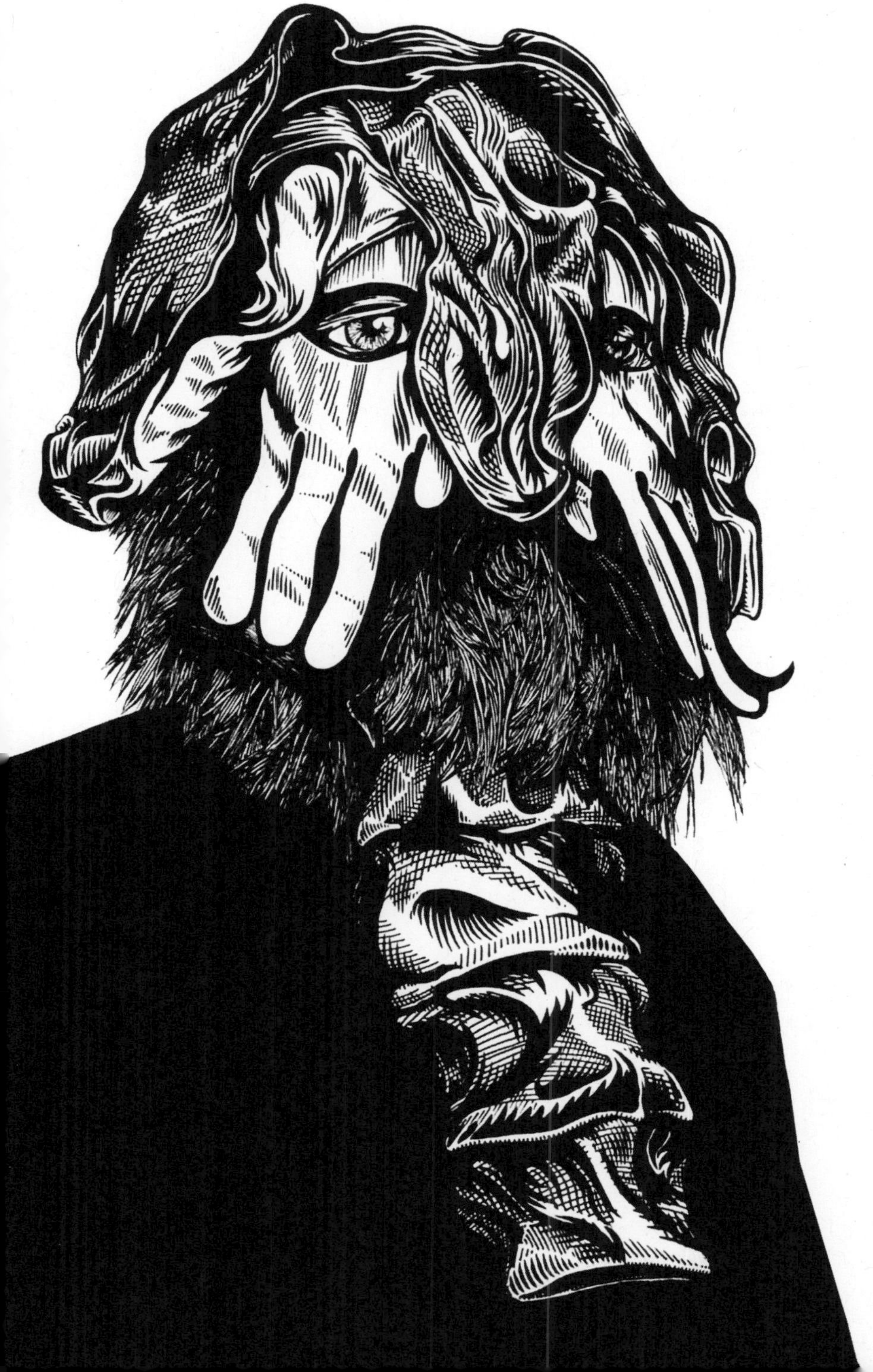

Return Journey
Natalie Ann Holborow

I'm not here, not now, but dividing myself
        with tectonic ease, my split reflection
signalling one desperate wave to the planets,
the other hand shaping my home,
        its neat wooden pier, salt-whistle, thick
snowfall of gulls on the track

it's frightening to learn how much sea
        the mind can yearn for, how many rolls
of sheer blue, weeds netting the waves
tightly, the sunlight harsh.
        You can see the lines of age on both
our faces and our eyes are swept open,

the hair lifting a faint swell across the brow,
        creased, reflecting. There
are words for this: an after-image bleeding
inkily into our shirt-sleeves,
        the lines of which stack themselves
into simple angles, a child's drawing of a house

or is it a new alphabet, the tongue lapsing
        awkwardly over sounds we can't
evoke? Old frost cribbing our tracks.
There are ways to return:
        the bridge with all its ropes
clattered out, thin-legged estuary warblers

and we're getting closer, arriving, not like
        the strangers we have been but easing back,
startlingly young until we're driving
through memory, pointing out these things:
        green-bowled valley, stumbling hill,
daffodils scorching the roadsides.

PS²

Belfast, Northern Ireland

Janie Doherty

Michael Hanna

Julie Lovett

Jan McCullough

Emily McFarland

PS²: An Introduction

PS² (= Paragon Studios + Project Space) is an artist-led organisation based in Belfast. Paragon Studios started in 1993 as an initiative by artists looking for affordable workspace after completing their MA course. The formally structured organisation was established by the group in a collective attempt to self-organise their own professional and artistic development.

Project Space was initiated in 2004 in a former shop on the same premises as the studios. It started in a playful way as a work- and show-room for invited artists and other creatives that was open to anyone passing by – much more a public visual rehearsal studio connected to the street than a 'gallery'. Not at ease with the exclusiveness of an indoor art space, Project Space soon extended beyond the shop space, undertaking interventions in public sites and engaging projects in temporary premises, shops, containers or caravans in and around Belfast.

Despite being forced to move premises regularly in recent years due to the pressures of city centre regeneration, PS² has grown up and become more professional and experienced. Though it remains stubbornly committed to an artist-centred ethos and a grassroots approach, it is furiously curious about art and creativity and is ambitious to fulfil and explore its two main functions: as a studio resource and network provider that facilitates affordable working space for 11 artists (at present) and a curator-in-residence scheme for emerging curators; and as an organiser and initiator of an engaged and year-round arts programme in its Project Space and / or in outside locations and neighbourhoods. Project Space has a fast turnaround of many diverse projects, reflecting a broad understanding of visual culture. The indoor projects offer an open, temporary workspace and showroom for invited or selected project artists, facilitating encounters for the general public to see, enjoy and participate in art in fresh and experimental ways. The outdoor projects, some of which are long-term, explore different forms of participation and co-production. This tandem approach underlies PS²'s core aim to connect contemporary art with society in a socially inclusive way and to a high artistic standard.

The Freelands Artist Programme dropped from the moon and landed in our open arms. Since then we have worked and played with it, together with the artists, on a pitch which isn't always 'ideal' and with hardly any seating for spectators. Art is played here on rough ground, but it will get better and as a consequence, so will we.

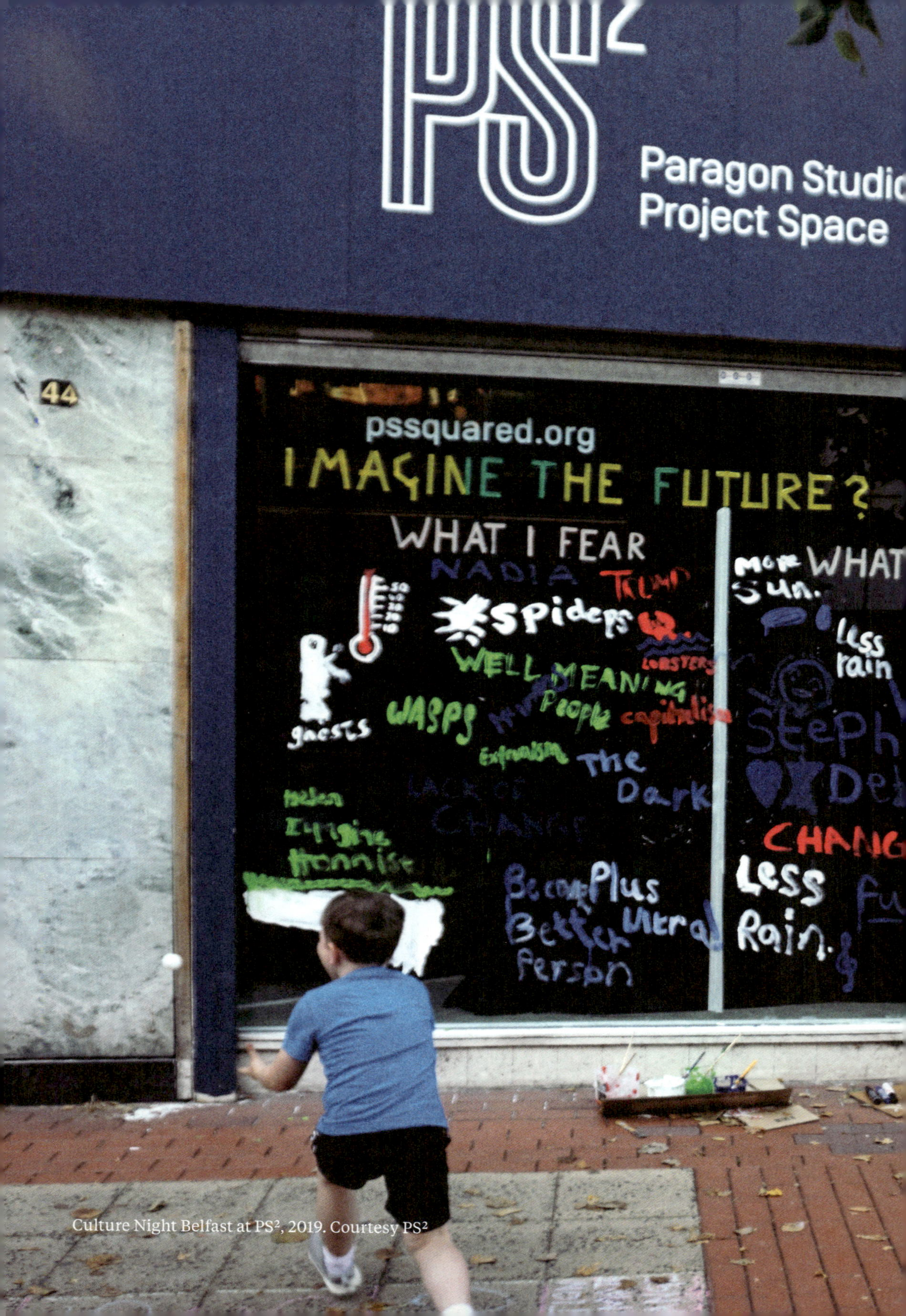

Culture Night Belfast at PS², 2019. Courtesy PS²

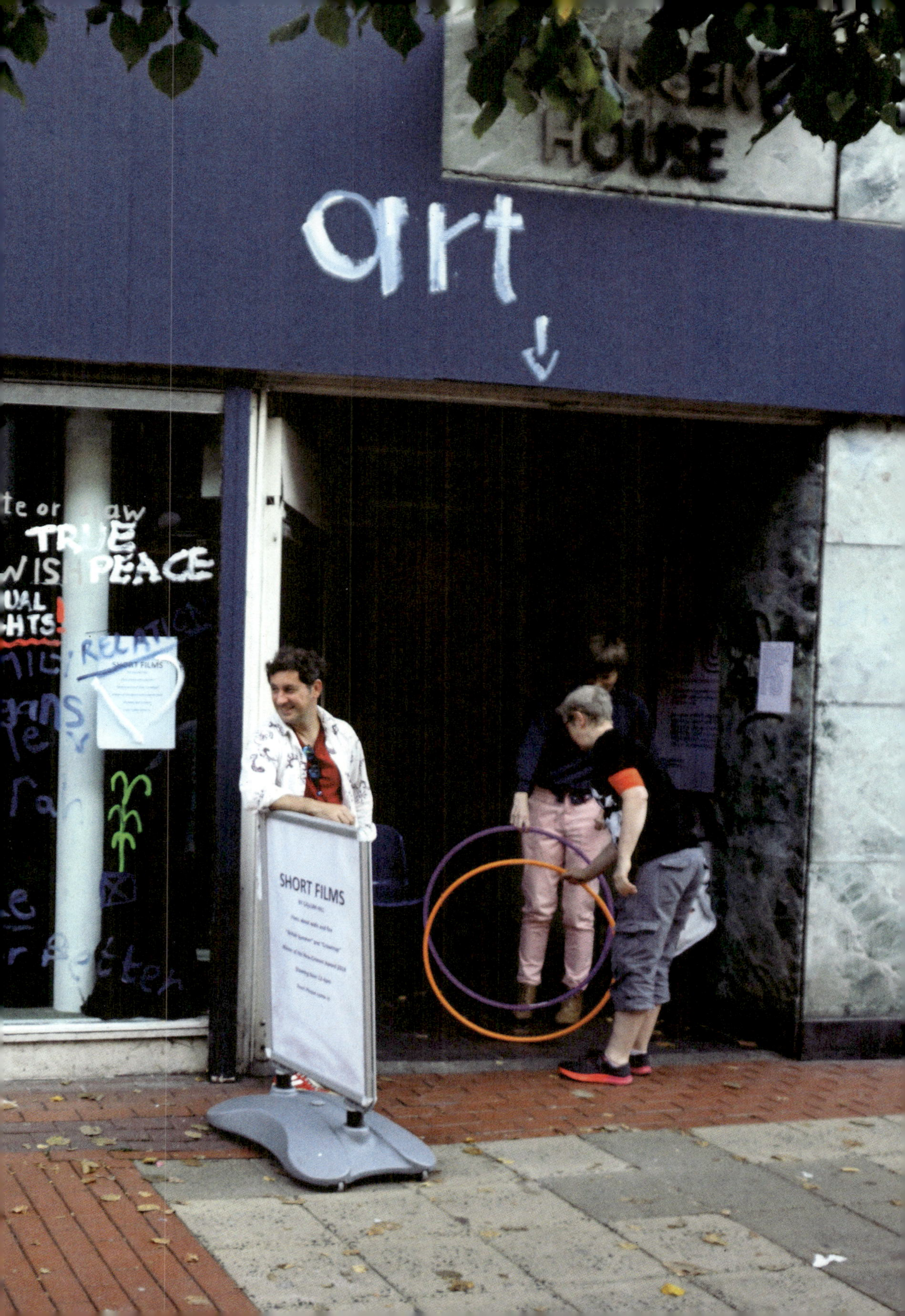
HOUSE
art
TRUE
PEACE
SHORT FILMS

PS² has appointed a curator in a part-time role who is dedicated to supporting the professional and creative development of the artists selected for the programme. This curatorial position takes a similar format to that of the artist cohort, as it will last for two years and will be rotated in order to maintain momentum and to increase opportunities for curators based in Northern Ireland.

The programme is tailored towards each individual artist's needs and aims to respond to their personal artistic and professional growth and to nurture any arising demands. As the scheme runs for five years, it allows the organisation to learn, to translate the experience into other projects and – hopefully – to mould and improve the wider arts ecology in Northern Ireland.

Alissa Kleist, Curator

It is the end of August 2020 and in four months I will conclude my term as PS²'s first Freelands Artist Programme project curator. Like our cohort artists, my two-year post was always designed to be time-limited. Since September 2018, I have accompanied our inaugural group of five (and later our second cohort of six) artists on their unique creative and developmental projects. There is something special about being the programme's firstborns. From making the initial inquiries and excursions to trying things out, we have been taking the first steps and setting the / a pace. We have been bolstered by the fact that these are collective firsts, shared by and with the other artists on the programme, the other partner organisations, and the Freelands Foundation too.

Like the artists, I am starting to reminisce, whilst simultaneously working on laying the groundwork for the next curator – and for the next cohort, to join us – as we are the first 'graduates' and prospective alumni of the Freelands Artist Programme's extended community. Our open call for artists to participate in the 2021–22 cohort is currently live, and the new project curator will soon be interviewed, selected and announced.

Despite the huge uncertainty caused by the COVID-19 pandemic, our artists are continuing to develop and finish their projects, which have had to adjust and shift to accommodate restricted and alternative ways of working. At times this situation has been lamented, at other times embraced, but always with the astounding levels of resilience possessed by artists, an attribute that is, sadly, compulsory in a sector where precarity and change are the order of the day.

Forced into exclusively online interactions during the lockdown, we have met virtually on a weekly basis since late April 2020. This new routine has had silver linings, fostering a closer group bond and subsequent new cross-cohort collaborations and connections that I trust will survive beyond December 2020, the end date of the programme for the first cohort and myself.

We all recently attempted a 'real-life' meeting – a catered picnic at a beach just outside the city. It was a fun activity for those who were able to attend. Others had to retreat into temporary self-isolation due to potential COVID-19 exposure, or were subjected to increased workloads as a result of shifting and postponed timelines, and so had to sit this one out. Going forward, this situation is perhaps characteristic of the new 'normal' we should perhaps expect (though I really hope that this part of the text, read a few years from now, will seem quaintly '2020').

There is an urgent need for us all to connect, as professionals and individuals. To be together, and to exchange information, gossip, tips, opinions, progress. The Freelands Artist Programme has augmented the most pleasurable elements of my profession: spending time with artists, and listening to and discussing their ideas. To coexist, momentarily, in a space where the air is thick with potential and unrealised possibility, and to support them in making things real. The programme has created an environment in which listening, trust, empathy, collectivity and solidarity are the modus operandi and driving force. What I have learned is that as well as financial support, what artists need most is what this programme offers: to be, and feel, valued.

Janie Doherty

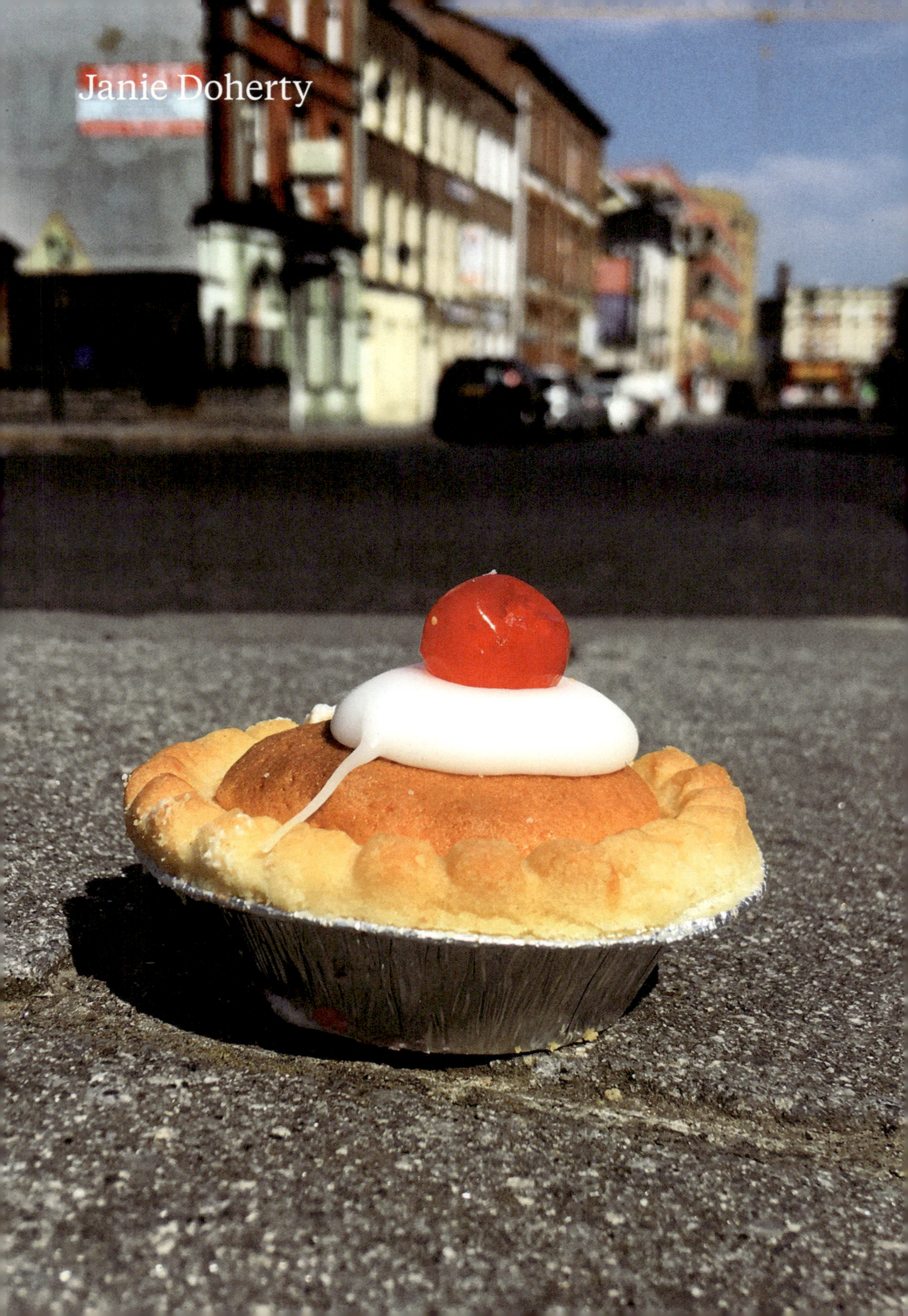

A Cherry, an Egg, Some Thighs

A bun a day keeps the blues at bay, so they say. Derry folk are mad for buns. And Janie Doherty should know, having worked in a bakery for a time. These buns – sticky, confected, larded – are a comfort as much as they are an indulgence, indivisible from the history and politics of the city. If bread be the stuff of life, then buns help sugar the pill. Slow down, take a pause. Exhale – maybe close your eyes. A moment on the lips. Doherty brings us here, if only for a short while.

Derry was deeply affected by the Troubles, as the site of Bloody Sunday.[1] Having grown up in Derry, Doherty feels the after-effects 'in the stonework of the city'[2] today. Trained as a dancer, her artistic practice mines the choreography of the everyday to unearth the somatic – how 'the body keeps the score';[3] that is, how the body expresses the mind, willingly and unconsciously. Where psychiatrist and author Bessel van der Kolks's landmark study explores how trauma is passed down through the body, Doherty's practice, through cathartic aesthetic experience, also works towards healing.

The symbolic daily ritual of going for a bun is the departure point for *The politics of comfort* (2018–). The work takes this simple act, small moments, turns of phrase, and builds a picture of resilience that has softness as its base. Hers is an act of listening, of observing, of empathising with the women at the bakeries serving the buns. We see beneath the surface of this brief daily event, often from the perspective of those who have lived through the Troubles. Doherty soundscapes their voices. Her camera moves through faces, hands, dough. A cherry, an egg, some thighs. It is a landscape of bodies, built on soft flesh and sugar. But in those bodies reside traumas which are not always evident.

Witty, and warm, these women serve the buns to customers, but they also console. Overtly or not. The work's vernacular is pure Derry: the craic and the sugared cream, the dark humour. The tone is bittersweet. You go to the bakery on a cold wet morning to stand in the warm, have a laugh, get served something familiar and delicious. 'There's no fanciness about buns here, you know. It's a comfort thing.'[4] Perhaps a kind of armour for the day ahead. But it is a fleeting balm. Coded social interactions such as these, where the bun is the stage, amount to a kind of transaction of care. This is historically – lamentably – a feminised, unpaid labour, built around empathy. The women's displays of strength are both performed and real, almost matriarchal. The performance – put a good face on and get out there – meets the real: don't cry because you'll not stop. Doherty's work is careful to honour these voices. What might they say now, in the post-conflict present?

This work is no documentary; point the camera and observe. Doherty speaks for and with these women and their communities. How? A strategy of empathy, starting from embodiment. She'll welcome you in, like she did at her performance at Centre for Contemporary Art (CCA), Derry~Londonderry. Come in and sit down. Are you comfortable? It's important to her that it's informal, familiar. Doherty's spoken performance oscillates between herself and the women from the bakery, inhabiting rather than acting. She is a Derry woman herself remember. Might some self-identification be taking place?

Doherty's work to sustain her art practice – dance facilitation, massages for elderly people – is an extension of her practice of empathy. Yet she understands the need for discomfort and catharsis too. Take her role with *Lady Magma* (2019–).[5] Five female dancers collaborate on an immersive visceral piece of dance theatre. The work is about female pleasure, pain and ancestral lineage; the body as gateway to the mind. The atmosphere is charged, heightened. You're up close to the dancers. They emit primal screams, drop to the floor. Embrace. Each dancer lets go, kills things off. Each woman's type of release distinct. They allow the audience to do the same through aesthetic experience. Might Doherty's *The politics of comfort* be operating in the same way? The soft close-ups of dough, the sensuality of skin, the sweetness of cherry, the humour. Whether visceral or seductive, we get to the same place – empathy, and ultimately, catharsis. Doherty wants others to feel comfortable, but also to heal – to do that is painful. The odd bun or two along the way might help.

29 May 2020

1 Also known as the Bogside Massacre, on 30 January 1972, 26 unarmed civilians were shot by British Army paratroopers during protests against Operation Demetrius, a policy of internment that saw 342 civilians arrested and imprisoned without trial.

2 In conversation with the author, Thursday 22 November 2018.

3 Bessel van der Kolk, *The Body Keeps the Score: Mind, Brain and Body in the Transformation of Trauma*, Penguin, 2015.

4 Janie Doherty, *The politics of comfort*, video, 2019.

5 *Lady Magma* is a performance event choregraphed and directed by Oona Doherty.

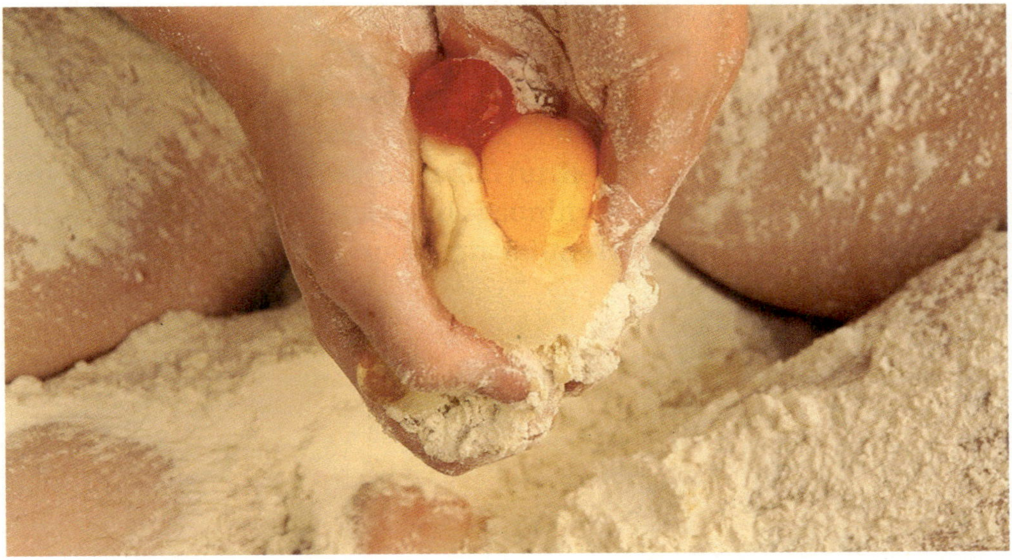

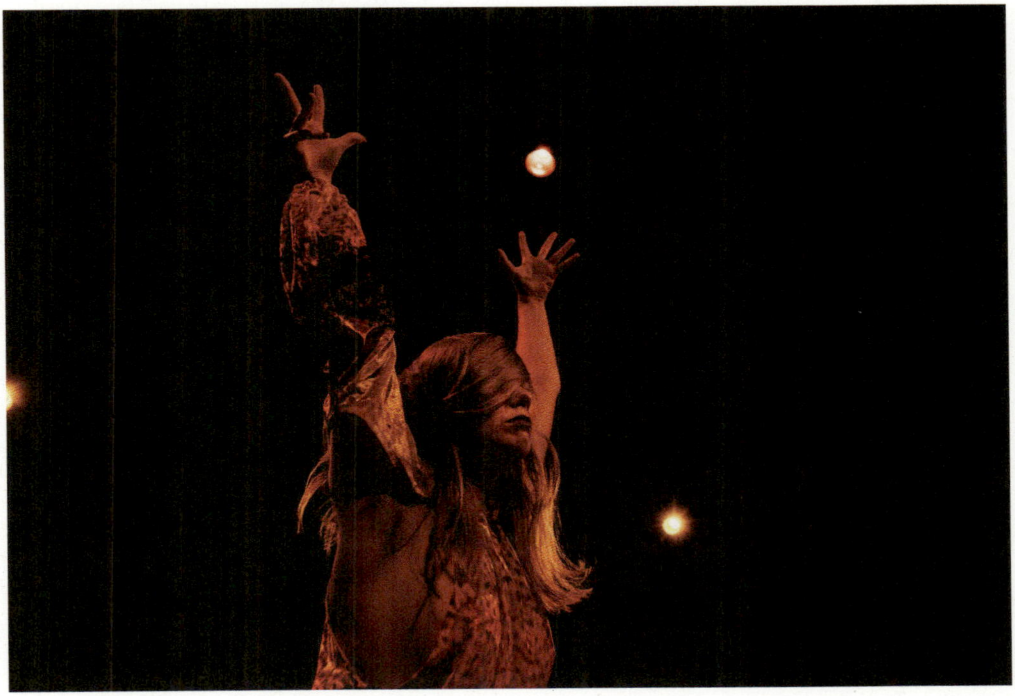

p.84: Janie Doherty, *The politics of comfort*, 2018. Photo: Alessandra Celesia
top: Janie Doherty, *The politics of comfort* (still), 2018. Photo: Aphra Lee Hill
bottom: Janie Doherty in *Lady Magma*, directed and choreographed by Oona Doherty, 2019. Photo: Luca Truffarelli
overleaf: Janie Doherty, *Bend in the River*, 2020. Photo: Locky Morris

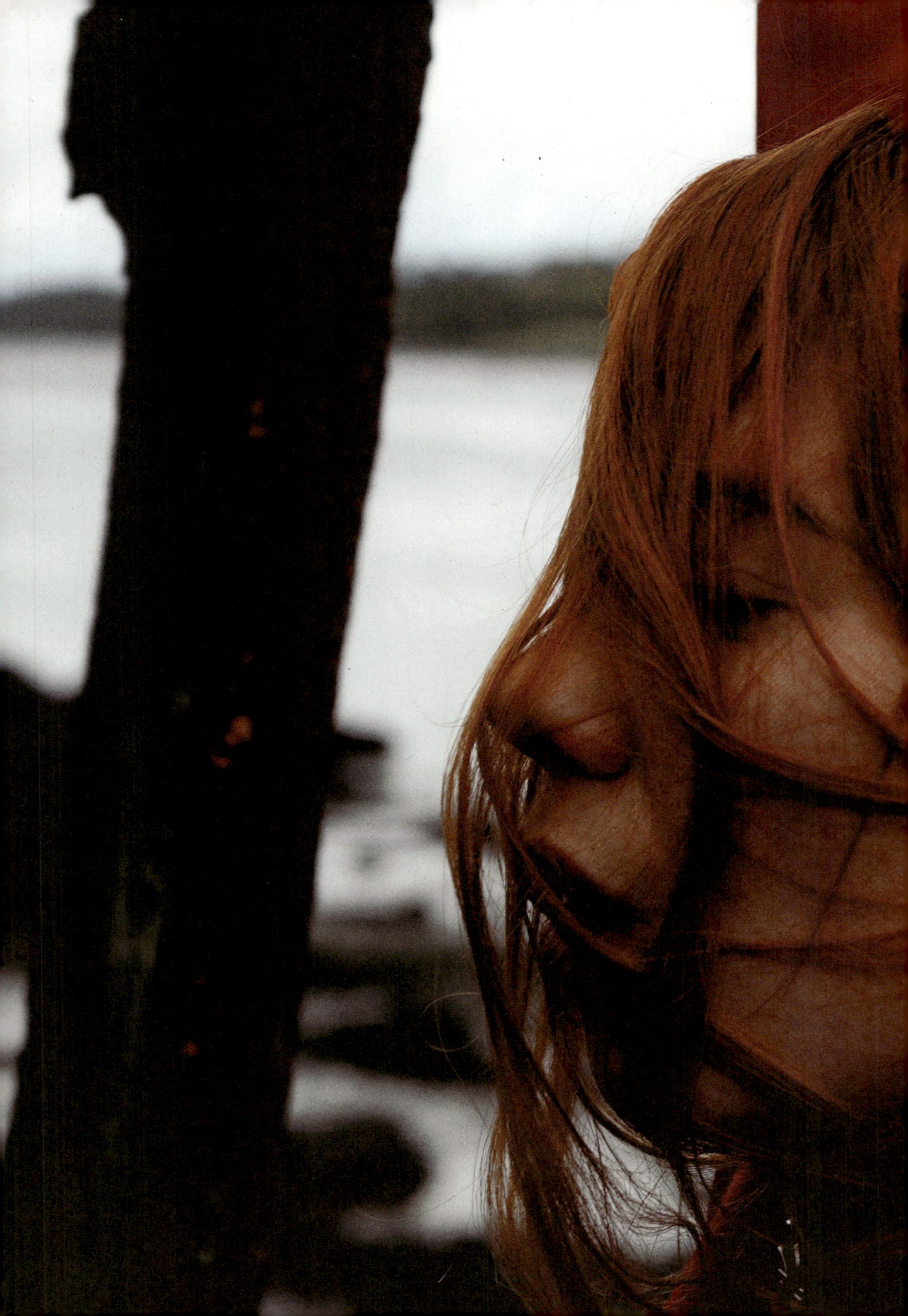

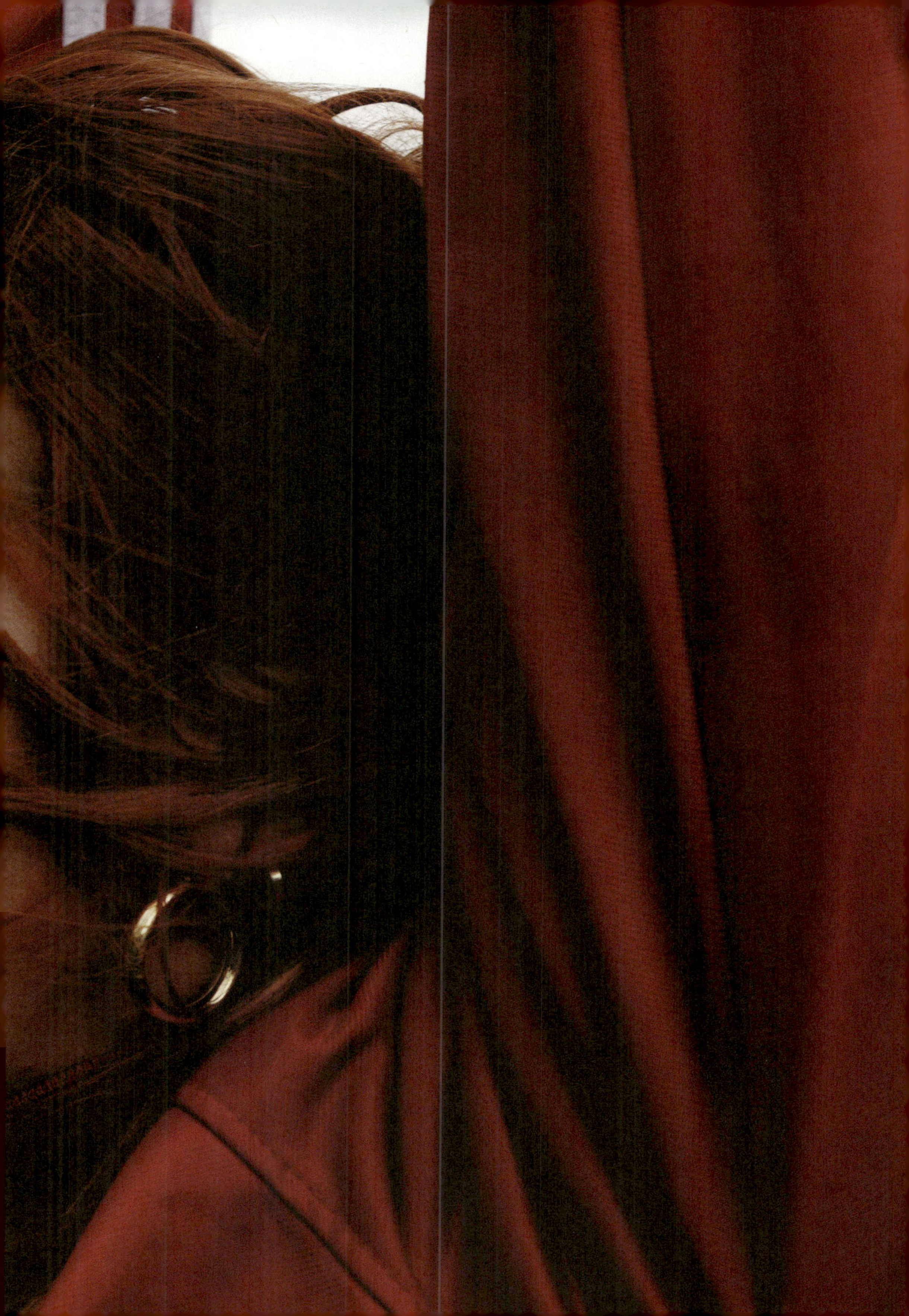

My name is Janie Doherty. I am an artist from Derry and now I live in Belfast where it is a bit more grey and industrial.

Here is some insider info you might not know and things that are swirling around for me at the moment.

Growing up post-Troubles, I was very aware that very bad things happened, and my family did a good job of explaining it all without being too one-sided, I think? When I came along, I had missed it, although it hung in the air like a bad smell.

My granny Annie Doherty was a tea leaf reader from the Bogside. She was quite famous locally and looked after the catalogues and helped people get what they needed. She held space for a lot of people there during the 1970s. My aunt Maureen brought up eight children and lost two sons to the Troubles. Her house was always immaculate, even the Imperial Leather soap never had any suds on it. I wonder if she used to clean the soap after each use to keep it looking so perfect? My mother was diagnosed with schizophrenia, although you would never know. She is reliant on pharmaceuticals to keep everything level, and she is the wisest and sweetest woman you could ever meet.

I grew up among women holding it together – putting on brave faces, looking glamorous, and hosting dinner parties. It is a beautiful quality that I have inherited, and I am great at it. However I am realising that if you keep holding shit together too much, you'll eventually get bowel cancer or become unwell; 'When the Body Says No', as physician Gabor Maté says.[1]

I have always danced and love being expressive in all ways. After graduating with a BA Hons in Dance at University of Ulster, I joined Echo Echo Dance Theatre Company as an ensemble member for six years and created work, taught on the outreach programme and was trained in a deep, authentic way of improvisation, coined 'poetic movement' by artistic director Steve Batts. These were my most informative years gaining knowledge of how movement is read on stage, through instantaneous composition and the detail of performance. Through my experience of facilitating dance in a variety of halls, rooms and other places, I have built up an acute awareness of how to guide groups in an artistic way, dancing through life with thousands of people of different ages. I believe that we all just want to be understood and loved for who we are.

I also worked in a bakery for a few years and fell deep into the bakery oven of robust life advice, community gossip, banter as a skill and the warmth of Derry women. My home town, my beautiful home place of Derry, where the fastest river in Europe flows through – which is closely linked to an extremely high number of suicides from mostly young men who have lost hope. The place is absolutely drenched in historical and political history and the people keep their spirits up to keep going. The charm and wit are so dry that outsiders often feel they can't enter into the humour.

I am interested in intertwining my personal life experience with my art in a deeply authentic and realistic way; in creating empathetic resonance in the audience, in storytelling and sitting around a table airing out problems with friends to detangle them in your own mind. A cup of tea is right for all occasions, big and small. I believe our lineage is carried in our bodies. We have embodied our ancestors and intergenerational trauma is passed down through us. It's there in the 12-year-olds building the bonfires with the same pride and shit they've carried on for their Das.

There is no separation for me between who I am at home and who I am on stage. Everything drips out anyway. I can choose to hide it or I can choose to become empowered by the vulnerabilities and strengths that are there. I am attempting to do justice to all the women who have held anything together, at any time of their life. It is local and universal; we all understand that as we all came out of a vagina. Can I create an environment where people feel like they can be settled in their own skin?

I qualified as a sports masseuse to wring out the flesh in others, to help shift pain, old emotional war wounds and sadness. To help others feel light. I believe our issues are in our tissues and I enjoy wringing it out because we definitely don't need the amount of shit we are constantly carrying, the shit that is weighing us down. It is a life practice. I am attempting to move towards pleasure and joy in all that I do.

Janie Doherty

1 Gabor Maté, 'When the Body Says No – Caring for Ourselves While Caring for Others', YouTube video, 6 March 2013, https://www.youtube.com/watch?v=c6IL8WVyMMs.

Michael Hanna

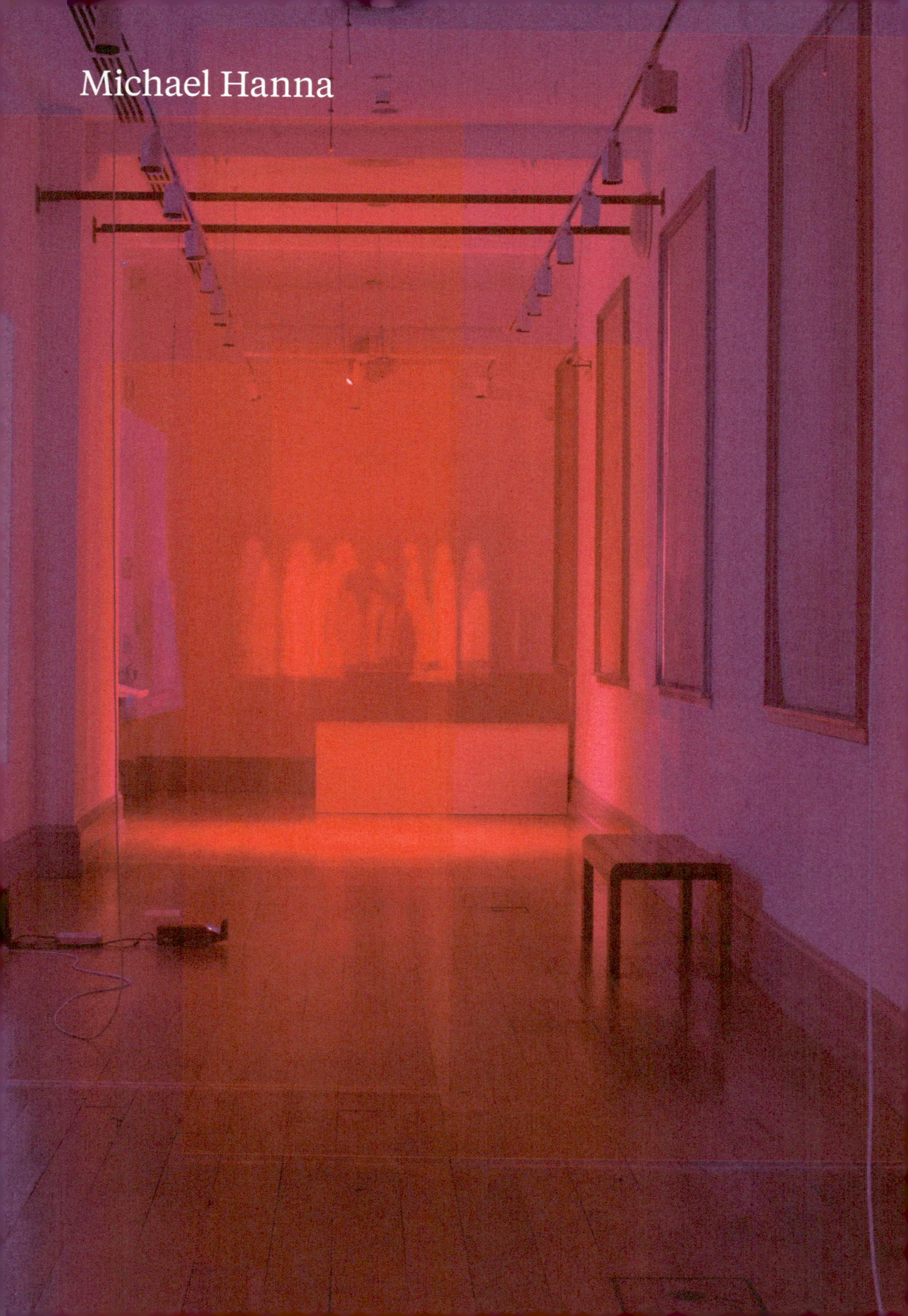

Plus or Minus Two

Michael Hanna operates at the edges of our conscious minds, laying out new pathways of affective experience. His work takes many forms, from text-based sculpture, to video and immersive environments with site-specific and responsive installations. He factors in disruptions to our ways of seeing and processing information, to how things operate – a spanner in the works. Glitches, occlusions, hypervisibility, overstimulation, dissociation, temporal slippages – to what end? Hanna teases out new lines of relation between sensory experience, psychology and society. His work sets in motion open questions about how our behaviour can be altered at micro and macro levels; how we make sense of the world.

Drawing on scientific methodologies of classification, Hanna's *Predictable Contact* (2017), which was shown at Naughton Gallery, Belfast, is a multi-channel video installation bathed in a synthetic magenta twilight. Thirty-two microfilms[1] focusing on optical perception are projected on to the wall at a scale that stretches beyond scientific testing standards. The uniform magenta hue – a colour Hanna drew on from the space itself and amplified sensorially – dissolves further the optical distinctions between each microfilm. It is generally accepted scientifically that the human brain can only store around seven items in its short-term memory, plus or minus two.[2] The eye therefore cannot take in all 32 microfilms at once, so focus waxes and wanes. And we can retain only a fraction of what we see. The work puts forth an affective sensory experience to test the limits of the visible and the perceptible in any given moment.

In Hanna's current project, *A Living Colour Index* (2020), he turns the experiment in on himself, while continuing his exploration of how colouration impacts cognition. The work is site-responsive in the most immediate way – a reaction to the lockdown directive to stay home brought about by the COVID-19 pandemic. An online project conceived with MAC (Metropolitan Arts Centre) in Belfast, over the course of seven weeks Hanna lights his home with a different colour each week, moving through the colour spectrum from red to violet. The project takes the scientific standard of controlled environmental conditions – his home – and refracts them through an acutely personal lens. Hanna posts a photograph of his home environment to the MAC Instagram account each day, and pairs it with a selected quotation taken from literature, colour theory, science fiction, the arts and philosophy – each quote broadly related to space, perception, time and memory. With routines, work, and life in general significantly disrupted, what does it mean to experience so much undifferentiated time at home? The logic of switching colours each week is to factor in some variance. As writer Joshua Foer has noted: 'Monotony collapses time; novelty unfolds it. [...] Creating new memories stretches out psychological time, and lengthens our perception of our lives.'[3] Hanna's project tests out these statements in real time, a 49-day durational performance-cum-experiment.

The project is developing a diaristic quality. Images so far range from a yellow-hued bedroom-turned-office, to an orange-tinged photograph on the wall, to a Mac computer clock, the dust-covered screen pixelated in a green hue. The steady accretion of images recalls filmmaker Chantal Akerman's early experimental work *La Chambre* (1972). In this silent, ten-minute film, shot in a single take, a constantly rotating camera unfolds a 360-degree view of a small room and the things it contains. Each completed rotation is its own chime of the clock, as it is with the passing colours of Hanna's *A Living Colour Index*. With both pieces, suggestions of artistic subjectivity emerge through the fixed formal properties of the work's construction. For Hanna, what informs the image choice each day? Does colouration preordain composition? And if so, does this aesthetic dimension belie a psychological state? Looking retrospectively at the project, I wonder if we might ascertain how each colour affected Hanna's rest, work, sleep and mood. Would a spate of blue-tinged photographs of screens connote the colour's capacity to aid focus, or to induce restlessness? Through this voyeuristic, indexical window into Hanna's lived experience, the present becomes cloudy – yellow's residual trace in orange's now – evoking philosopher and critic Roland Barthes's conception of the photograph as 'that-has-been', a 'superimposition [...] of reality and of the past'.[4]

Hanna's recent exhibition *Looking Backward* (2019) at PS² in Belfast was drawn to this same temporal collapse, envisioning the promised futures of utopia through a historical text. The exhibition draws its title from Edward Bellamy's 1888 novel of the same name, then a bestseller and since largely forgotten. Written at a time of significant wealth disparity and socio-economic turmoil, its utopian premise sees the narrator awaken in the year 2000, fresh from a 100 year-long sleep, into a promised new land where wealth is evenly distributed, social justice is the rule not the exception, and banks, money and political parties are obsolete. Hanna is drawn to the social,

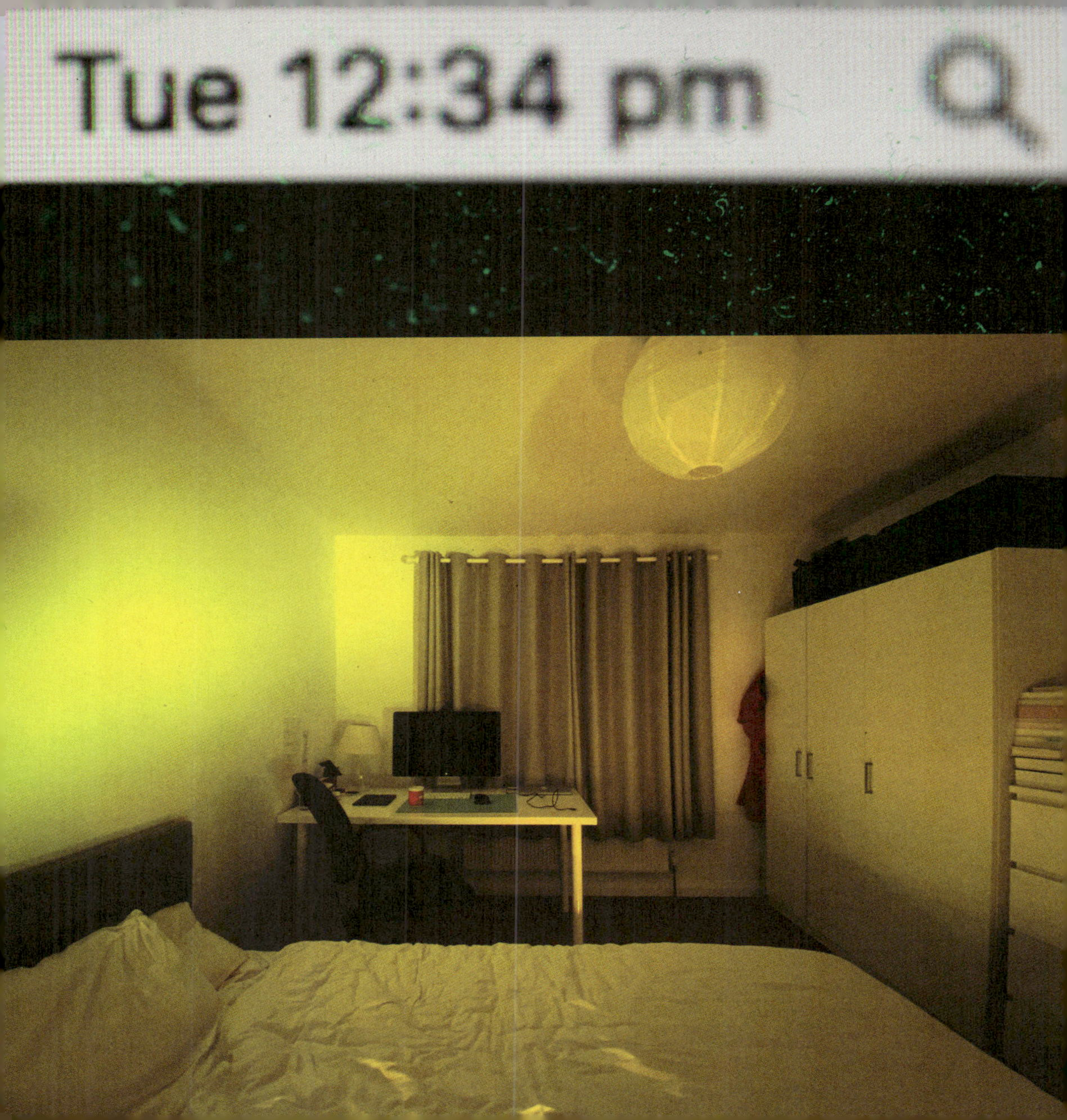
Tue 12:34 pm

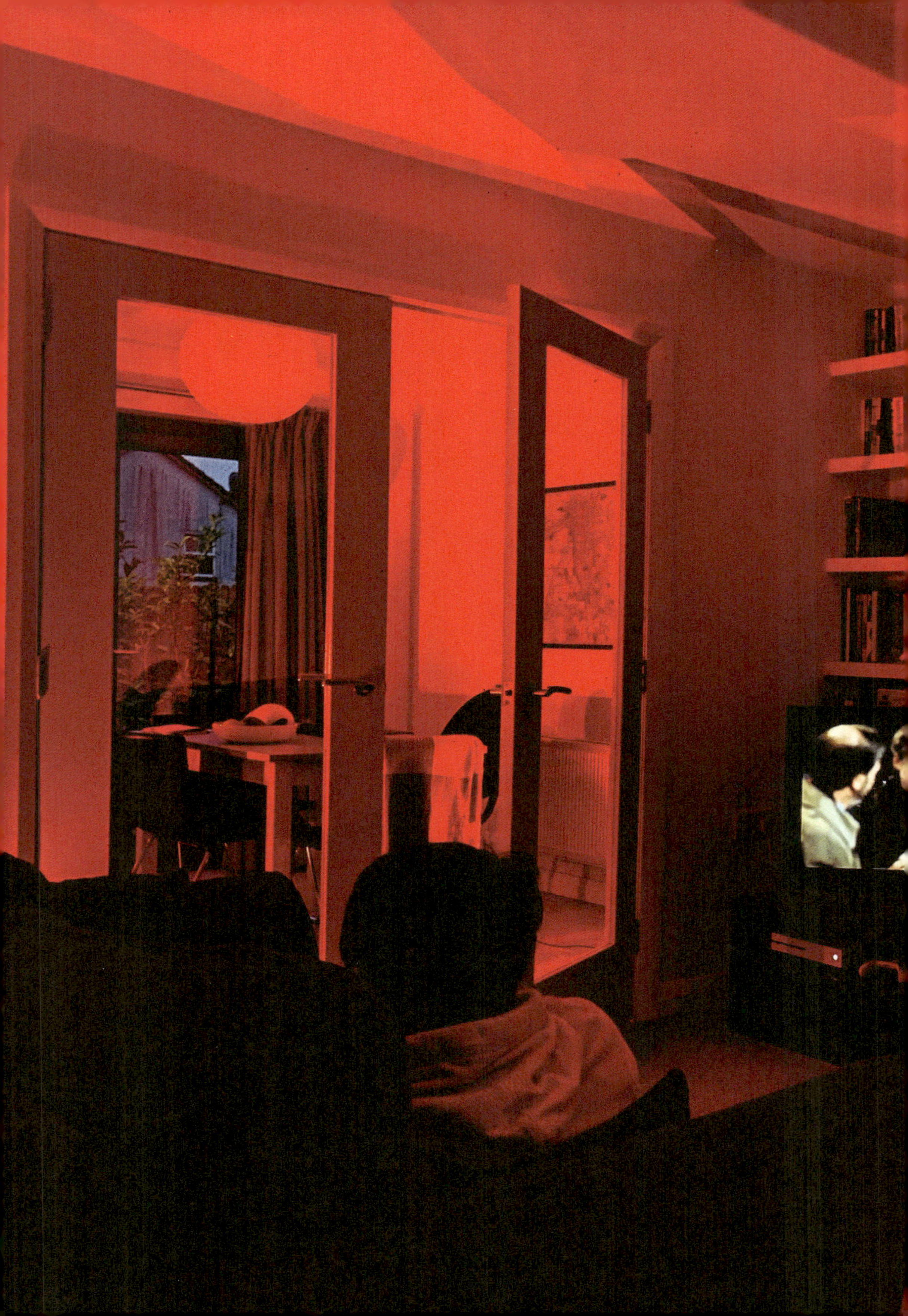

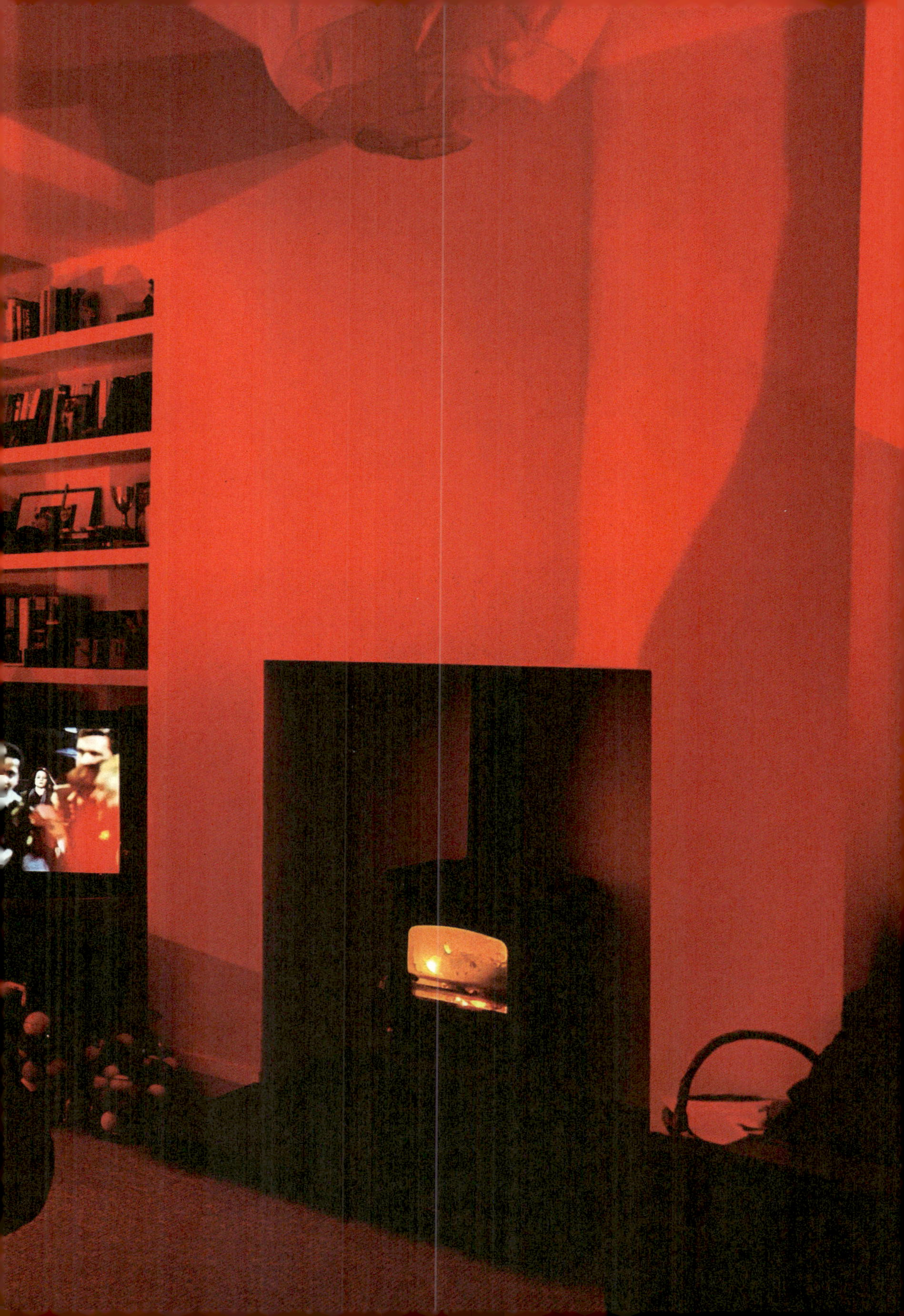

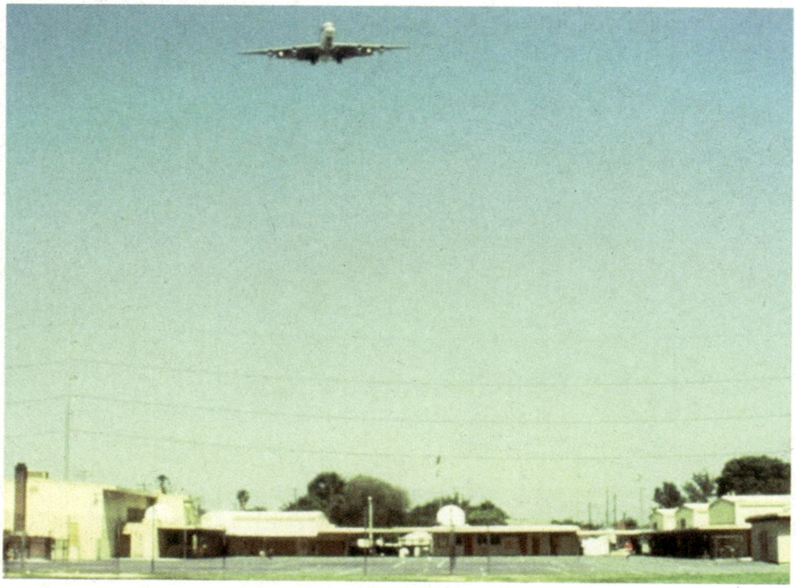

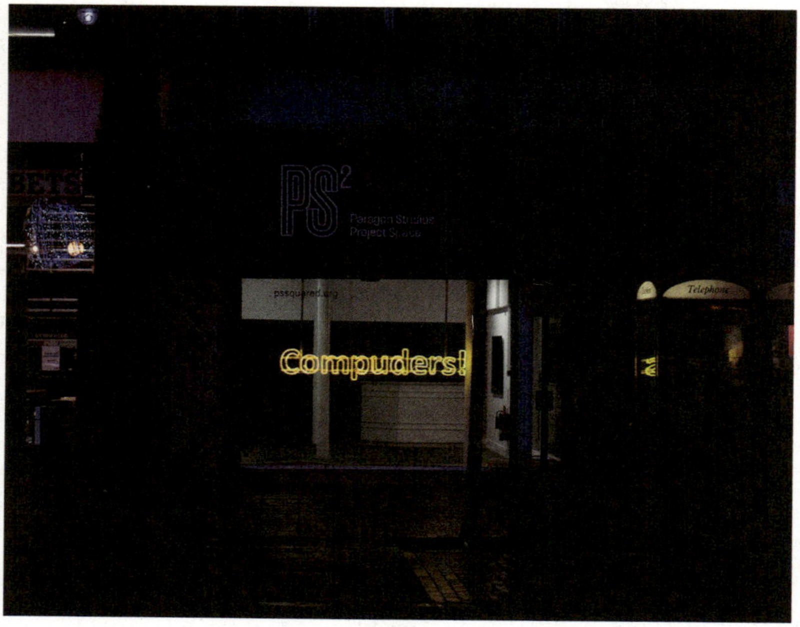

p.92: Michael Hanna, *Predictable Contact*, installation view, Naughton Gallery, Belfast, 2017
p.95 top: Michael Hanna, *A Living Colour Index (Green Tuesday)*, 2020
p.95 bottom: Michael Hanna, *A Living Colour Index (Yellow Saturday)*, 2020
pp.96–97: Michael Hanna, *A Living Colour Index (Red Wednesday)*, 2020
top: Michael Hanna, *The Ones Who Walk Away*, 2019. Found image
bottom: Michael Hanna, *Compuders!*, *Looking Backward*, PS², Belfast, 2019

political and imagined architectures of utopian vision, but also to how utopian ideals fail and become outmoded.

Through photography, text, painting and moving image, *Looking Backward* mimics these structures of Bellamy's utopia in its somewhat wistful aesthetic of future's past. A neon text work, *Compuders!* (2019), hangs in the gallery window facing on to the street, a seeming relic of once-newness; the withering language of technological innovation. *The Ones Who Walk Away* (2019), two photographs of aeroplanes flying above a depopulated urban landscape, installed in a deliberately quiet way, evokes another possible fade into obsolescence. We might now wonder: will air travel ever be the same? The short-circuited future of Concorde haunts these images, whose once-bright possibility caught the imagination of artist Wolfgang Tillmans in his 1997 exhibition *I Didn't Inhale* at Chisenhale Gallery, London. Tillmans staged a vision of a world he would like to live in. Concorde was one such emblem. Hanna looks to his own future's-past, too, installing a painting from 2007, *The Diagnostic View IV.* The work directly copies painter Luc Tuymans's *Der Diagnostische Blick IV* (1992), which Hanna had re-made for an application to an anthropological art school in Germany, highlighting other, more personal, avenues that did not come to pass. The future as we think or imagine it never truly arrives, which brings us back around to perception – we can only hold so much in our minds at once.

26 May 2020

1 The artist's term for short individual films or animations.

2 See Wayne Weiten, *Psychology: Themes and Variations*, Wadsworth Publishing, 1989, which references George Miller, 'The Magical Number Seven, Plus or Minus Two: Some Limits on Our Capacity for Processing Information', a paper published in the *Psychological Review* in 1956 that outlines the brain's limited capacity for short-term memory.

3 Joshua Foer, *Moonwalking with Einstein: The Art and Science of Remembering Everything*, Penguin, 2011.

4 Roland Barthes, *Camera Lucida: Reflections on Photography*, trans., Richard Howard, Jonathan Cape Ltd, 1982, p.76.

Julie Lovett

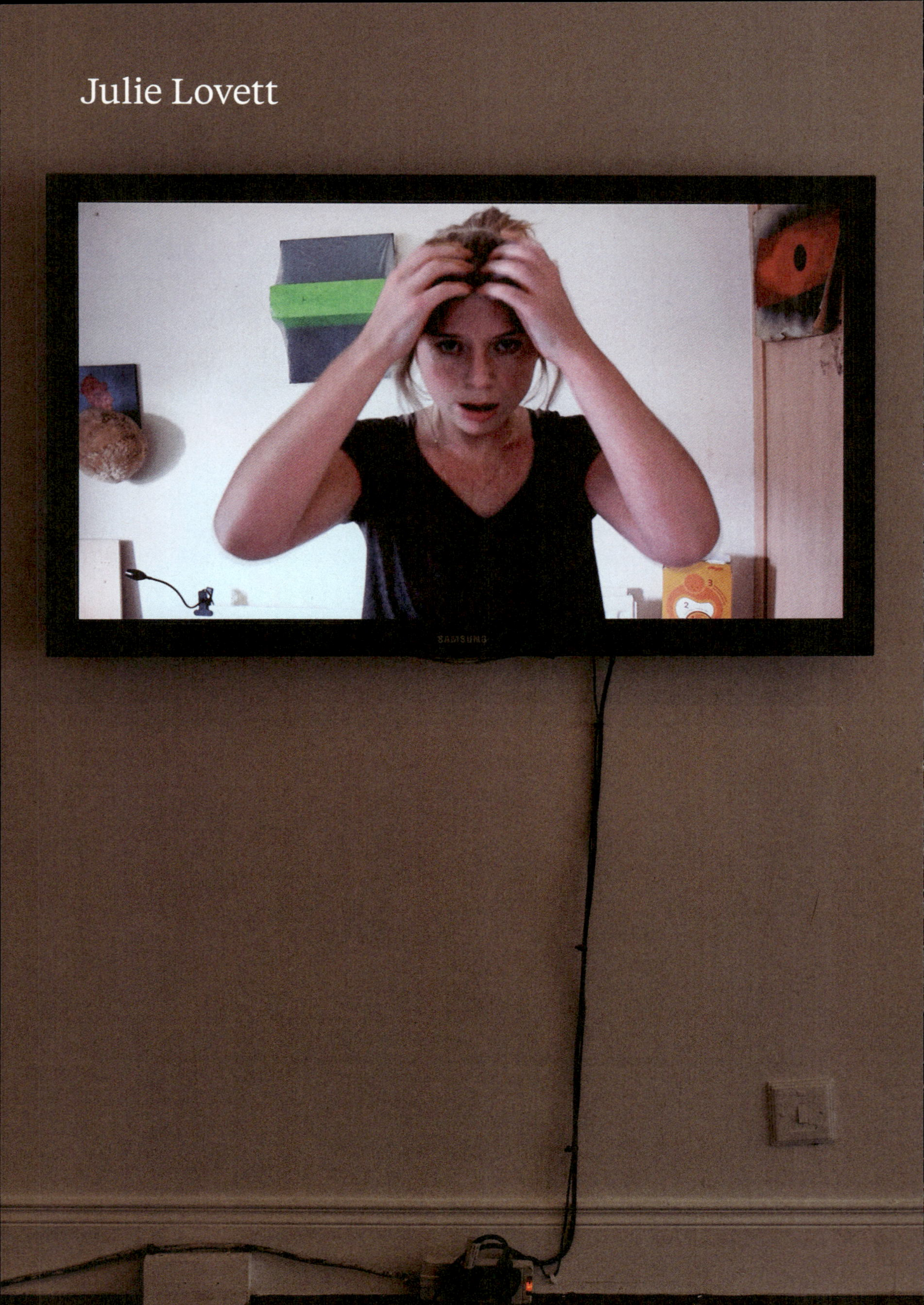

Real Life: A Professional Essay

Truth is, Julie Lovett makes me laugh.

Right off the bat, Julie Lovett wants you to know that Julie Lovett is a professional photographer. 'Hi there, my name is Julie Lovett and I am a professional photographer', she deadpans to camera. Hers is a 'story-based', 'action-based' and 'painterly' practice, working with what's at hand: 'milking clusters and the *plein-air*'.[1] Besides this sharply observed professionalism, her humour mines the subtle comedy of daily life, and how we perform ourselves.

Comedy and tragedy tend to come as a pair, and Lovett understands how the comedic belies deeper, sometimes colder truths. Through video, performing and painting, Lovett's work is finely attuned to the world around her – to what 'real life' is. What is the real life of Julie Lovett the professional artist? Lovett toys with the complex idea of authenticity – is what we see the whole story? But she is no unreliable narrator. There is never the intention to trick or to wrongfoot. I've wondered if her work might be a kind of realism. But if it is, it is a realism that understands the inherent artifice of art-making – something that lies between performance and a life. She doesn't hide, but nor does she put it all out there. You have the sense of watching Julie Lovett trying to make sense of things in real time, with all the attendant stops, stumbles and repetitions. Occasionally, too, there's a knowing nudge at the fourth wall.

Lovett's recent exhibition *The truth always comes out in October* (2019) at PS² in Belfast comprised six loosely episodic monologues to camera, alongside sculptural elements and props which had appeared in the videos. Filmed between Belfast and County Kerry in Northern Ireland, where Lovett grew up, the exhibition oscillated between the two contexts in an expanded act of self-identification. The whimsical video titles, such as *By late morning, those who eat breakfast perform better both physically and mentally* (2019) and *In your mid 30s activity and performance will become more problematic* (2019) reference those affirmations found in outmoded self-help books, but also something curiously prescient to today's online self-improvement culture. Each video is from a fixed camera source, only lightly edited. Lovett repeats herself quite a bit. The aphoristic quality of her phrasing, and her playful approach to cliché, suggest that the easy explanation can only ever really be a partial truth.

In the second monologue, Lovett seems to be practising the art of confidence. *I am perfectly at ease*, she wants us to know. She stands at the entrance to her studio, effortfully conveying a relaxed body language. We never quite settle on inner truth or artifice. She waves us in, 'this is where all the magic happens'. Lovett quickly dismantles the image of the artist as genius, constantly struck with inspiration. She also seems to enjoy the awkwardness of the studio visit set-up. Is she delivering a sales pitch? In another video, Lovett reappears in the shot with a paintbrush tucked behind the ear. Despite the seeming editorial looseness of the six videos, watch closely and they loop back into one another. In the first monologue, the camera pans to one of Lovett's paintings on the wall that hangs next to a ticking clock. The visual gag – what does an artist do all day? – effaces something more universal. Was Leonard Cohen right? Are we all just looking for something to do between meals? Lovett may be an artist, but she still watches the clock, still breathes the same *plein-air* as the rest of us.

Lovett draws from conventions we all seem bound to encounter at some point – the studio visit, the job interview. 'I have a wide range of skills',[2] she lets us know, while running a figure of eight around her parent's farm courtyard, positioning life as a kind of eternal treadmill. A dog lolls around in the foreground, a car drives right through the shot. The minutiae of home life can intrude on the images we have of ourselves out in the world. Not a great deal happens in these videos, but there is a subtle accumulation of small details, and an emotive complexity just below the surface. That feels like real life to me.

Lovett recently moved back to Kerry, and from here is exploring the act of 'moving to the countryside'. Is a professional artist in the city the same as a professional artist in a rural setting? In a series of Instagram takeovers of PS² and Freelands Foundation (2020), Lovett homes in on the dynamics of small-town life, continuing her use of the video diary as an artistic format. These short clips have more of a fly-on-the-wall feel to them. In the first video for PS², she satirises the artist ego. 'Does he not know that I am an artist?'[3] Lovett trills, as her brother tinkers in the garden, interfering with her carefully constructed video composition. With this, all the inherent tensions of how to transplant a life in Belfast into a new environment with very different concerns creeps in. Lovett doesn't supply the whole picture, but she doesn't need to. These are gaps for us to fill in if we choose.

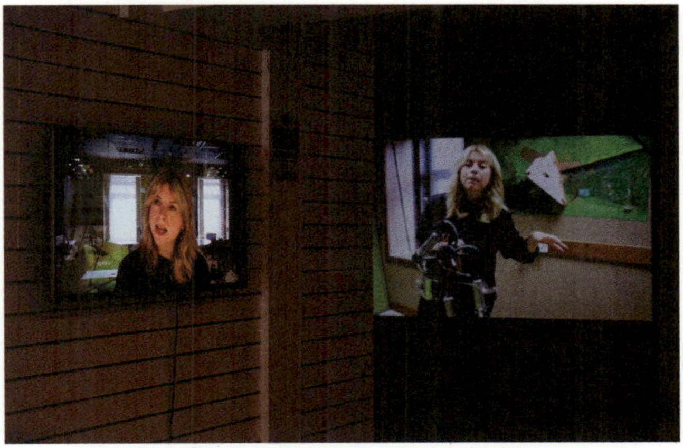

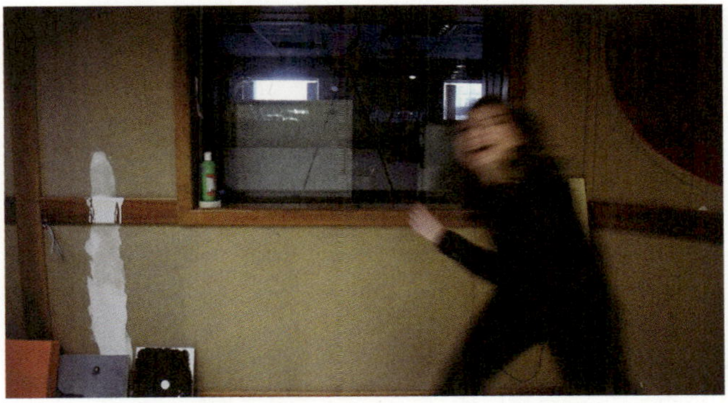

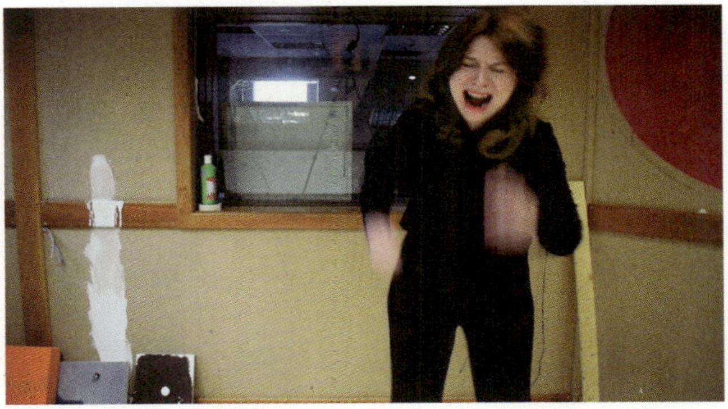

p.100: Julie Lovett, *Take me to the countryside, solve all my problems and make my life easier*, video (still), 2019
top: Julie Lovett, installation view, *Remain upright. Hide all facial expressions. Don't check your watch*, video (still), 2019 and *In your mid 30s, activity and performance will become more problematic*, video (still), 2019, *The truth always comes out in October*, PS², Belfast, 2019
middle and bottom: Julie Lovett, *City studio laughing series to be continued in the country*, video (still), 2020

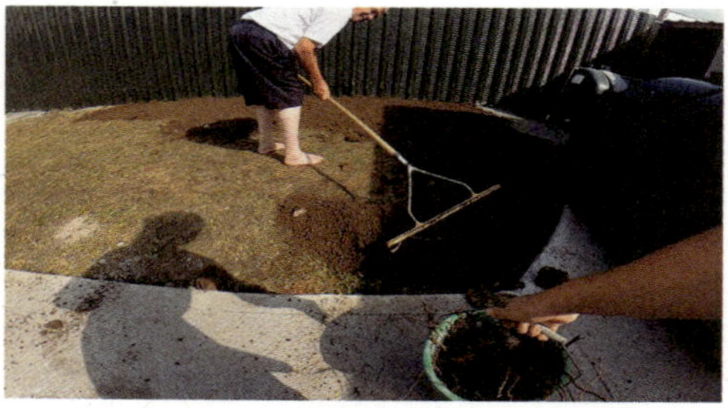

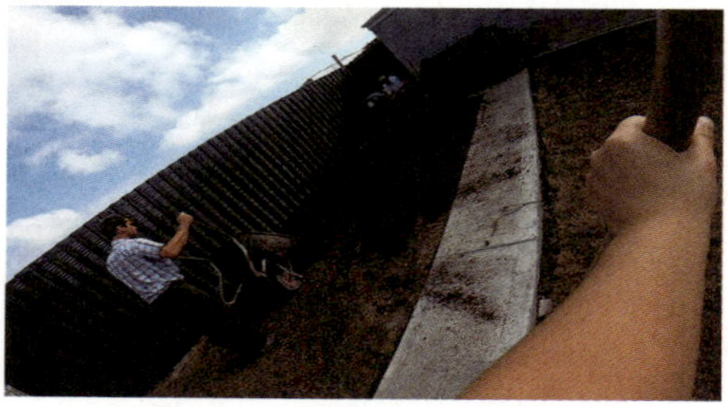

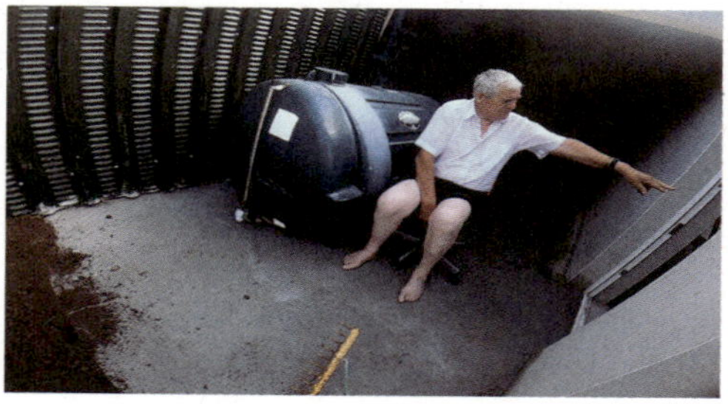

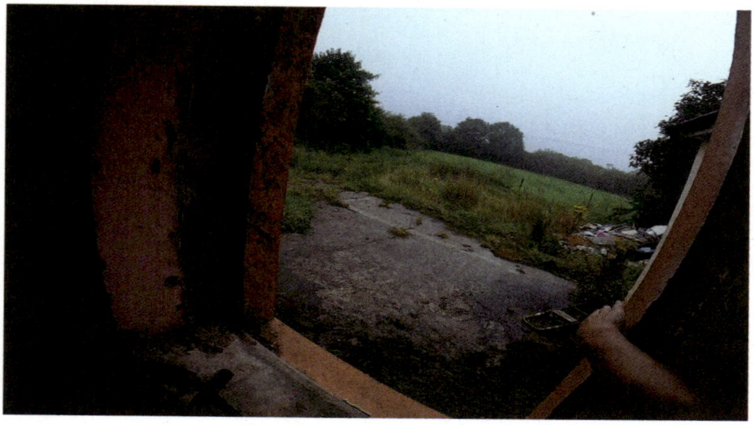

top three images: Julie Lovett, *Collaborating with the father by building shelves from Lidl / Lidls*, Go Pro video (stills of work in progress), 2020
bottom: Julie Lovett, *6am cycle to the woods, beating the traffic, looking for the fog*, Go Pro video (still of work in progress), 2020

The unresolved and episodic nature of Lovett's videos intertwines the process with the outcome. For Lovett, the research is the work is the process is the product. Take her final post on PS²'s Instagram: a watercolour of toilet rolls, strategically – or randomly – placed in a series of locations around her home and the local town. Is this painting a prop? Is it the 'real' work, the end product? Or are the videos that precede it where the work is? Lovett upends, or at the very least complicates, the idea of the object as the end result.

Lovett's repetitive approach is something of an oscillation between different states, phrases, objects and contexts. She seems to alternately accept and push back from the conditions she finds herself in. She has a heightened consciousness of her immediate present and surroundings. But just as you think she has settled on something, we pivot to another shot, or a quick turn of phrase reveals what we saw wasn't the full picture. There is the recurring theme of the double in Julie Lovett's work. The real and the performed. The professional and the personal. The rural and the urban. The process and the product. I wonder if that double is the artist known as Julie Lovett and Julie Lovett herself.

19 May 2020

1 Julie Lovett, *Being physically comfortable on the job (Part 2)*, video, 2019.
2 Julie Lovett, *ibid*.
3 Julie Lovett, *Freelands 2*, video, 2020.

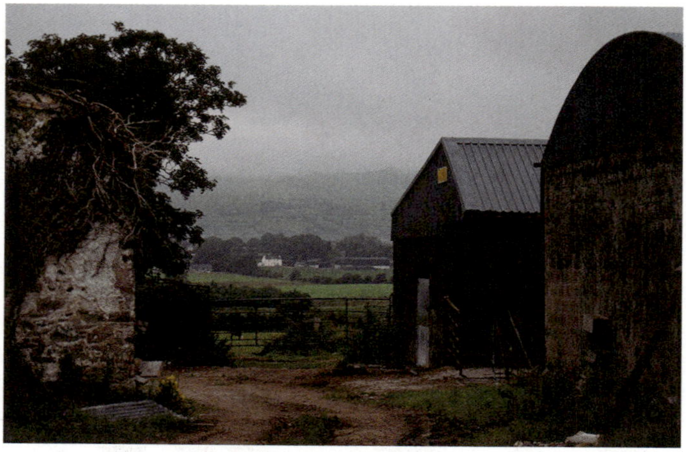

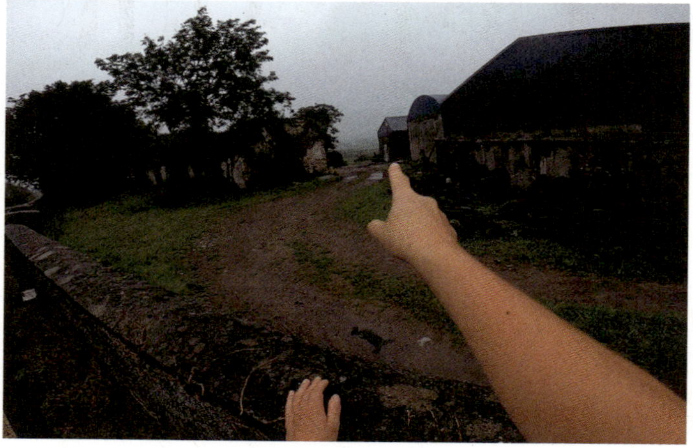

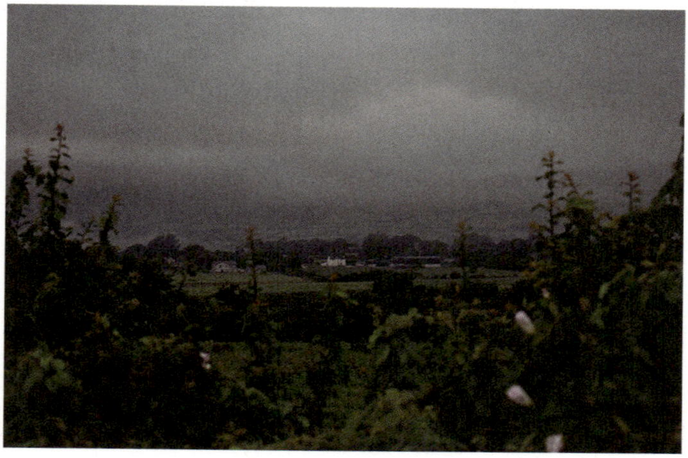

Julie Lovett, *Attempting to capture my house in the distance from the perfect angle with the perfect fog on the way to the woods*, photo series (work in progress), 2020

In the countryside of Kerry, I am adapting my practice to recreate ideas of common artistic working conditions which I previously practised and played out in the city of Belfast. Focusing on 'the artist's studio', I have taken the traditional idea of a physical studio space and mentally positioned it on to the confinements of Castlemaine, my home village.

Through conscious planned activities, such as durational recordings of daily morning cycles to the woods and attempting to capture the perfect photograph of my house in the distance, to carrying out domestic farming duties with my father, these new performance and filmworks focus on responding to my own circumstantial frustrations by fictionalising, layering and compiling repetitive past and present narratives, incidents, local happenings etc. into the dialogue and production of new moving image works.

By treating the village, its natives and landmarks as an expanded artistic space, I am aiming to push the possibilities of what collaborating and self-made opportunities can be in an Irish country village.

Julie Lovett

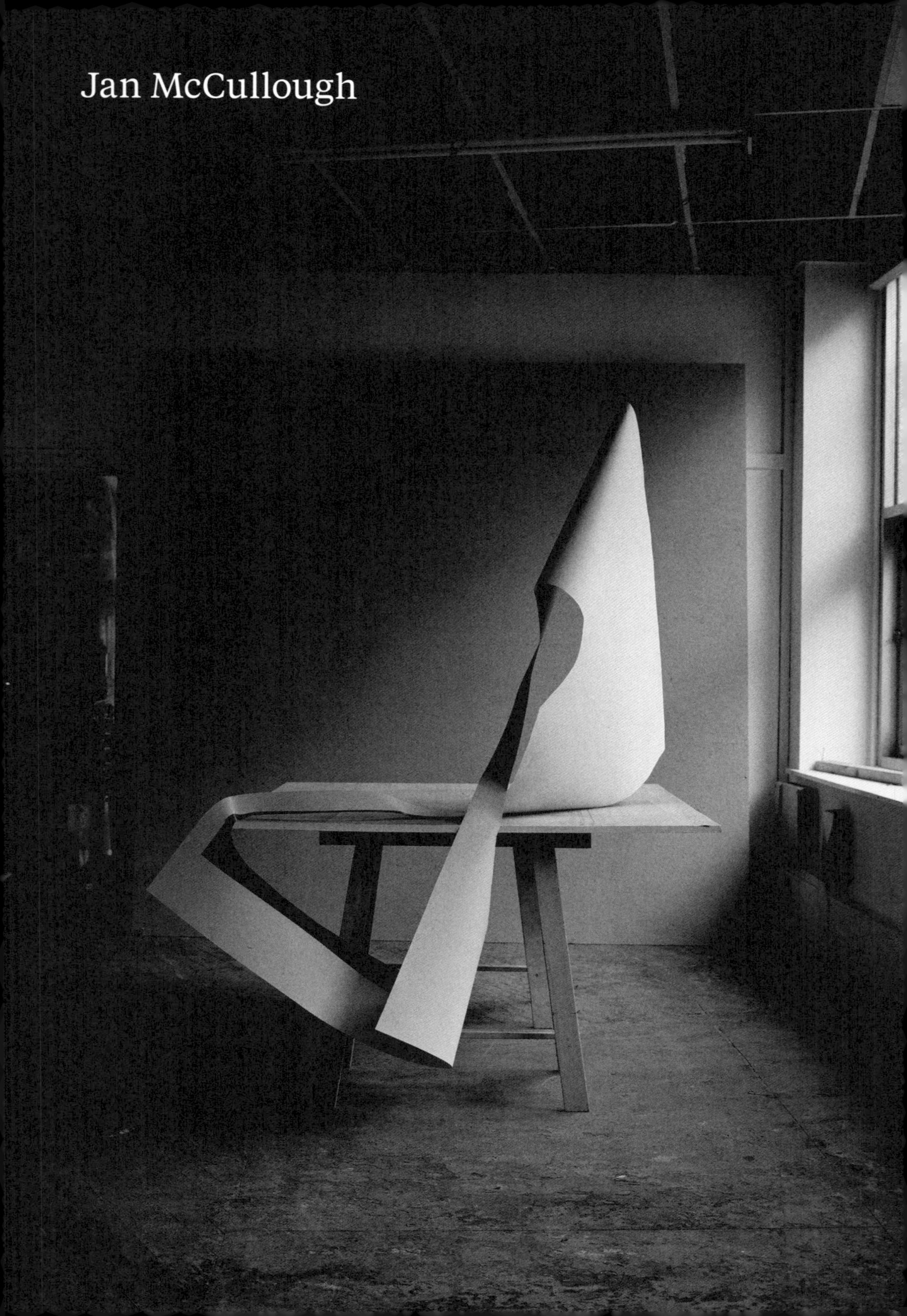
Jan McCullough

A Design for Life

Jan McCullough is something of an anthropologist, drawn to how we use photography to construct and imagine ourselves, and in turn, how the world of images shapes us – circling around us through the mediums of television, magazines, online and advertising. McCullough likes to work somewhere between these two poles: in the slippery zone between our own unconscious wants and what we are 'produced' to want. That could all sound abstract, were McCullough not so profoundly engaged with materials, and the processes we employ to shape our desires into materiality.

I call McCullough an anthropologist because of her intention to 'live in the field' – her way of submitting herself to processes of lived experience as a research method. In an early work, the publication *Home Instruction Manual* (2014–16), McCullough drew inspiration from 'Do-It-Yourself' culture and the ways in which we see our homes as an expression of ourselves. She typed 'how to make a home' into Google and was directed to an online chatroom where self-described experts would exchange highly detailed advice on any and every aspect of home renovation. McCullough then rented a house in Belfast for two months and carried out other people's detailed interior design instructions to the letter. The work's highly procedural material process constructs a patchwork of identities – all belonging to someone else – from scratch. Then, once the rental contract ends, this idealised life is taken down part by part. That the end result of the project is a book – a manual – is an enjoyably absurd twist on the folly of aspiration. McCullough spent two months inhabiting and manifesting desire, only for it to disappear.

Home Instruction Manual is a photography book resulting from a process not unlike durational performance. McCullough works primarily with photography, but from a conceptual terrain: as a desire mechanism, as a methodology. In the publication, McCullough pairs her photographs with corresponding online instructions. She also mimicked the aesthetics of DIY culture in her compositions, through poking fun at what she has dubbed 'estate agent photography'.[1] 'What makes an amateur and what makes a professional?' her style asks. McCullough makes space for other voices, but the only moment we perceive the artist's hand – sometimes quite literally – is in the photographs, which seem to ape the somewhat comedic styling tips provided by members of the online forum, such as how to make the house look 'lived-in'.

The COVID-19 pandemic has compelled us to stay home and live our lives increasingly from this one environment, engaging with the world through video communication software. Interactions with others now frequently oblige us to construct an image of ourselves in our homes, which is not so unlike the logic of McCullough's project. How to express taste – and therefore identity – in articulating the language of our home on-screen? What we read, what colour of Farrow and Ball paint we have selected for the upstairs study, whether to show orange tulips or white lilies – our reflection through a computer screen codifies who we are perhaps more than ever. Keeping up appearances, studiedly curating what the *New York Times* might term the 'semiotics of the bookshelf'.[2]

Yet our homes are just one aspect of how we construct ourselves, both privately and in public. McCullough's more recent, and related, work, *Vision Board Party* (2018) focuses on how social ties and connections might shape our image of the self. Vision boarding is a kind of tactile collage process of manifesting desires: cutting up magazines and photographs to create a patchwork of hopes and aspirations for the future. Perhaps there is a related aesthetic interest for McCullough too – the teenage bedroom, the homespun; highly individualised. McCullough's own artistic process frequently involves collaging and constructing mood boards to visualise and expand out from her research. Here, the artist was intrigued by the social aspect of the vision board: the increasing popularity of 'Vision Board Parties', where small groups of people come together to each craft their own vision boards from a collective pool of magazines and images. The resultant work is a 12-minute video which follows host Kaya, as she enthusiastically leads a Vision Board Party. McCullough's camera watches on, observing the group as they cut and paste and form their ideal lives in real time. Her camera seems interested in the tactility of how photography is used, with close-ups of hands and scissors as they form new shapes and meanings. Judiciously chosen observations by Kaya overlay the scene: 'You also get certain pictures that people look for ... one of the typical ones is a happy couple.'

This particular interest in materiality – as a material manifestation of desire – has led McCullough towards her current, ongoing body of work. Where previously the artist was drawn to the DIY processes with which we might construct an image of ourselves, for her forthcoming exhibition, *Tricks of the Trade*, at Centre for Contemporary Art (CCA) Derry~Londonderry,[3] she is focusing on the material qualities of DIY cultures and spaces of production. Mood boards and manuals – present in McCullough's previous

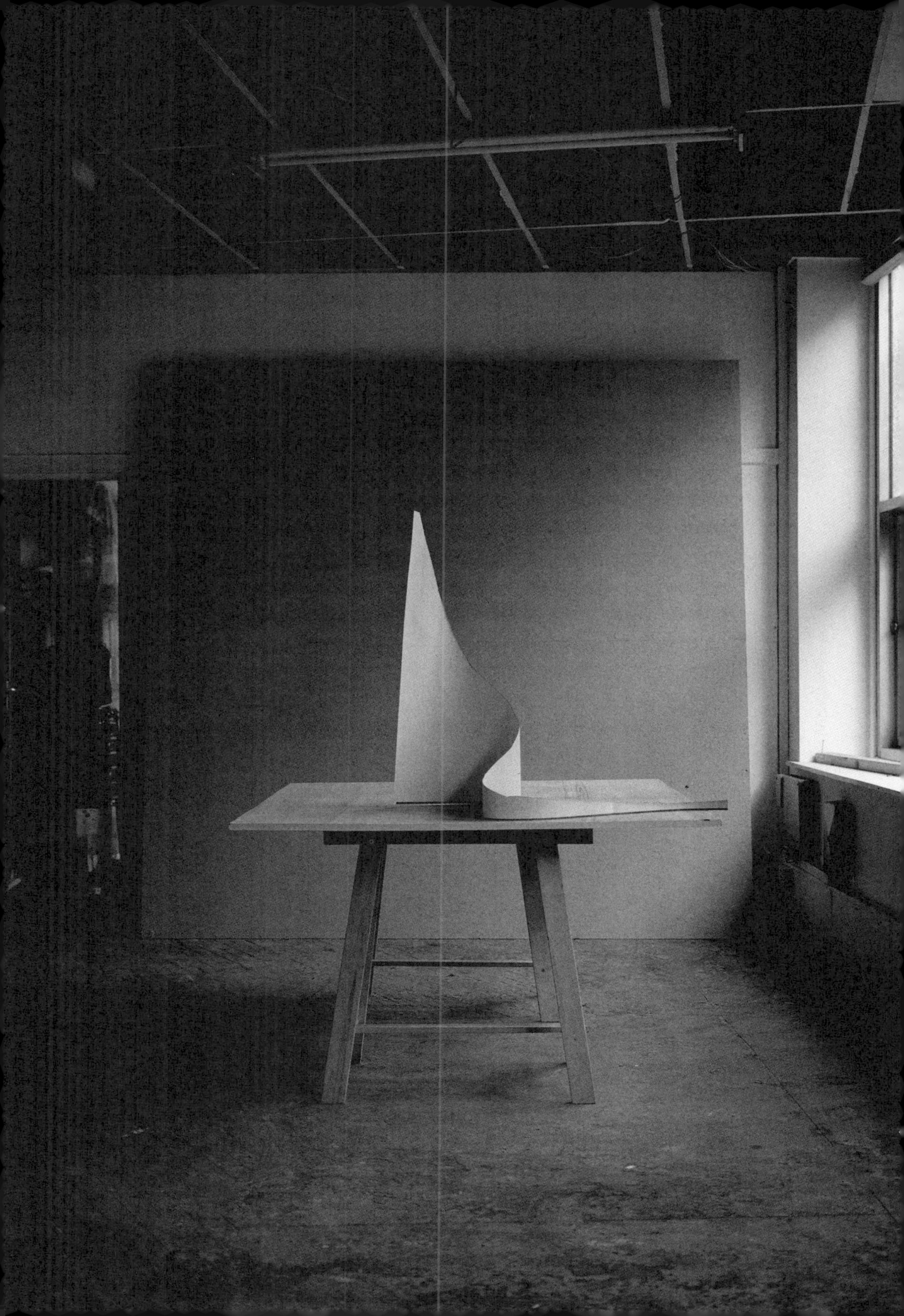

enquiries – each require idealisation and interpretation to become physicalised. The title, *Tricks of the Trade*, takes pleasure in the specific vocabularies that develop around such interests – the time-saving devices, the expert tips, the shortcuts.

McCullough has been photographing spaces such as hardware stores, garages and sheds for a number of years,[4] building up her own incidental archive. For this exhibition, the artist is translating aspects of those images into sculptural environments, seeking to capture the effects that photography alone cannot capture – the texture of the wood, the smell of varnish, the cool of the steel. The three rooms of CCA will become three different production areas, three different processes: the factory floor, the studio, the hardware store – evoking their distinctive atmospheres throughout the galleries. McCullough's work is always invested in the specific futurity that plans, ideas and dreams offer – and her work meets these imagined worlds in the present, in the processes of their manifestation.

26 May 2020
Updated 2 October 2020

1 In conversation with the author, Thursday 22 November 2018.
2 Amanda Hess, 'The "Credibility Bookcase" is the quarantine's hottest accessory', *New York Times*, 1 May 2020, https://www.nytimes.com/2020/05/01/arts/quarantine-bookcase-coronavirus.html.
3 At the time of writing the exhibition is due to open in November 2020.
4 In conversation with the author, Thursday 1 October 2020.

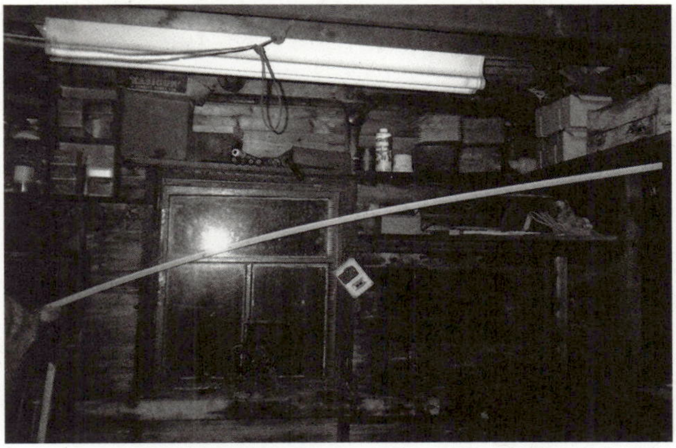

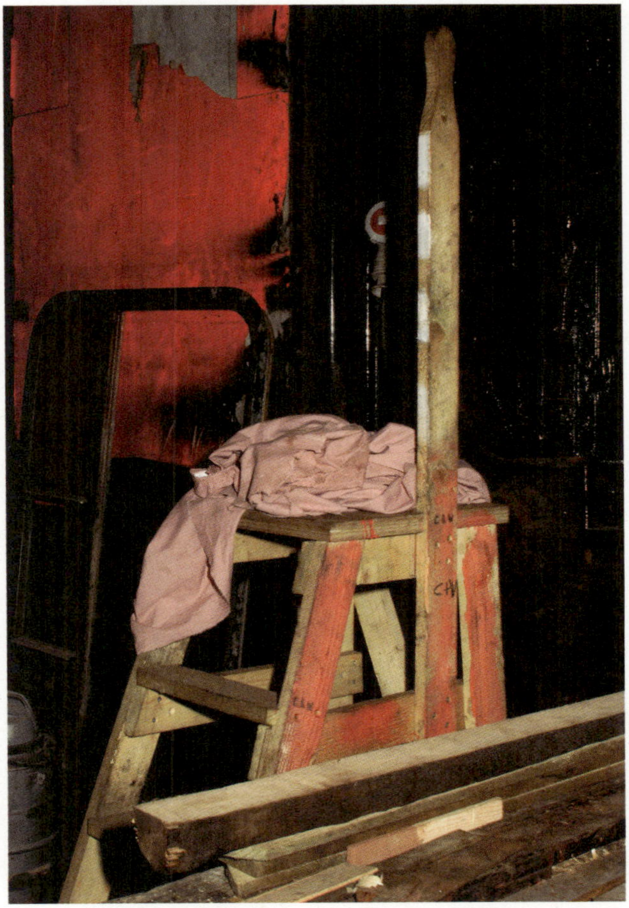

pp.108 and 111: Jan McCullough, *Constructions*, 2019
top: Jan McCullough, *Garage*, photographic print, 2020
bottom: Jan McCullough, object from studio, 2020

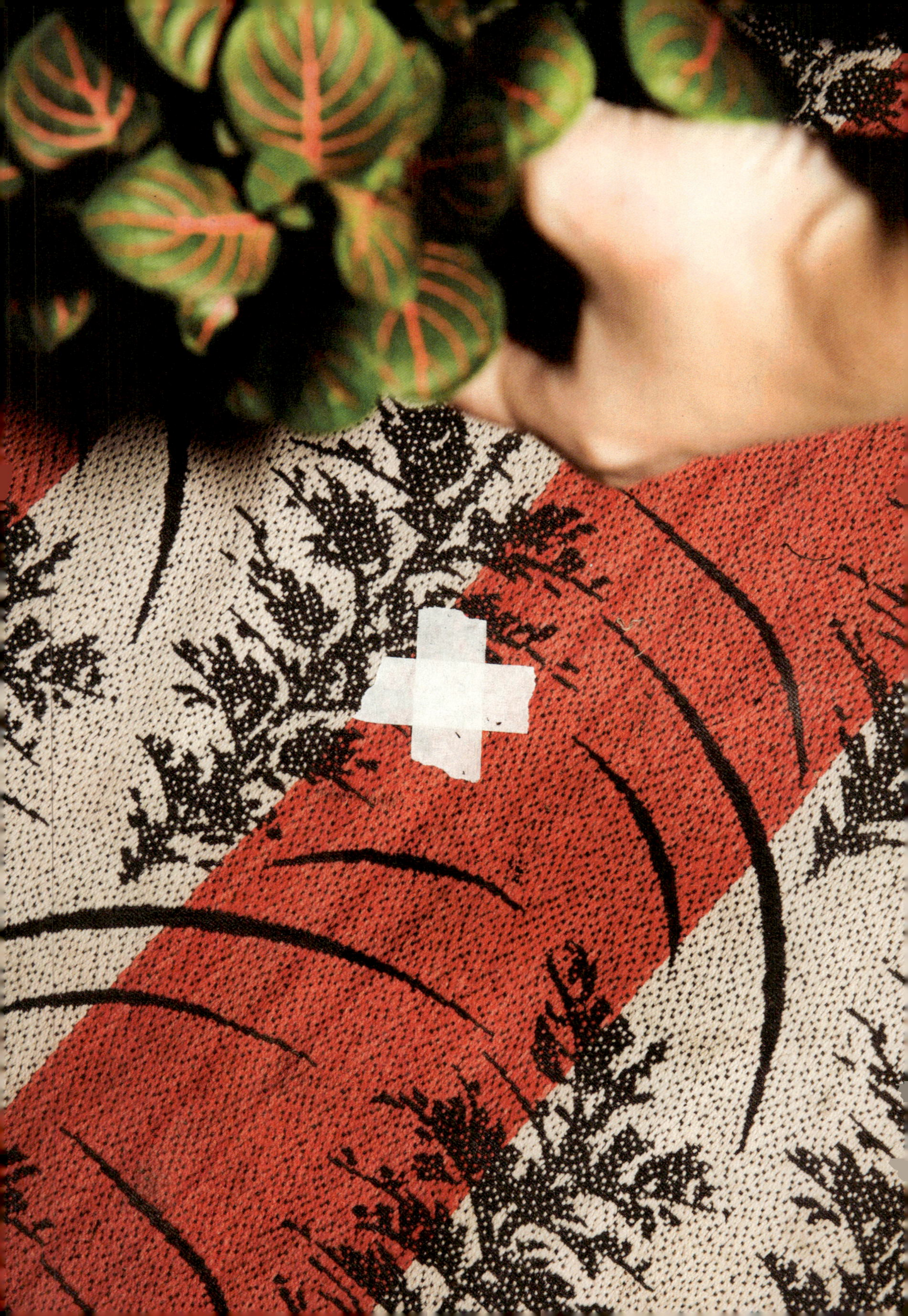

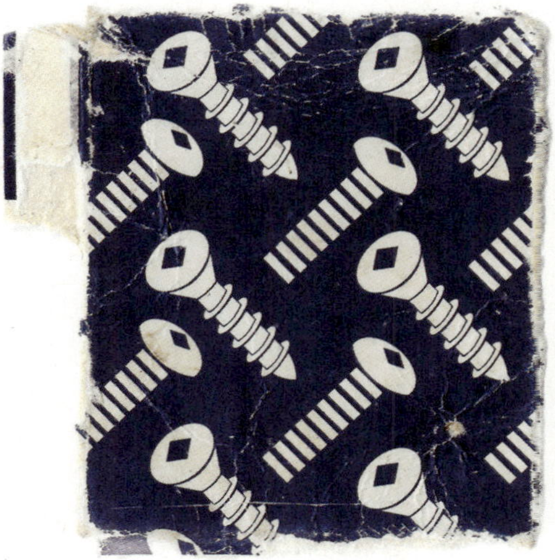

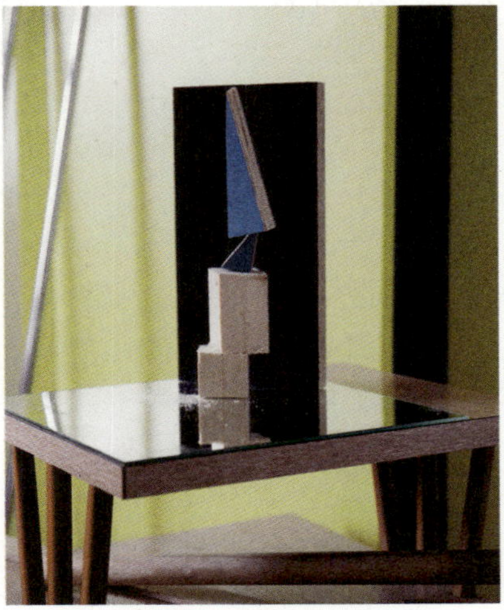

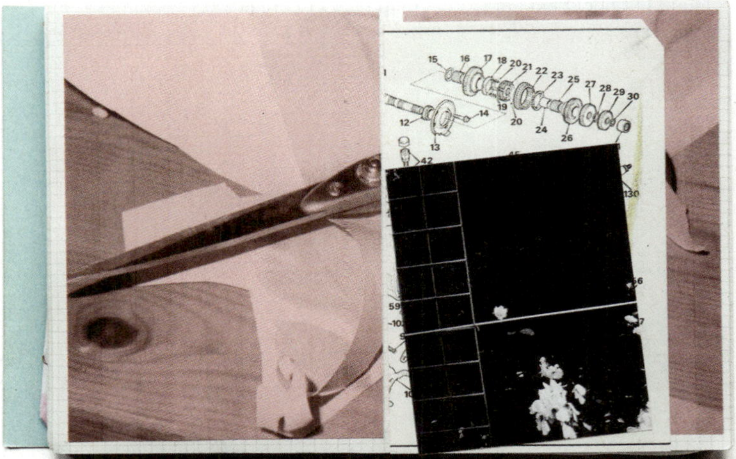

opposite: Jan McCullough, from the series 'Home Instruction Manual', 2014–16
top left: Jan McCullough, Screwbox, object from studio, 2020
top right: Jan McCullough, Maquette, 2020
bottom: Jan McCullough, Sketchbook, 2020

Emily McFarland

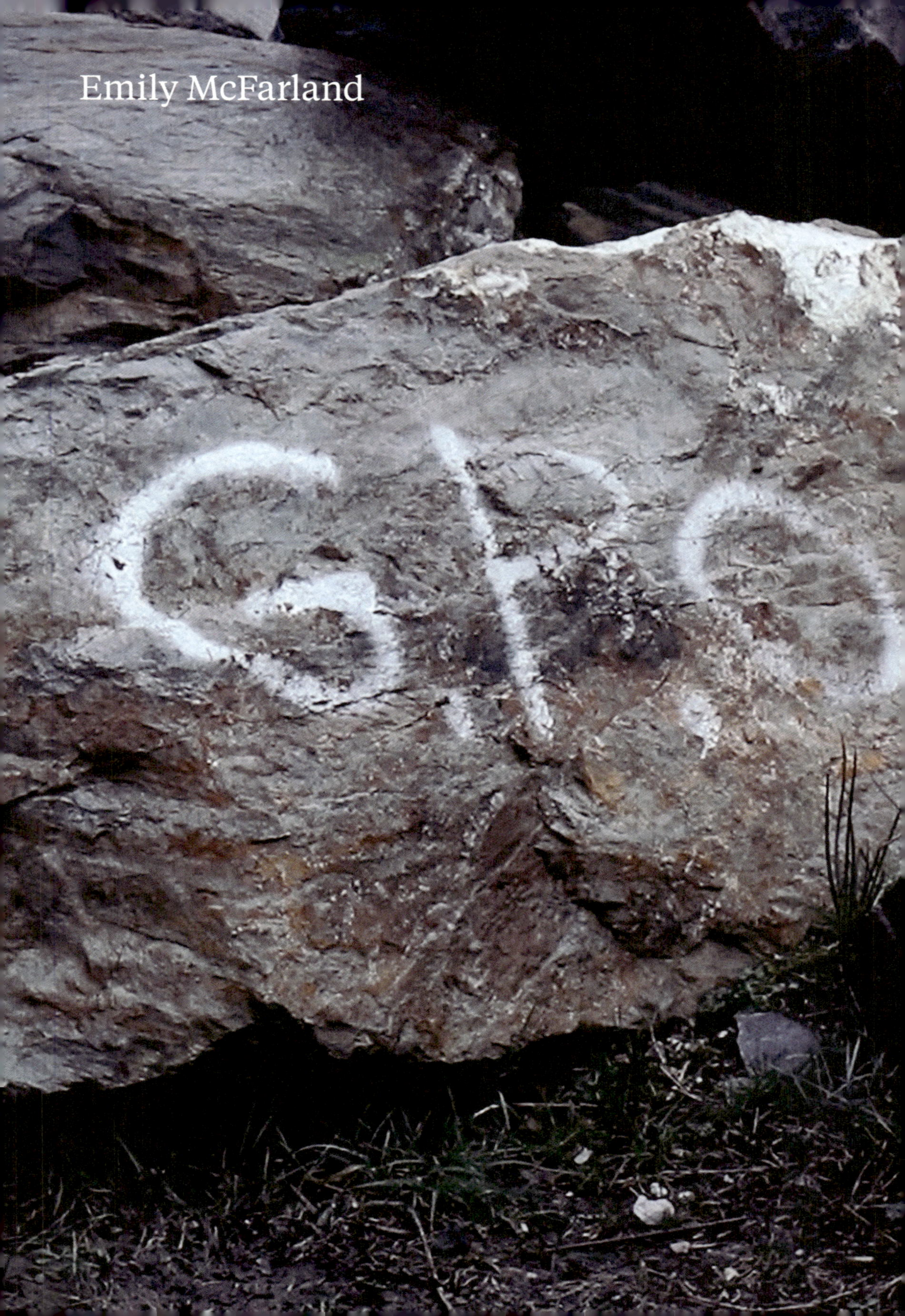

The Rock and the River

The camera lingers on a small rock on the riverbed, and the slow attrition taking place; a minor detail in an embodied memory of the land. Emily McFarland's recent moving image work *Curraghinalt* (2019–20) unfolds a slow chorus of ecologies, histories and myths held in the earth – a ground-up approach to community and place. The work is the first in a connected series of films exploring the gradual creep of extractive global capital on a local landscape.[1]

McFarland began filming in and around the townland of Curraghinalt in County Tyrone, Northern Ireland in 2018. The surrounding Sperrin mountain range is an Area of Outstanding Natural Beauty, and also the site of escalating tension between the local community and Dalradian Gold, a Canadian prospective gold mining company. With potential gold deposits worth billions held in the ground, in 2017 a planning application was lodged by Dalradian to build an underground mine and the associated surface developments, including a processing plant. In this context, environmental damage is just a casual corollary to substantive economic gain – with the use of poisonous chemicals such as cyanide for prospecting irreparably contaminating the water supply. Toxic liquidity in action. Curraghinalt is the rock in the riverbed, a community holding firm to stem the flow of the substantive Dalradian legal and financial resources seeking to dislodge them. Kinetic force tends to win out in the end.

McFarland's filmmaking indexes moments of testimony in specific places at particular moments. In *Curraghinalt*, she recorded conversations with local community organisers across a single day at the Greencastle People's Office (GPO) – a collection of caravans high in the mountains overlooking a valley of farmland. Conversations range from personal accounts and shared experience, to the local history of the area and worries for the future. The single-channel video weaves together dislocated sound, voice and image, like a wave lapping the shore. One scene gives way to another. Colloquial speech, rich with local knowledge, overlays images of the landscape. The work pulls apart documentary form: fragmented narratives and details don't accumulate, don't build a 'full picture'. McFarland's formal and conceptual approach finds connection with artist Isaac Julien's film installation *PLAYTIME* (2014). This seven-screen work tracks the dislocating, nebulous flow of capital and the impossibility of its representation. Julien's

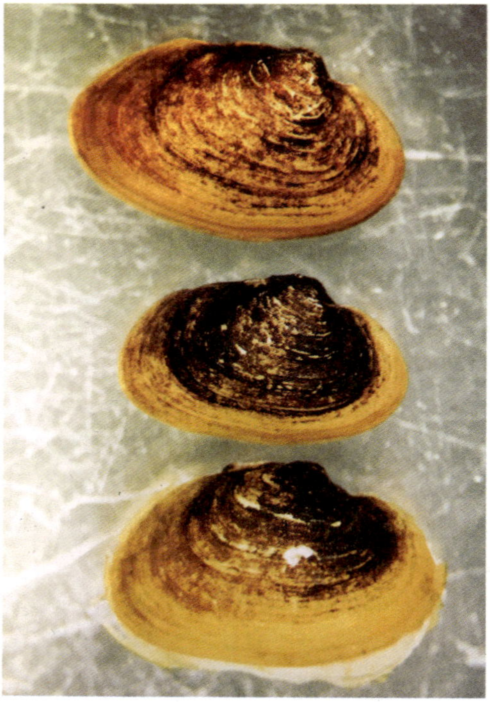

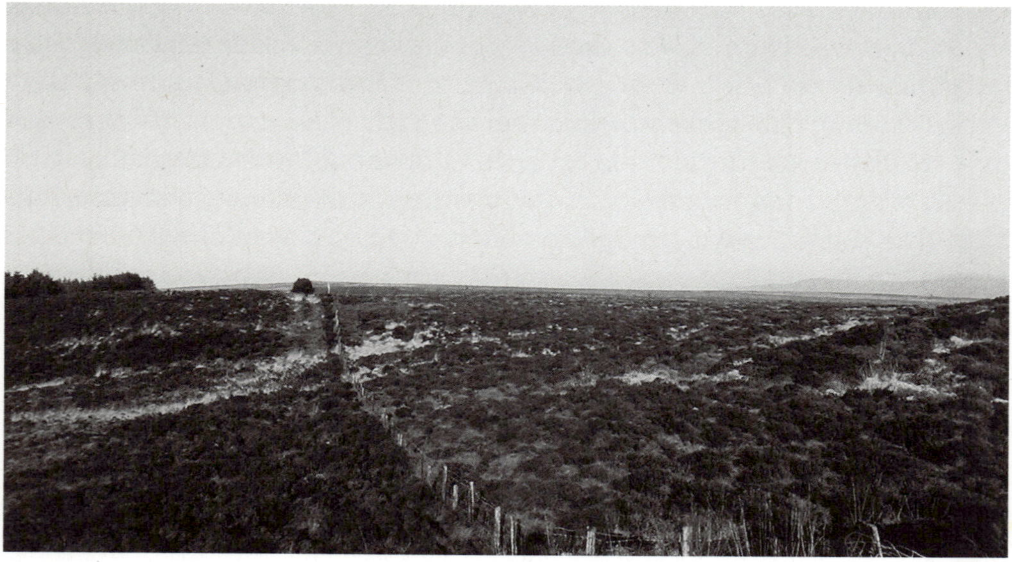

p.116 and bottom: Emily McFarland, *Curraghinalt*, HD video (still), 2019–20, exhibited as part of the 39th EVA International – Biennial of Contemporary Art
top: Emily McFarland, *Margaritifera Margaritifera*, C-type print, 2020
Courtesy Frank Michell and the artist

display strategy employs metaphors of liquidity and formal techniques of montage and chorus to track the flows of global capital across the cities of Reykjavik, Dubai and London. Satellite-like surveys of different environments intermingle with short, partial studies of those caught in the global capitalist slipstream. It is an ambivalent portrayal. Although *Curraghinalt* does not editorialise, our vantage point is clear: the land and those who live there. Our positionality is from Curraghinalt: a specific geographical voice, built on local, generational knowledges and ecosystems.

The cultural theorist Donna Haraway defined the term 'situated knowledges' to articulate that all knowledge comes from positional perspectives,[2] and McFarland sites herself here, a space from which we might discern a lens-based ethics. In *Curraghinalt*, the filmmaker isn't telling their own story. Instead, film emerges as a container for different knowledges, subject positions and ecologies to reside together without submitting to an overarching narrative. In the gaps and ellipses, counter-narratives can develop, from which political potential emerges.

In previous works, McFarland has explored the cinematic staging and depiction of revolutionary action. In her solo exhibition *The Complex Seer* (2017) at Centre for Contemporary Art (CCA), Derry~Londonderry, McFarland 'cut up' segments from films, focusing on representations of small groups of people who live and organise in opposition to mainstream society. These films range from *La Chinoise* (1967) one of Jean-Luc Godard's most political works, and *Zabriskie Point* (1970) by Michelangelo Antonioni. *Curraghinalt* self-reflexively asks questions of its own cinematic conventions: how is community action depicted here? A lingering close-up shot of a large rock spray-painted with 'GPO' posits the rural as a site of protest, a place of assembly. The initials become a slogan, inviting a reading of solidarity. The acronym GPO can also be traced back to the General Post Office in Dublin, site of the Easter Rising of April 1916. The Rising was launched by a group of Irish Republicans to end British rule in Ireland and establish an independent Irish Republic at a time when the United Kingdom was fighting the First World War. McFarland's film gives space to this lineage. A group of community organisers working under the same acronym as a historical anti-colonial uprising highlights the Dalradian project for what it is: an extractivist and colonial land grab. McFarland doesn't make this statement, it is visually revealed as the testimonies build.

Across a planned series of films, McFarland's camera windows on to specific places and circumstances. The rich aquaculture of Owenkillew river, which rises in the Sperrin Mountains, is another such site, home to Northern Ireland's largest population of rare freshwater pearl mussels. McFarland has been in conversation with a man who breeds this endangered species, which can live for up to 200 years. The mussels inhabit the silted sand of the river, but if the river becomes clogged or contaminated, they will suffocate. This film situates us from the perspective of the land and the water, a long view beyond human life span; highlighting that all filmmaking is to mark a time and place. Developed alongside this is a new, parallel, work, *Three Acts* (2020–), which sees McFarland think through the historical retellings of the Greek mythological play *Antigone*, as transformed across cultural life spans. Antigone is the heroine who recognises her familial duty, taking radical action against societal infringement on the individual. Across all of McFarland's projects are common themes of unravelling, and ultimately, resistance. In *Three Acts*, McFarland asks: how can a character function as a series of questions? In turn, McFarland positions her own filmmaking as space for potential. Her work marks moments in time, but is attentive to lineage, knowing that there will be future retellings.

Is McFarland's filmmaking its own form of solidarity? In conversation McFarland has referenced the Zapatistas movement in Mexico – a community also fighting against mining companies. The movement understands cultural production as a form of resistance. McFarland's ongoing projects gather voices, stories, accounts of generational knowledge, landscapes – contributing to a collective memory of place. Her work, as cultural production, says: We were there.

7 June 2020

1 Emily McFarland is one of the artists selected for the Platform Commissions, 39th EVA International, Ireland's Biennial of Contemporary Art, https://www.eva.ie/platform-commissions-39th-eva-international/.

2 Donna Haraway, 'Situated Knowledges: The Science Question in Feminism and the Privilege of Partial Perspective', *Feminist Studies*, vol.14, no.3, autumn 1988.

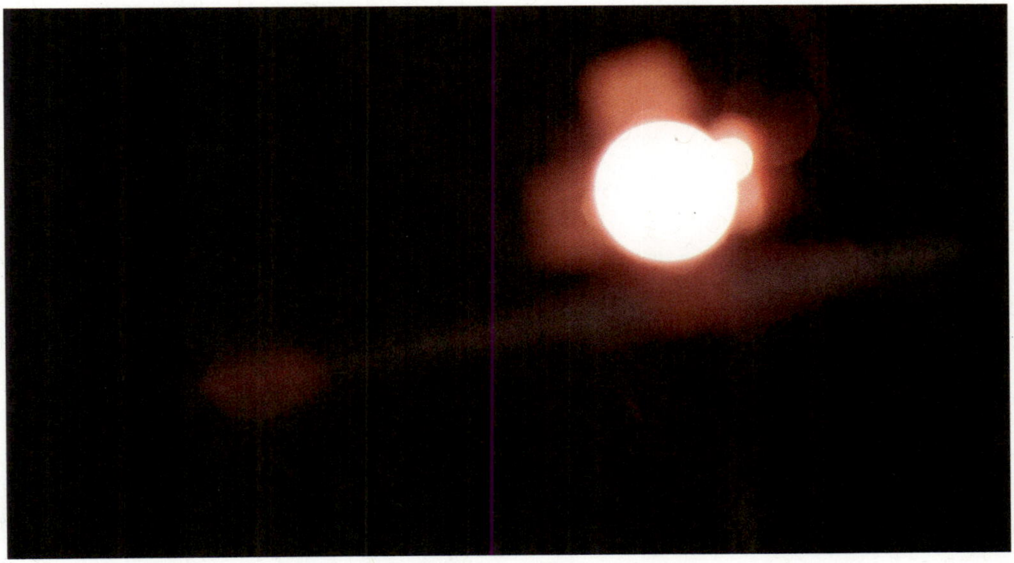

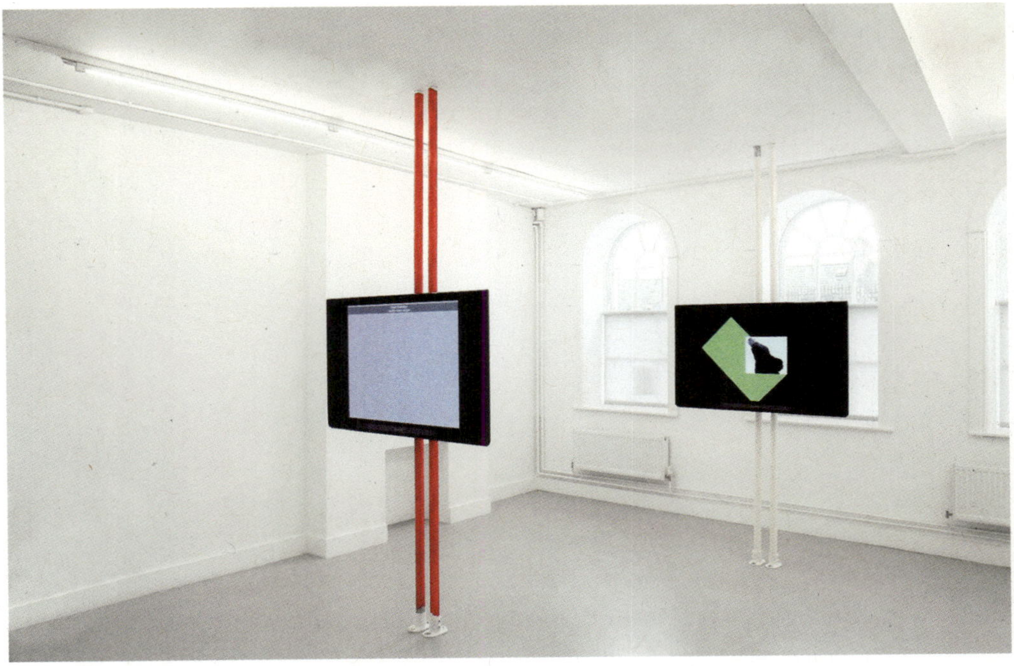

top and overleaf: Emily McFarland, *Afterplay*, HD video (still), 2020
bottom: Emily McFarland, *The Complex Seer*, installation view, CCA Derry~Londonderry, 2017. Courtesy CCA Derry~Londonderry and the artist

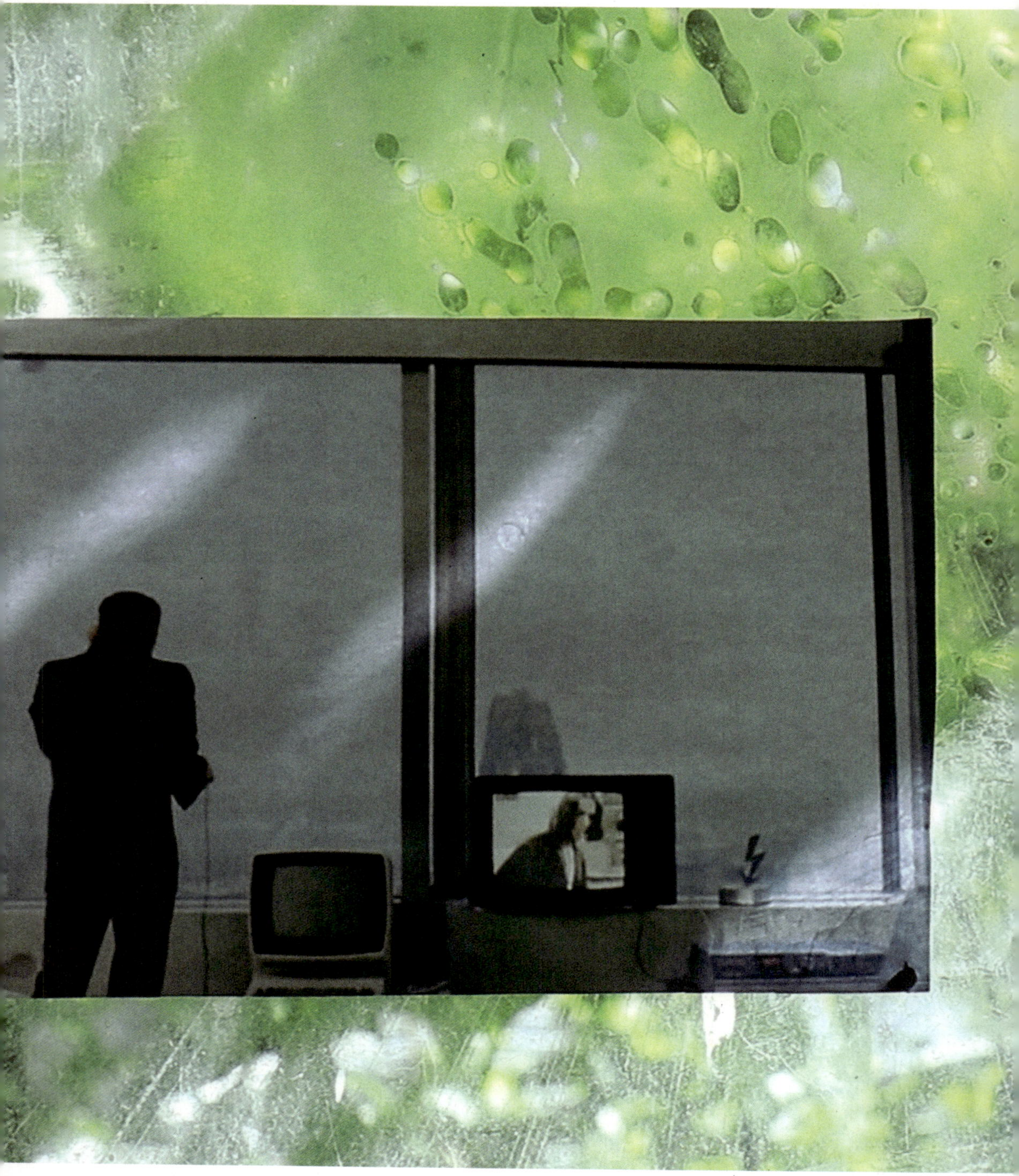

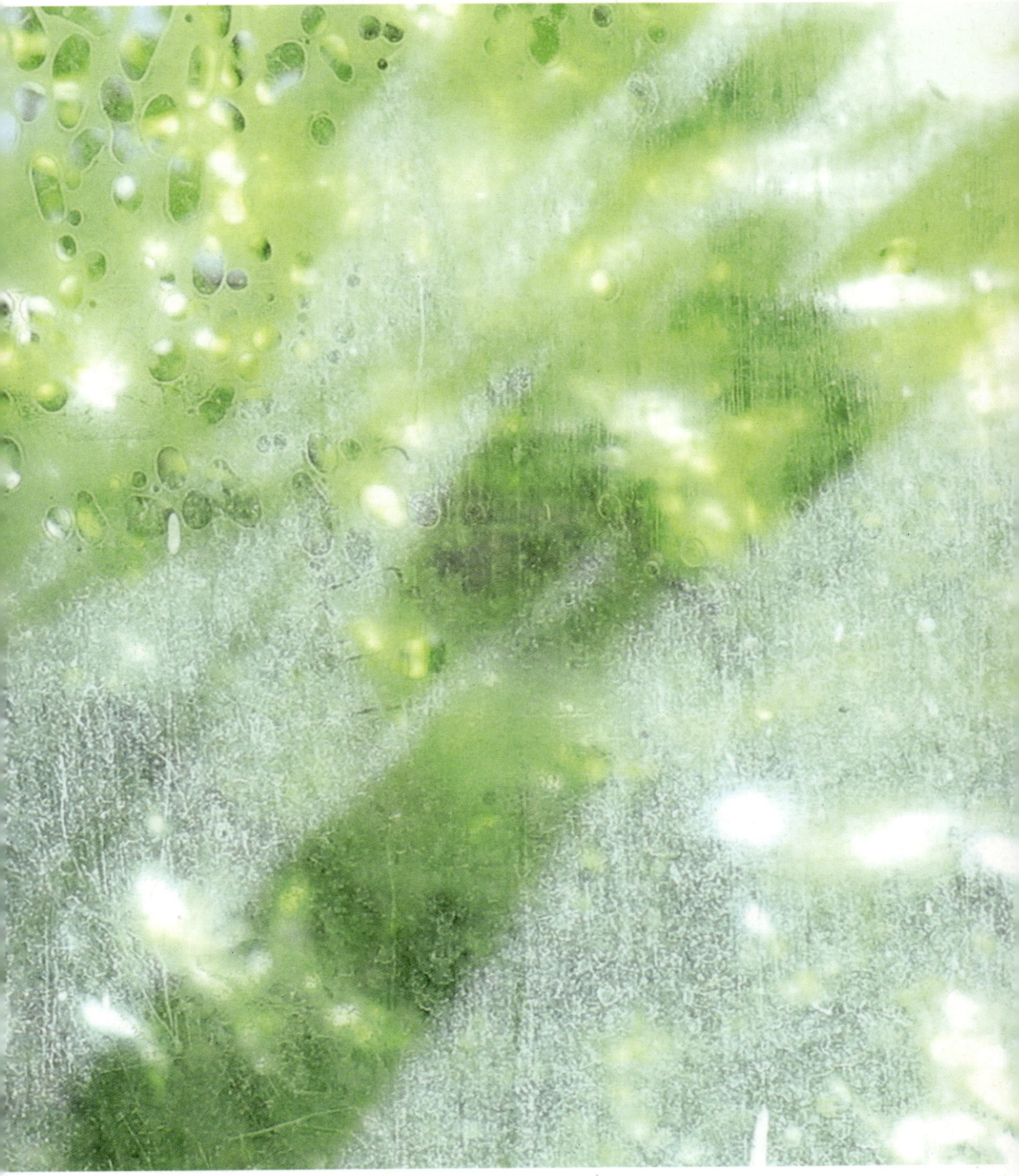

Troubling the Water

Jan Carson

The rumour about the Templemore Baths was essentially circular in shape. Which is to say, this one told that one, that one passed it on to the next and, within a few days, it had made a complete circuit of the 'Knit and Natter'. Nobody could've said who started it, though Agnes was the likeliest candidate. Agnes had a source in the Council: a great niece in Cleansing Services. She was the group's go to for complaints about missing wheelie bins or the dog dirt which appeared in the bus shelter, each deposit individually bagged like a portion of butcher-bought mince.

Kathleen suspected Agnes was the instigator, although it had been Mary who'd called to ask the lend of her magic loop, (*she'd seen a thing on Facebook, looking hats knitted for preemie babies and wanted to give it a whirl*), and to let Kathleen know the paramedics were in with Marty 'round the corner, (*not Marty Barr, the other Marty, the one with the leg*), and to tell her the forecast was bad for the weekend and chocolate digestives were on two for one in SuperValu, oh and, on the off chance, had she heard anything funny about the Templemore Baths? Kathleen knew, from the slight change in pitch, that this was the real reason for Mary's call.

It was not the first time Kathleen had encountered a rumour like this. People assumed it was only country folks who went in for the weird stuff; that if you lived in a city with modern conveniences such as satellite television and all-night Tesco, you'd be too sophisticated to go in for such nonsense. Not a bit of it. The East was full of old ladies who spun tall tales: Margarets, Maureens and Marys, (pronounced Meery to rhyme with cheery thus differentiating them from the other sort of Mary, the ones named after the Mother of God). Mother of God, these women loved to gossip. The more unlikely the story, the quicker they took to it, spreading word of strange happenings by phone, by text, by street corner chat, by carrier pigeon if such a vehicle came to hand. There was no keeping a good rumour down and Kathleen had heard a fair few good ones in her time.

There was the one about the young fella in Ballybeen who'd been knocked down dead by joyriders, only to wake up on the undertaker's slab, bruised and confused, but ultimately, grand. They claimed a miracle for that one. Apparently, the granny was a champion prayer; a tight wee Baptist woman with a beret permanently clamped to her crown. They said, her earnest petitions had brought the wee lad back. In certain circles you could still say that sort of thing and be believed. Then, there was the lady who walked amongst the headstones in Dundonald Cemetery and the equally dead RUC officer, (half his face missing from a car bomb), who frequented the back corner of the Park Avenue's lounge. There was the woman with the cure for asthma in Ballyhack, and the auld lad who sat on the bench next to McDonald's drive-thru. He'd do your future for the price of a Smarties McFlurry. He was accurate, they said, but wouldn't give racing tips no matter how much you offered. Officially, the Protestants didn't go in for all that supernatural shite. It was the other sort who done the weeping statues and miracles. Pragmatism might well have been preached from the pulpit, but in the streets and fussy wee living rooms of East Belfast, folks still believed in things unseen. There wasn't much else to hold on to round here.

The Templemore Baths had been clinging to the end of Templemore Avenue since 1893. Red bricked, chimneyed and blessed with a somewhat incongruous spire, the structure didn't immediately scream swimming pool. The passing stranger – and there were very few strangers passing through this part of the city – might well have taken the building for a Victorian cloth mill or a place of worship. Inside, the facilities remained reassuringly old-fashioned. The stench of bleach and chlorine sat crisply on every tiled surface. Drafts swept uninterrupted from one end of the building to the other and all the heating pipes were crusty. A deep, rectangular pool dominated the inner sanctum. The ceiling above was high, windowed and impractically arched, so the air above water remained permanently icy. In winter, the swimmers could see their breath fogging in front of them as they crawled and butterflied up and down the lanes.

Individual changing cubicles lined the pool's edge, so it was only a short swimsuit-clad shuffle from the door to the water. The old ladies appreciated this. They didn't like to be observed – varicose-veined and bulging – in their saggy one pieces and clip-beneath-your-chin caps. The old boys didn't give a rat's ass how they looked in their trunks yet still swam in the Baths because they were cheap and handier than bussing across town to the big municipal complex on the Boucher Road. Through the day, when the weans were in school, it was really only old ones who swam there. Yes, you might stumble across the odd pregnant lady or a young mum dragging a toddler across the shallows, clumsy and howling in orange armbands. And there was, of course, the rougher element: young fellas on sticks like bandy-legged lambs hobbling to the pool's edge, lowering themselves painfully in. The physios said swimming was good for them – *low impact, and all that* – there was very little else you could do, exercise wise, with the kneecaps taken off you. It was a pity of these young fellas. Or was it? Sure, they only had themselves to blame. The old women gave them the side-eye as they swam past and knew not to bring anything valuable down to the pool. You couldn't really trust a locker, could you? Those kind of lads would be in and out and away with your purse before you'd even got your key out.

The Knit and Natter ladies were Templemore regulars. They came for aqua aerobics on Tuesday morning and afterwards retired to a coffee shop 'round the corner. The place was staffed by ones with special needs. Though the coffee wasn't as good as Costa and sometimes you'd have to go up and repeat your order to the supervisor, the ladies liked to be seen to be doing their bit. Tuesdays weren't an official Knit and Natter session. These took place on Thursday afternoons and Monday mornings. They were held in the Community Centre and presided over by Julie, who was employed to run projects for older people. The ladies could count on Julie to keep them well-supplied with tepid mugs of Nescafé, Jammy Dodgers and the inevitable evaluation forms which appeared after every session. Nobody ever joined the Knit and Natter. Though, to its credit, they'd only ever lost two members: Marlene, who'd died, and Susan, who was doting now and had moved in with her son in Bangor. This bothered Julie. It didn't bother the Knit and Natter ladies one wee bit. All eight of them had known each other since girlhood. They'd no desire to recruit outsiders. They met twice a week to knit and gossip, taking advantage of the Community Centre's central heating. All but Linda, (who was constrained by her oxygen tank), reconvened on Tuesdays for their subsidised swim.

It was Wednesday when Mary phoned Kathleen. They wouldn't be back in the Baths for almost another week. Mary wasn't saying Kathleen should make a point of going down there unscheduled or anything. Mary wasn't even claiming there was any truth in the rumour. She was simply letting Kathleen know what people were saying. She was just being a good friend, for she knew Kathleen was crippled with the arthritis, not to mention poor Bill. To be honest, it was Bill she was really thinking of. She didn't like to put it so bluntly, but Bill didn't have long left. And daft as the whole thing sounded, sure there was no harm in trying. You'd try anything when it came close to the end, wouldn't you? Hadn't she put her own dying mother in the car and driven her all the way up to Ballymena to see that faith healer? It hadn't made the blind bit of difference but at least Mary could content herself knowing she'd tried. There was a comfort in knowing you'd done everything you could.

The conversation went on like this for several minutes. The telephone receiver began to sweat uncomfortably against Kathleen's ear. Mary's calls were always delivered in a similar roundabout style. There was a nugget of news in there somewhere, you just had to wait patiently until it emerged. Kathleen caught Bill's eye across the room. He was a good sort. He'd muted the TV as soon as the phone went and rolled his wheelchair up close to the screen so he could read the subtitles. She mouthed the word *Mary* to him and pointed at the phone. He rolled his eyes ceiling-wards before returning to the News. The light from the screen drew the colour out of his face. He was particularly pallid today. The last round of treatment had left him wild papery looking. Kathleen needed to get Mary off the phone so she could get him up to bed before he was too exhausted to help her.

'What are you going on about, Mary?' she asked, interrupting the other woman mid-flow.

'There's a girl swimming at the Baths on Friday mornings', said Mary, 'a foreign girl.'

'What sort of foreign?'

'I'm not sure. Eastern European, I think. It doesn't really matter. Anyway, they say this girl's got some kind of cure. If you're in the water when she's swimming it comes off on you.'

'Bollocks', said Kathleen. Bill was starting to fall asleep and she was running out of patience.

'Honest to God, Kathleen. Our Liz was down there last Friday when the girl went in and afterwards there wasn't a speck of psoriasis on her. You know yourself she's been plagued for years. And the young one on the butcher's counter at Spar said his wife took their baby in when that girl was in and it fixed her squinty eye. I even heard somebody over on the Beersbridge Road got rid of their cancer.' She dropped her voice to a whisper as she spoke. This was clearly for Bill's benefit, though Bill was flat out by this stage and snoring. 'I'm just saying', she continued, 'don't rule it out, Kathleen. If I was in your position. I'd try anything.'

'It's not true', said Kathleen. 'The thing about the pool and getting healed is in the Bible. It's one of Jesus's miracles.'

'Is it? I don't know that one. Well, if it's in the Bible then it must be true.'

'Aye, for Bible times maybe. Not for now, in East Belfast.'

'Ah, you're probably right there, Kathleen. If Jesus was going to do a miracle nowadays he'd probably go somewhere a bit classier than the Templemore Baths. There's that waterslide park over in Lisburn. The grandweans love it. He'd probably go somewhere like that.'

'He would indeed', said Kathleen and, shortly after, hung up.

She tried to put the Templemore Baths to the back of her mind. She knew it was nonsense. Or pure coincidence. Swimming was good for sick people. Doctors were always banging on about gentle exercise. Everybody felt better for having been to the Baths. It was nothing to do with the foreign girl appearing. Nothing at all. But then again, what if the rumours were true? They were living in strange times. Bill was only after telling her a fella in England had given birth to a baby and in the States, there were holy rollers claiming they could raise the dead. Sure, you didn't know what to believe any more. At the end of the day, thought Kathleen, was there any real harm in taking Bill to the Baths? Better to chance your arm and be disappointed than miss out for fear of looking daft. She didn't sleep a wink all night for considering it and, by breakfast time, had decided, yes, they would go down there on Friday morning, though she'd have to make it look coincidental; like it was nothing to do with the girl being there.

Half the Knit and Natter had had the same idea. By the time Kathleen got Bill out of his chair, into his trunks and transferred into the special hoist, the other ladies were emerging from their own cubicles. Agnes, with her blood pressure. Mary, who suffered with lumbago. Deirdre and Evelyn, who had so many complaints between them, Kathleen could never keep track of who was crippled with what from one week to the next. They lingered round the pool like elephants toeing the edge of a watering hole. Nobody wanted to be the first one in. It was important to maintain an air of nonchalance. You couldn't let the others see you'd come here looking to get healed, for you'd only feel a right eejit when it didn't happen. There'd been a similar stand off last November when Poundland ran a Black Friday special on selection boxes. They'd all turned up at ten to nine, ready to grab enough for every one of their grandbabies and, confronted by the others, felt the need to mask their desperation. They'd made a sterling attempt at pretending to be there for toothpaste or toilet cleaner and only stumbling upon the selection box offer by chance.

This morning they eyed each other suspiciously across the water and mumbled their excuses. Agnes was trying to lose a bit of weight. Mary had mixed her days up and come down to the Baths thinking it was aqua aerobics day. Evelyn and Deirdre claimed the doctor had prescribed swimming to ease their various complaints and, spotting a perfect opportunity, Kathleen jumped on the back of their excuse. She said the specialist had told Bill the very same thing. She looked to her husband, hoping for an alibi and, when he didn't offer one, stood lightly on his naked foot, so he got the message. Yes, he said nodding, the specialist thought the water might help with his pain. The specialist had said no such thing but the two of them had been together long enough to understand when back up was required.

Kathleen hadn't told Bill that she hoped a dip in the Templemore Baths might cure his terminal cancer. She'd found herself incapable of voicing the words. Though they seemed almost plausible in her head, out loud she knew they'd sound limp and ludicrous, like the punchline to a bad cracker joke. Instead, she'd appealed to her husband's romantic side. As teenagers they'd spent many hours down the deep end of the Baths. The East, with its tiny houses, stacked one on top of the other, offered very little privacy for courting couples and they'd soon learned how to keep their faces casual and impassive, whilst beneath the waterline they touched each other through their swimsuits in blatant disregard of the sign forbidding heavy petting. Kathleen and Bill had fond memories of the Baths. She'd asked him for one last dip, for old times' sake; afterwards she'd take him to S D Bell for a fancy cup of coffee and a bun. It was not like Kathleen to ask for anything, so Bill conceded immediately, and had been somewhat baffled to find the other Knit and Natter ladies intruding upon their wee moment together.

It was obvious that all five woman were waiting for the foreign girl to appear. Kathleen understood their logic. She'd done her homework; fished the old King James version out of the bookcase and read the story before leaving the house. If this girl was anything like Jesus – and that was the assumption to end all assumptions – they'd have to wait for the spirit to trouble the water. Or, in local parlance, the cure wouldn't take if they were in the pool before her. If Agnes's furtive glancing was anything to go by, the girl was already here and changing in the cubicle furthest from the entrance. Kathleen could picture her in there dragging her hair up into a high ponytail, contemplating a wee cappuccino after her swim, not for a minute anticipating six senior citizens waiting to suck the power out of her the instant she hit the water. Poor wee lassie, thought Kathleen, the young were never fully aware of their own capabilities.

When she emerged, the girl was plainer than she'd imagined; a bit hefty round the thighs and just as pale as a local. She did not look like a miracle. She looked like the kind of girl who cleaned toilets for a living. Still, you couldn't judge people on looks alone. Kathleen herself had been at school with a girl who ended up a novelist, and a more homely looking girl she'd never seen. She glanced across the room. Agnes was already inclined towards the pool's edge; her weight resting on her front leg like a runner poised at the starting blocks. Mary was all business too; her face folded in grim concentration. So, it has come to this, thought Kathleen. They were pitching themselves against each other, for it was only the first to hit the water who'd get the good of the miracle. Everybody else was just going to get wet. Kathleen's dying husband didn't seem to give her any natural advantage. It was every Knit and Natter lady for herself this morning. Damn them all, she thought, I deserve this. As the girl curled her toes around the pool's lip and prepared to dive, Kathleen wrapped her arms around her husband's flabby belly and, with all the strength she could muster, jumped.

They hit the water a split second after the girl. The other four followed immediately, plopping dully into the pool like dropped stones. For a second the water was white with froth. It puckered then settled slowly as the five grey heads bobbed back to the surface, spluttering wildly. Agnes. Mary. Deirdre. Evelyn. And Kathleen. They blinked the chlorine out of their eyes. They looked like they wanted to stab each other though their lips were smiling, and their mouths were saying, 'that was some splash, wasn't it? It's a wonder there's any water left in the pool.'

Bill was not so buoyant. Bill would require some assistance from the lifeguard and oxygen and a long weekend in ICU. Bill would not see the end of the month. Poor Bill. The Knit and Natter ladies noted his declining condition and did not ask Kathleen if the Baths had helped at all, if there was any truth in the rumour. They felt bad for having given the poor woman hope. They'd be more careful in future about what they passed on.

Kathleen felt bad too, but her guilt was different. It was not so easy to dismiss. She'd done her best to help Bill. Or had she? Perhaps some selfish part of her had wanted the miracle for herself. Her body had rushed ahead of her good intentions and it had been her heels that pierced the water first, her legs, arms and aching arthritic limbs which soaked up the cure. Kathleen had been healed. Bill hadn't. She could not even bear witness to the miracle for the awful shame of it.

Symposium

Introduction

The first annual Freelands Artist Programme Symposium, held over three days in June 2019, was hosted by Site Gallery in Sheffield. It brought all participating organisations and artists together in one location, in some cases for the very first time.

As the first formal gathering of those involved in the programme, workshops and sessions developed with guest speakers were designed to produce a series of open-ended questions to be continually addressed and built on across the duration of the five-year programme.

Workshops by Helena Reckitt, Grace Ndiritu, George Clark and Kunsthalle Lissabon introduced subjects such as the thematics of care, community-led practice, refusal, and radical hospitality. Each of these sessions have informed new textual material, which is published overleaf.

Curator and researcher Helena Reckitt introduced her proposition of 'Productive Refusals', drawing from her work on care and artistic labour. Her workshop looked at what it might mean to say 'No' as a productive way to change existing habits and systems. The workshop also foregrounded important ethical questions around issues such as pay, labour, and exploitation in the art world. Reckitt's essay contextualises the workshop within her wider research and details a number of artistic practices pertinent to such concerns.

A group session following this workshop focused on a commissioning model of parallel practice, originated by Witte de With Center for Contemporary Art in Rotterdam.[1] In 2017, the museum invited artists Ahmet Ögüt and Goshka Macuga to examine each other's practices through conversation, and to subsequently realise two collaborative exhibitions together.[2] For the Symposium Grace Ndiritu and George Clark – two artists engaged in film and community-led practice – were invited to discuss the many parallels in their work, before the 20 Freelands Artist Programme artists were paired up to have conversations of their own. Although Grace Ndiritu and George Clark had met briefly once before, this was their first opportunity to formally connect and talk. What follows is an edited transcript of their conversation.

Kunsthalle Lissabon is an exhibition space in Lisbon, Portugal known for its original and dynamic curatorial approach that places 'radical hospitality, which it defines as sociability, solidarity and generosity, at the core of the institution. Celebrating its tenth anniversary in 2019, Kunsthalle Lissabon took the radical act to give away its entire infrastructure – website, budgets, office, gallery space – to four invited guest institutions, with the host organisation 'disappearing' in the process for the duration of the project. This workshop addressed how friendship can be thought of as a relevant political category to imagine and produce other ways of operating as an institution. Kunsthalle Lissabon, at this vital moment of rethinking itself, presented its space as an empty vessel, on to which the four guest groups were invited to project their own institutional desires. A subsequent questionnaire with Kunsthalle Lissabon co-directors João Mourão and Luís Silva sees them reflect on this act of withdrawal, as well as the enforced act of withdrawal – the closure of the gallery – brought about by the COVID-19 pandemic.

This central section holds a space for reflection: how might these ideas, introduced in 2019 and developed further in these pages, continue to influence further iterations of the Freelands Artist Programme?

30 July 2020

1 The institution is currently undergoing a process of renaming due to its name's past colonial associations, but was titled Witte de With when the session took place. The new name will be adopted on 27 January 2021 following collective public discussions.

2 Ahmet Ögüt and Goshka Macuga, Episode 1 & 2, Witte de With, 17 June – 20 August and 8 September – 31 December 2017.

Productive Refusals

Helena Reckitt

Over the past decade, stepping aside and saying 'No' to conventional requests and expectations has become a prominent tool of subjective and political resistance. Highlighting society's dependence on undervalued labour and unsustainable resources, practices of negation challenge the status quo, leading to new intimate and professional habits.

Within the cultural field, various tactics of refusal have emerged. Artists have declined invitations to speak at art fairs that pose as community gatherings, or on panels whose academic premise they disagree with. They have asked not to be nominated for prizes based on identity criteria with which they prefer not to be linked.[1] When they are shortlisted for prizes, they have rejected the demand that they treat other artists as competitors, dividing the spoils amongst themselves instead.[2] They have refused to exhibit in museums sponsored by foundations and corporations that perpetuate exploitative practices, in turn prompting some art institutions to sever long-term philanthropic relationships.[3] Cultural workers have rejected working gratis, or for inadequate pay.[4] They have questioned the contradictions that lie at the heart of many artistic projects and institutions, demanding that organisations pursue progressive practices that match their rhetoric.[5]

Within my milieu I have encountered various instances of productive refusal. An artist refused to provide an image of her work to accompany an article I'd written, asking why she should subsidise a profitable academic publisher. A message to a cultural worker prompted an 'Away from emails' automated response: it featured their rules for 'Extraction October', 25 directives, starting with 'No doing work on commutes' and ending with 'We don't repeat the hyper-delivery-care-deficit-fatigue ever again.'[6] To my invitation to perform in Toronto, an artist explained that instead of flying from London they would take the less physically and environmentally damaging option of participating via Skype.[7] Recently, lecturers on short-term contracts at Goldsmiths, University of London, where I teach, announced a staff wildcat strike, protesting the College's decision not to renew their contracts during the COVID-19 pandemic, an act that disproportionately affects precariously employed People of Colour.

In contrast to these overt acts of withdrawal, refusal can operate in less visible or public ways, such as continuing to show up while participating 'otherwise'. Minimising unwanted surveillance and control, this approach can prove necessary in situations where it is impossible, or too risky, to walk away. Working to rule, fulfilling the terms of employment yet withholding the extra labour upon which the system relies, is a tried and tested tactic. In *Garments Against Women,* Anne Boyer enacts a form of 'not writing', detailing the very conditions – from temporary employment and lack of healthcare, to single parenthood – that contribute to her economic vulnerability, undermining her ability to write. Virginia Woolf advocated the cultivation of indifference as 'a form of quiet revolt, the disruptive power of choosing not to care about what we are enjoined to',[8] as characterised by Maria de la Puig Bellacasa. The radical feminist Shulamith Firestone in 1970 advocated a smile boycott, 'at which declaration all women would instantly abandon their "pleasing" smiles, henceforth smiling only when something pleased *them*'.[9]

For workers employed to provide care, attempting to separate their 'true' feelings from those expended for pay might be necessary to protect their personal affects and relationships from being exhausted.[10] Such efforts constitute a Bartleby-esque stance of 'preferring not to', where refusal does not entail quitting, but replaces ingrained habits with unorthodox forms of behaviour that unsettle expectations. Bartleby disarmed his employer by continuing to show up for work and staring out of the window at a brick wall instead of performing his expected tasks.[11]

The readymade artist collective Claire Fontaine describe such flights from convention in terms of Human Strike. A movement of 'desubjectification', Human Strike stages 'a strike against oneself, an exit from one's identity (of a good mother, diligent worker, loving wife, active citizen) and all that sustains it.'[12] Disidentifying from stereotypical roles and obligations can lead to 'a new state, less defined, more uncertain, but freed of the weights that burdened the previous identity and perpetuate the status quo.'[13] As a rallying cry from the 1970s Italian feminist movement states: 'We don't believe what they say about us.'[14]

Rather than constitute literal withdrawal, refusal changes the focus of attention, prompting a reappraisal of value. As a participant at a workshop on curating and care recently observed: '"No" is not compromise but conversation. "No" becomes "not this way". If you always say "yes" you suppress the reality of the situation and therefore justify it (it becomes naturalized).'[15] Art workers at another gathering in Paris declared, 'Our proposition is instead of agreeing to provide to what is demanded, we turn the conversation around to work on what is really needed.'[16]

The Land of NOPE

The development of subterfuge and withdrawal as survival strategies has a long lineage within Black theory and practice. The political scientist and historian Françoise Vergès describes 'the loopholes of retreat' forged by enslaved Black women, which entailed 'creating one's own forms of freedom, endurance, perseverance, fortitude, as well as cunning', including 'learning to play stupid, deaf, and blind to gather information in order to distract those in power'.[17] Not opposing one to another, Vergès asks, 'how do we develop a politics of visibility *and* invisibility both for fighting in the open and for building spaces of retreat away from the constant racial-sexist gaze of State surveillance and control?'[18]

Essentialist assumptions about identity and representation imposed on members of marginalised groups constitute damaging forms of tokenism. People of Colour question the supposed benefits of being included as representatives of ethnic groups and as evidence of institutional inclusivity. They indicate that they routinely carry out labour that exceeds their paid roles, from providing extra mentorship to Black and Brown students who seek them out as role models,[19] to using their personal networks to encourage members of culturally diverse communities to attend white-dominated art institutions.[20] Yet People of Colour in the art and academic sector are disproportionately employed at lower ends of the pay scale or on short-term and part-time contracts. Expected to share their stories of vulnerability and pain, their presence in white-centred organisations bolsters institutional optics around representation and diversity, as a UK collective of artists and arts workers recently objected.[21] Sought out to develop community-engagement and education programmes in museums and galleries, too often this involvement does not translate into broader institutional support for their professional development or artistic practices, thus marginalising them and their work.[22]

Nowhere is the exploitation of People of Colour's labour more visible than when their criticism of institutions is used by those very organisations as evidence of their progressive culture. This is the paradoxical situation that Sara Ahmed faced when she exposed the systemic racism and sexism that she encountered at Goldsmiths, where she was a professor and diversity officer. 'The work you do to expose what is not being done is used as evidence of what has been done', she pointedly explains.[23] Likening her experience to that of facing brick walls, Ahmed resigned her post. Ahmed practises another form of productive refusal in her writing. Reversing academic habits of 'citational privilege', where the same intellectual precursors are referenced time and again, in *Living a Feminist Life* Ahmed does not cite a single white man; instead she highlights those feminist and critical race practitioners whose work has sustained her.

In another form of strategic withdrawal, artist E. Jane's *NOPE (a manifesto)* rejects demands that their identity and subjectivity be deemed visible, stable and knowable. 'We are beyond asking should we be in the room. We are in the room. We are also dying at a rapid pace and need a sustainable future.' Resisting the colonial occlusion of 'identity and representation', E. Jane affirms their place 'outside of it in the land of NOPE'.[24]

Passionate Work

At the 2019 Freelands Artist Programme Symposium at Sheffield's Site Gallery, I led a workshop on 'Productive Refusals'.[25] I started by highlighting some of the problematic work conditions common to the cultural sector, symbolised by the many invitations that we receive (and perhaps give) to participate in projects gratis – for the opportunity, exposure, or contacts. I asked those present to recall a time when they agreed to something that, in retrospect, they should have refused, as well as an incident when someone saying 'No' to them proved generative.

This exercise was adapted from a proposition that I developed with artist Alex Martinis Roe as part of a feminist workshop that formed the basis of her 2016 film *Our Future Network*.[26] Following my account of being expected to pay to register and travel to an academic conference at which I was speaking, Martinis Roe described having invited the philosopher Luisa Muraro to participate in an artwork inspired by her research into the Milan Women's Bookshop collective, co-founded by Muraro. When Muraro declined, on the basis that Martinis Roe was her teacher in this situation, what might have felt like rejection ended up empowering Martinis Roe, who found the source of authority within herself, rather than externally.

In subsequent role-play sessions in Sheffield, one group examined the need for clarity on project budgets and artist payments, while another explored how to turn down an exhibition invitation from a friend. Some participants objected to what they understood to be the exercise's underlying premise, which pitted artists and representatives of arts organisations against one another. Their work in artist-led culture would never happen if they waited for funding to be in place, and for everyone to receive fair pay, they argued.

While I agree that financial reward is often the last reason why we choose to participate in the arts, unfortunately the assumption that we work for love, rather than pay, perpetuates the field's poor labour conditions. Cultural workers, like others who occupy feminised roles, risk being treated as sources of infinite support. Such expectations reflect extractivist attitudes that treat nature, like maternal love, as a free, boundless resource. Consequently, the subjectivity demanded of cultural workers, which emphasises flexibility and mobility, communication and overwork, can be even more emotionally draining than that required of conventional 9–5 employees. The Freelands Foundation workshop explored how to stimulate more reciprocal relationships, based in solidarity and mutual recognition, between artists and those holding institutional roles.

Cultural workers are often in a double bind. Faced with reduced programme and institutional budgets in the wake of austerity measures, they carry out the socially reproductive labour of maintaining an institution's smooth operations and positive public image. Internalising the pressure to operate in an opportunistic and entrepreneurial fashion, they feel unable to demand better conditions. A passionate commitment to artists and projects can ultimately jeopardise their own, and their collaborators', flourishing, as well as their ability to nurture non-professional relationships and care responsibilities.

Sociologist Arlie Russell Hochschild discusses the emotional splitting amongst flight attendants and other employees whose jobs entail managing other people's feelings while suppressing their own.[27] Citing Hochschild, curator Jenny Richards explores the tendency of arts workers to downplay problems and emotions. Richards aptly describes the phenomenon of the 'coping curator', an inherently feminised figure, with perfect haircut and lipstick, denying her fragility and reliance on others to present the perfect show in the perfect white cube. Contesting this tendency for self-exploitation, while at Konsthall C in Sweden, Richards and her co-director attempted to make their working conditions visible, emphasising how their roles encompass multiple tasks including those of 'janitor / chef / cleaner / therapist / friend / organiser / builder / teacher / administrator / artist'.[28]

Empty Gestures?

Many cultural workers share Richards's concern about the impact of neoliberal pressures to be endlessly busy, productive and in demand. The toll of staying au fait with the latest art world developments puts an unsustainable burden on human as well as environmental resources. Having diagnosed these norms, we must move beyond analysis. This is not to underestimate the challenges arts workers face when they attempt to change rigid, top-down institutional dynamics. Instead it recognises the need to nurture collective acts of refusal that can stimulate subjective and structural change: urgent in an art culture that often courts the performance of radicalism and criticality, without attempting to transform exploitative and unsustainable working conditions.

While I have emphasised refusal's productive potential, I also want to note that withdrawal can encompass 'unproductive' gestures of inefficiency and uselessness. 'Generative' rather than 'Productive' might be a more accurate description for the processes of refusal I have described here. Stepping aside can be a valuable act of self- and collective-care in the face of widespread burn out, exhaustion and other forms of ill health. Challenging networked culture's emphasis on spectacle, speed and shareable content, it can engender 'pointless' acts of pause and *détournement*, pleasure and play. For it is in moments when we choose not to perform as expected that '"I am not what you see here" gives rise to "Let's be another possible now."'[29]

Helena Reckitt thanks Sharon Kivland for her editorial work on this essay

1 See artist Jesse Darling's 'Thank you for thinking of me: Correspondences 2014–2017', in which redacted details of specific invitations that Darling has turned down are presented. In one letter, Darling explains, 'I wish to practice [*sic*] this politics of protest and refusal in the sense of "putting my money where my mouth is" and in this sense it would be disingenuous for me to continue.', *Unbag*, End, winter 2018, https://unbag.net/end/thank-you-for-thinking-of-me.

2 Examples of the prize-winning artist dividing the award include Theaster Gates at Artes Mundi 6, 2014, and Helen Marten at the Turner Prize and Hepworth Prize for Sculpture, both in 2016. In 2019 the four artists nominated for the Turner Prize asked the judges not to select a winner, but to treat them as one collective and divide the funds between them.

3 One prominent example is Nan Goldin's threat to withdraw from an exhibition of her work at the National Portrait Gallery, London in 2019, if the museum accepted a £1m gift from the Sackler Family, owners of the pharmaceutical company that makes the prescription opioid painkiller OxyContin.

4 See Precarious Workers Brigade, *Training for Exploitation? Politicising Employability and Reclaiming Education*, The Journal of Aesthetics & Protest Press, 2017. The California-based curator Astria Suparak publicises times when she refuses to work for inadequate pay on her Facebook account. In September 2019, Suparak posted that she had said no to jurying an artist residency programme, because the fee constituted less-than-minimum wage. She subsequently updated her post, explaining that the fee had been increased, the employee explaining how Suparak's refusal enabled them to pressurise the institution to increase its budget allocation.

5 I learned of a great example from artist Hayley Newman during the '(Un)Learning Habits of Care' workshop that I organised with Grace Ndiritu at Studio Voltaire, London, September 2019. Newman, who has a long history of environmental activism, explained how she has grappled with the contradictions of being included in events with environmental concerns, to which she is expected to travel by air. Having flown only once since 2007, Newman often subsidises her travel by train. In an email to me she aptly described the pattern by which 'Artists who work for cultural change do so in our own time and at our own cost (financial and personal/emotional) and without credit.'

6 Devised by artists Sophie Chapman and Kerri Jefferis as part of 'Extraction October' in 2017.

7 Raju Rage, 'Yeah But Can We Listen Tho?' performance, part of 'Care Crisis, Care Connective: An Open Forum on Cultural Work', organised as part of the series *Take Care*, Blackwood Gallery, University of Toronto at Mississauga, September 2017, for which I curated the exhibition *Habits of Care*.

8 Maria de la Puig Bellacasa, 'Introduction', in *Matters of Care: Speculative Ethics in More than Human Worlds*, University of Minnesota Press, 2017, p.5.

9 Shulamith Firestone, *The Dialectic of Sex: The Case for Feminist Revolution*, Bantam, 1970, p.90.

10 This argument is made by De La Puig Bellacasa, *op.cit*.

11 Herman Melville, 'Bartleby, the Scrivener: A Story of Wall Street' (1853) in *The Piazza Tales*, Dix & Edwards, 1856.

12 Claire Fontaine, 'Existential Metonymy and Imperceptible Abstractions' in *Human Strike Has Already Begun and Other Writings*, Mute Books and Post-Media Lab, Leuphana University, 2013, p.56.

13 *Ibid.*, p.56.

14 From a lecture by Fulvia Carnevale, 'And they ask for her help more than they are ready to help her', Goldsmiths, University of London, 16 March 2015.

15 Participant notes from 'Curating and Caring,' a workshop which I devised and which I jointly led with Christine Shaw, Blackwood Gallery, University of Toronto at Mississauga, September 2017.

16 From propositions written during 'Take (Back) Care,' Cité de Culture, Paris, which I developed with Christine Shaw to accompany the exhibition *Take Care*, La Ferme du Boisson, May 2019.

17 Françoise Vergès, 'Politics of Marooning and Radical Disobedience', *e-flux journal*, #105, December 2019, https://www.e-flux.com/journal/105/305244/politics-of-marooning-and-radical-disobedience/.

18 *Ibid*.

19 See Akanksha Mehta, 'Teaching Gender, Race, Sexuality: Reflections on Feminist Pedagogy,' *Kohl: A Journal for Body and Gender Research*, vol.5, no.1, 2019, pp.23–30, on the affective labour she carried out as a teacher of colour, and her students of colour, on a UK university module about the intersections of race, gender and sexuality.

20 See Teanne Andrews, 'Hypocrisy, fake solidarity and glass ceilings: My perspective working at the William Morris Gallery', weareparable.com, 2020, http://www.weareparable.com/hypocrisy-fake-solidarity-and-glass-ceilings-my-perspective-working-at-the-william-morris-gallery/?preview=true&fbclid=IwAR0ivcAAd5EoCpOSwrR-Cd0F5gZxVzT-aSzhSiMRdxnJ2DfadKwISTTqB34.

21 Arts collective including Jade Montserrat, Cecilia Wee, Michelle Williams Gamaker and Tae Ateh, 'We need collectivity against structural and institutional racism in the cultural sector', *Arts Professional*, 24 June 2020, https://www.artsprofessional.co.uk/magazine/article/we-need-collectivity-against-structural-and-institutional-racism-cultural-sector?fbclid=IwAR0lwrTL1mRmG2F83673mENmA7AiNhRzCeGHBRFfEme-MUyrtHuui187QJ4.

22 'While we do not dispute the essential impact we may bring to this specific agenda, this is an active restriction on our creative capacities which prevents us from becoming more deeply involved within these organisations', Montserrat et al, *ibid*.

23 Sara Ahmed, *Living a Feminist Life*, Duke University Press, 2017, p.110.

24 E. Jane, *NOPE (a manifesto)*, 2017, http://www.e-jane.net/#_=_.

25 Available to listen to at https://soundcloud.com/user-682181597/helena-reckitt-freelands-artist-programme-symposium-day-1?in=user-682181597/sets/freelands-artist-programme.

26 Our proposition, together with those of the other participants, appears in Alex Martinis Roe, *To Become Two: Propositions for Feminist Collective Practice*, Archive Books, 2018.

27 Arlie Russell Hochschild, *The Managed Heart: The Commercialization of Human Feeling*, University of California Press, 1983.

28 Jenny Richards in Victoria Horne, Kirsten Lloyd, Jenny Richards, Catherine Spencer, 'Taking Care: Feminist Curatorial Pasts, Presents and Futures', *OnCurating*, issue 29, May 2016, https://www.on-curating.org/issue-29-reader/taking-care-feminist-curatorial-pasts-presents-and-futures.html.

29 'Sonogram of a Potentiality', first published in French as *Échographie d'une puissance in Tiqqun #2*, 2001. The English translation was published by Pétroleuse Press, 2011.

GN Maybe we should first say that we've only ever met once before, briefly, a month ago in Ghent, at the 2019 Courtisane film festival. George was showing some films and then afterwards we spoke, and I felt we had a lot in common.

GC I've known about you and your video work for more than ten years through the broader community around LUX.[1] At Courtisane it was a great reconnection and also fascinating to find out about your processes and work, and to realise that we both came through LUX.

When we were talking earlier this morning, we realised that we both live and work in a nomadic fashion, partly by design, partly by necessity, and partly by kamikaze attitude [laughs]. One of the things I was really interested in is your decision to make this shift: to move out of the city and to work in a rural space, and to look at different sorts of communities and try to find different models of working.

GN I think it's a shift I've had since I was a kid. My family are from rural Kenya, so I kind of grew up in Kenya and also in working-class Birmingham, and I had this back and forth movement between things since I was a small child: meeting different types of people, different cultures, classes... When I was quite young, this 'airport lifestyle' just felt very natural, but as a teenager I felt like I should choose. I went to school here in the UK and so I became a teenager in England. Then after that I started to feel a bit lost again, because the nomadic side of me needs to be nomadic, so I started to travel a lot independently, sometimes with friends, sometimes on my own. I studied abroad as well, in Amsterdam at De Ateliers.

For many years I had a weird double life doing a lot of esoteric things: having gurus and going on meditation retreats, while also having a contemporary art life, but keeping these two worlds separate. At that time people weren't very open to that kind of knowledge. About six or seven years ago I decided to open up and bring these two lifestyles together, which is how projects like *The Ark*[2] came about. *The Ark* is a project where I decided to start my own community. In 2012 I decided I would only go to the city when it was necessary, otherwise I would always live in rural places, and I ended up living in a lot of alternative and New Age communities but also with the Hare Krishnas, or in a forest or in a van, all sorts of places...

I was doing informal research myself at the time and using my intuition – I was filming things but I wasn't really doing it for a purpose. After a few years when I'd gotten together all of this information, I thought I should do something with it. The obvious thing was to do an exhibition, but actually I thought, 'Why not start a community?' I was interested in thinking about group dynamics and individual dynamics and how in communities the problems of power – and a lot of problems that we have in the city such as sexism, racism, classism – can be replicated in communities; the idea of community as 'Utopia' and the problems with that was also interesting. So I decided to make an experiment and I invited artists, scientists and spiritual people to live together in this community that was called *The Ark*.

GC Is *The Ark* constituted geographically, or is it a project that can move around, where the communities reconfigure themselves in different places?

GN No, it was in a fixed place and time, in Paris in 2017. A lot of these people I had already met in different communities at different times, or were people I had met on my travels or through the internet, etc. I was thinking, 'Okay, I'm going to do this community – what do I need? I'm going to need a biologist, an economist.' But early on I had already met this sociologist Petra Carman and she had done a lot of studies on cults, and there is this joke: 'What's the difference between a cult and a community?', which was also intriguing. How does it go from being a community to a cult? This idea of power – that was a big thing. So Petra and I made this experiment and created two badges – one badge said, 'Working Together for a Plant Based Future' and was all about cooperation and working together and peace, and the other one said, 'Charismatic Cult Leader'. You were allowed to choose when you would wear these badges. At the beginning of the community everybody wore the 'Working Together' badge [laughs]. Every day was structured around waking up with the sound of a gong and then we'd have a silent breakfast, like at a retreat – and then we would have some spiritual exercise, followed by an academic talk from a biologist for example, which was always connected to the current world problems. In the afternoons we would work on art, and we made some costumes for the public part of the project that would happen at the end of the retreat.

When it came to people's own individual workshops, they would sometimes put the 'Charismatic Cult Leader' badge on, and it would feel empowering to say that, but then afterwards people would feel guilty, take it off and put the other one on [laughs]. By the end, some people had both badges on!

GC I'm really interested in this idea of the double life that you mentioned, which I think many of us function in. Often we might say we're an artist-writer, but we wouldn't necessarily say we're an artist-barista, or any of the other things we do to support ourselves. Perhaps you wouldn't talk about your involvement in alternative communities in an arts context, but would you talk about your involvement with the art world in these alternative communities?

GN It wasn't that I was ashamed of alternative communities in art – it was more that most people at that time would just take the piss when I said I did meditation and yoga. So it was because I didn't like feeling bullied for doing something that I believed in!

Western culture is very materialist – I don't mean materialistic, rather, in the sense of thinking there's nothing more than 'this'. And in your own work, as you have understood from spending time in Asia, Animism is an important concept – that is, the world is a living being. It's only in the West that there's this kind of deadening of objects. That's what I found very confronting, especially in the art world, where you would think it would be the opposite because art is all about creativity. Yet there wasn't that room or space available at that time. That's why I came to separate the two, but equally, if I was at a monastery – I lived in monasteries for a while – I would talk about being an artist and going to art fairs, and some people were judgemental. And then I would have to justify that part of my life. There was always a justification of both parts, which was kind of frustrating for me as a person, but I just knew I had to go through it because that's how I felt anyway as a kid. To me it's a natural way of being, being nomadic. It makes sense to be interested in and curious about people.

GC Yes, why would you *not* want to do things with others?

GN Exactly! But you can see right now in the news in 2019 – Trump, Brexit – we're closing in. There is this lack of curiosity. Why don't you want other people to come to your country?! [laughs] Because they bring other things. And isn't that a good thing? It's that fear of the Other. I would be equally interested to know your sense on this – what made you have that impulse, as an English person?

GC I'm from West Yorkshire, right on the Pennines. I grew up in Marsden, a small former industrial textile village. I was interested in cinema, but there was no cinema there. I was interested in the world, but it felt very far away. You had video shops, but there would be one shelf of World Cinema [laughs] and I was much more interested in that shelf – that was where I wanted to be. It felt like going to London was to have access to that. London was access to cinemas, to the screen, to other languages and other cultures and other people. I don't know why, but I wanted to be part of this thing that felt like it was distant, and it felt hard to do that here in a rural context. When I think back to that time, I was such a country boy! I would go to London and go to Piccadilly Circus and then be confused as to why there wasn't a circus there, things like that [laughs]. For me, cinema was this access, this route to elsewhere.

GN Why not anthropology?

GC I think it's images for me – I'm also dyslexic, so language wasn't a route into other places like images were. Sounds were the route. The first film I saw at a film festival was *Daisies* by Věra Chytilová[3] – this incredible experimental feminist film made in the former Czechoslovakia in 1966. I had to take three buses to get to Bradford to see it, and there were about three people in the cinema but I thought, 'Wow: this is worth the journey.' I had no idea what the film was about, but I knew I was in the right place. And that kind of desire, to put myself in that place, to confront myself with other types of knowledge is something I was always drawn to, and cinema was the most expedient way to do that.

But back to this double life question – I studied at art school, I studied Fine Art, and as part of that, I also wanted to see lots

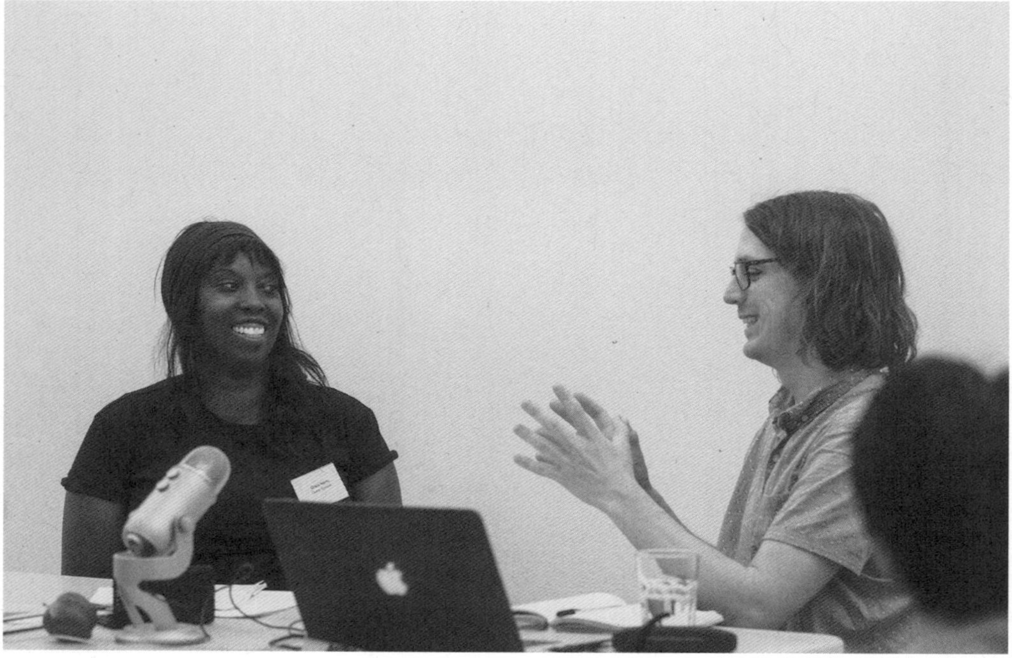

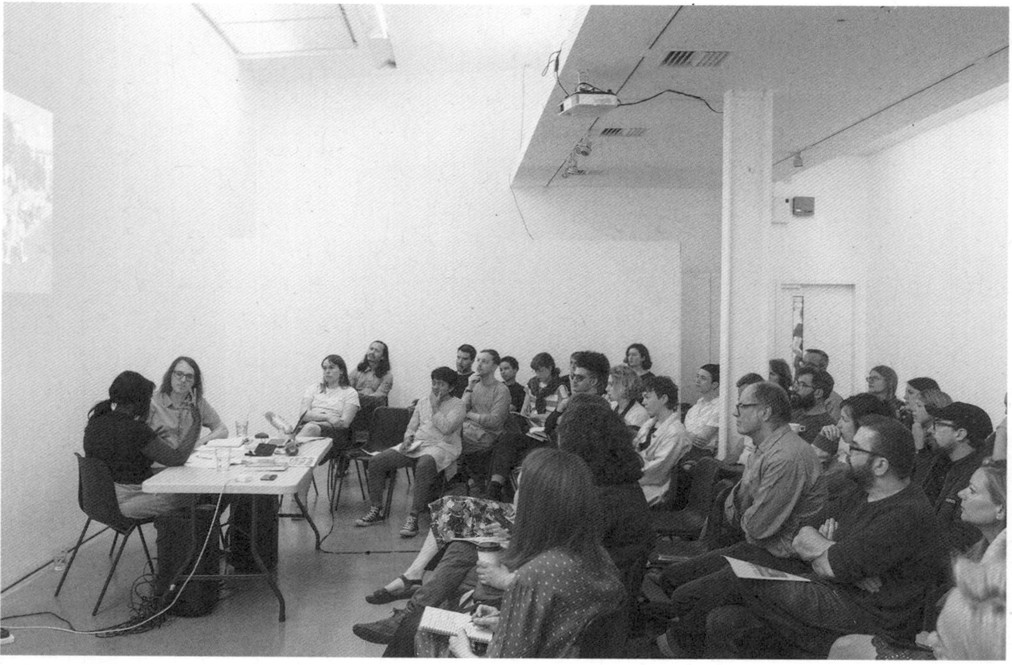

Grace Ndiritu and George Clark in conversation, Freelands Artist Programme Symposium 2019, Site Gallery. Photo: Mark Howe

of things, so I started a film club at the art school. We had one rule – we would only show things that weren't available on DVD or video. I had already started falling into curating and other things like that around the same time. For me, writing about work, curating work, making work, they're all part of this same continuity – they are all layers of being engaged with other people, with making things. But then at some point I crossed over this line, and I was no longer an artist, I was a curator.

GN So you were an artist and a maker first?

GC Yes, and for me they all felt like the same thing, but maybe it was easier to get paid as a curator [laughs]. It was also quicker to show other people's films than to make them all myself! I came to work across different institutions in London, and I felt like people kept talking to me like I was a curator and not as an artist. I needed to leave London to try and re-orientate both how I work in terms of balance, of the different aspects of what I did, and also where my work could be situated – in terms of geographies and different kinds of centres of practice. This decentring was essential for me.

GN And you chose to move to Los Angeles?

GC Yes, I thought I would move to Hong Kong, but that proved harder to achieve. With LA I thought I would go for a month and it ended up being three years. Which was incredible. I realised that to be in LA was also to be adjacent to the Pacific, and also then to shift from an Atlantic European worldview to a Pacific worldview was really essential to me. From there I would then start to travel more and to work in Taiwan, Hong Kong, Thailand...

GN From LA?

GC Yes, and also work in New Zealand and Chile. I began to re-orientate myself and become interested in the Pacific context. What's interesting is that a lot of these decisions are in a way pragmatic and kind of lucky ... I'm terrible at making decisions!

GN Is that part of the pull? That there are too many options? ...a lack of focus that you've used to your advantage as an artist, to follow your natural instinct.

GC Yes, when something was happening, I would already be thinking: 'What next?' When I worked more in curatorial practice, if someone was showing something, I would think: 'Great! I can show a different film and bring something else into the discussion.' In a way, I got involved in artists' film because it was the hardest stuff to see in any other context. In that respect it made it very easy to decide what to do. Something in mainstream cinema would be on for a month, whereas this one film was only on once. For me this connects to the idea of liveness – cinema is not this thing that is always available, it's only available at this particular time.

GN It's about the moment, the immediacy. That's why I also started, and the way I made my films in the first place. It would just be me and the camera and it would be very immediate, that relationship: I would put myself in a trance and perform, and then afterwards I would look back on what I had done. There was this sense of a real mind-meld between the camera and the body that could only happen in that moment. I think that's part of Process art isn't it? Even if it's on film.

GC Yes, it's contingent. And in a way it's easier to think about certain practices within moving image which are more aligned with performance and liveness, or which are more aligned to community, or organising modes of assembly. That idea of the screening as an event – film as a reason to bring people together. I wanted to ask you about your relationship to ritual, of this kind of performance as another mode of cinema.

GN I also wanted to bring up that we both love Raúl Ruiz![4] His idea is that film is a poetic object and not just an industrialised piece of art.

My background is in Textile art, and I studied at Winchester School of Art. Afterwards I just started making films myself. I had a Super 8 camera and I was experimenting. I wasn't making textiles in the sense of printing, I was making installations and conceptual work. When I moved to Amsterdam,

I carried on making videos. I was self-taught. But this idea of craft ... in film school you learn how to storyboard. But I had learned how to mood board, coming from a fashion and textiles perspective. And out of that I would make the work. So there was no narrative exactly, but I would set up a scenario. From my esoteric studies that I was doing at the same time, I was very interested in different states of being and how film is a living medium. Video is very visceral, and I was very interested in how to transcend that medium. But it wasn't until I started doing all the esoteric stuff that I understood what my kind of performance was. Because I'm not interested in the theatrical – I like the idea of spontaneity. In trance anything can happen. It's part of the process. And in terms of ritual, I wanted to ask you about your project you were talking about at Courtisane: an outdoor projection event in a cemetery.

GC I'm interested in projection as a type of performance and as a type of assembly. The UK has a long history of expanded cinema and different ways of showing films to challenge what the screen might be. What film might be. The act of projection itself as a kind of creative thing. The film maybe doesn't happen on the wall but happens in between this space. I started to travel and to look at other models of sited cinema that maybe wouldn't be described within an art historical term of expanded cinema, or would come from other types of ritualistic practice.

In Taiwan in particular there has been a strong Animist tradition, shared across South East Asia, of showing films for ancestors or for the dead. The main audience is the ancestors. This is an outdoor mode of projection that has a completely different way of thinking about what the audience is. This related really well to a reading of Raúl's work, and to the idea of a cinema that is more multivalent.[5] Raúl has this idea that every film contains many other potential films. He said that we make 'zero audience' films, that is, if we make films for no one, then if one person comes it's a huge success! Maybe that person could be living or dead.

GN Raúl wrote an essay called 'For a Shamanic Cinema', and I did a screening at the Centre Pompidou using that title.[6] I did a live trance possession before the screening started and then showed films that went with that title. It's very powerful, and I don't think his work has really gotten the credit that it deserves.

GC Also powerful is his writing on cinema: reconceptualising that film is not about the production of a static object. This for me also related really strongly to your essay, 'Healing the Museum'.[7] In a way we can think about cinema as a museum structure, an institution that brings with it similar problems to the art museum, the gallery, the ethnographic museum, in terms of this treatment of the audience relationship – how the object is treated and how people are associated with it. Raúl's approach is very expansive – it tries to treat the separate elements of the film so that they have their own autonomy and are valued as such. It's not about a conflict-based model of construction – it can open up and be expansive rather than be closed down. For me, as a way of working, a type of assembly, this would lend itself very naturally to say that film is not just an object, but also that maybe the production of a film, the preparation...

GN ...the behind-the-scenes, the back story of the making of the film...

GC ...and then the film doesn't have to contain all these things, and in a way it's better – the film can point to all these other things around it. Shall we talk about your essay?

GN The essay I wrote a few years ago called 'Healing the Museum' is part of a wider project with the same name, and it's really about how I felt museums are dying, because they are disconnected with what's going on out in the real world, both politically but also energetically. How it's not just about bringing different audiences but a different mindset to the museum, whether it's a contemporary, ethnographic or an art historical museum. I wrote a second essay in 2017 called 'Ways of Seeing', after John Berger's book,[8] and the subtitle is 'A New Museum Story for Planet Earth'. This is really about how the Western mind looks at objects as dead objects, so it means that with everything that is collected the value is always first the monetary value, then the cultural value, and then down the list it's the spiritual value.

In ethnographic museums that's a problem because most of those objects were made for spiritual and social-cultural reasons, and money was the last reason why the object was made. Our way of collecting, using and handling objects is causing issues for the objects themselves. Museums don't necessarily have the sensitivity to understand that. For example, totem poles were made to be outside – they need the elements, nature and the wind to be activated and to fulfil their purpose as totem poles. So when you put them inside you deaden them. This is also affecting our relationship with them.

GC One of the other things we began with was a shared interest in ecology. When I moved to LA, as well as trying to make more films I also grew a garden. It's brilliant in LA – things grow all year round. When I was in Taiwan, I made a new garden during a residency I had there. For the residency exhibition we invited all the people who came to also plant new seeds, so the garden became a kind of clock throughout the exhibition. Visitors would write down what they had planted and when they planted it. What would grow was based on who came to see the show. For me the garden was a great way to do everything that I was interested in with film, but without having to make a film – it was about time, it was about landscape, it was about light, about habitat. Also I was spending too much time on my computer [laughs] or in the dark – that's the problem with being interested in cinema! So I wanted to think about how to do these things but to do them outside or with other people.

To then find projectionists who would project these films outside revealed to me how cinema doesn't need to be this deadening thing – how cinema can be aligned with more organic or ecological methods. I became very interested in this parallel history of cinema and in a different way to think about the act of projection, which is about the act of making these things active and present again. In Taiwan I had a difficult time on a project. I had a whole plan for an exhibition, I had a title and we'd published the catalogue but I had a difficult experience with one of the collaborators and eventually had to cancel everything, and destroy all the material we had printed and completely change the exhibition. I suddenly thought that I was going to make a failed project. Although I remembered that Raúl actually tried to make a film in Taiwan himself in the mid 1990s, which was lost, so I thought I would make my own failed film. As with growing the garden, I really wanted it to be a living thing.

GN You wanted it to be real.

GC And also, to try and see what had happened to this failed project with Raúl: to see why it didn't materialise, to see if there was a way to maybe retrieve it or develop a working relationship to it. Part of that then was to think about how this film was never finished and we can't see it, but we shouldn't see that as a negative, as this lost thing. Maybe that's just a different state of that film. Is this simply a film we can't see? There are many films we can't see, many artworks we can't see that we know about, which are vivid even though we can't see them. That's not a negative thing. My question was how to make this absent film more tangible.

GN Can I ask – when you spoke to Western people about these ideas, what was the reaction? How did you contextualise it?

GC The premiere of my film *Double Ghosts* (2018) about Raúl's lost film took place in a cemetery in Taiwan, and the cemetery was the commissioner of his film originally. The projectionist I remember asked me: 'Do you really want to show the film in the cemetery?' Yes – it's a gesture, an offering in a way people understand. Cinema is weird: everyone together in the dark watching these flickering images. It's already a strange ritual. You're in this interstitial space, so in a way it doesn't take much to push that a little further and say actually cinema is always a ritual whether we think about it or not.

GN Whereas if it was an object, you think it would be more difficult? Because people have stricter ideas.

GC Exactly. With film archives you can have a room full of film print but you can't see it. There is this idea that films are only live when they are being shown, they have to be activated. You don't go to the archive to look at these empty film cans! Cinema relates very clearly – it needs activation, it needs to be shown, it exists in time. With cinema, too, often we're watching dead people anyway. So already it's a very metaphysical thing.

Freelands Artist Programme Symposium, Site Gallery, Sheffield, 19 June 2019

1 LUX, artists' moving image agency, https://lux.org.uk.
2 Grace Ndiritu, *The Ark: Center for Interdisciplinary Experimentation*, Les Laboratoires d'Aubervilliers, Paris, 2017.
3 Věra Chytilová, Czech filmmaker (1929–2014).
4 Raúl Ruiz, Chilean filmmaker (1941–2011).
5 See George Clark, *Double Ghosts*, 35mm film, 31 mins, 2018.
6 Raúl Ruiz, 'For a Shamanic Cinema', *Poetics of Cinema 1*, Dis Voir, 1995; Grace Ndiritu, *For a Shamanic Cinema: Alternative Strategies in the Practice of Performance*, Centre Pompidou, 2013.
7 From 2012 onwards Grace Ndiritu developed a body of work titled *Healing the Museum*, including essays and performances, such as the performance event and film at Printemps des Laboratoires, Paris, 2016 and Thalielab, Brussels, 2018.
8 John Berger, *Ways of Seeing*, Penguin, 1972.

Edward Ball Can you describe what Kunsthalle Lissabon is, and how the institution constitutes itself?

KL Kunsthalle Lissabon is a contemporary art institution operating both locally and internationally. It was founded in 2009 as a reflection on what possible institutional models we can imagine and collectively produce, as a direct response to the world to which we are inextricably tied.

The diagram opposite presents a tentative model of institutional activity that positions a hijacked understanding of radical hospitality at its core. Rather than being a normative model, prescribing how institutions should act, it reflects Kunsthalle Lissabon's ongoing commitment to imagining other ways of 'instituting'.

At the centre of the diagram, and therefore of the institution, lies radical hospitality, which is defined by ideas of generosity, solidarity and sociability. If we consider this model an economic one, these factors can be considered the raw materials that the institution needs in order to operate. The outcomes, or end results of institutional activity perceived in this way, exist outside of the institution, in the world, and can be understood in terms of criticality, friendship and production. Criticality is the ongoing reflection / speculation that may or may not materialise in the form of production. Friendship is the long-lasting relationship the institution establishes with its constituency (audience, artists, writers, technicians, sponsors, etc.). Finally, production relates to the public output of the act of instituting, whether in the form of exhibitions, publications, discursive programmes, or any other public activity. These three categories of institutional activity are hierarchically equivalent, and in this mutual equivalency of relevance lies a possibility for thinking about the world differently.

EB You recently celebrated Kunsthalle Lissabon's tenth anniversary and instead of throwing a party, you made a decision to withdraw entirely for a year. At that time, what did you think might happen?

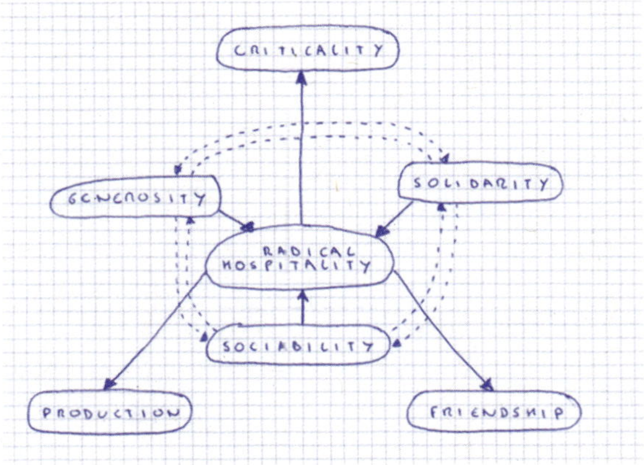

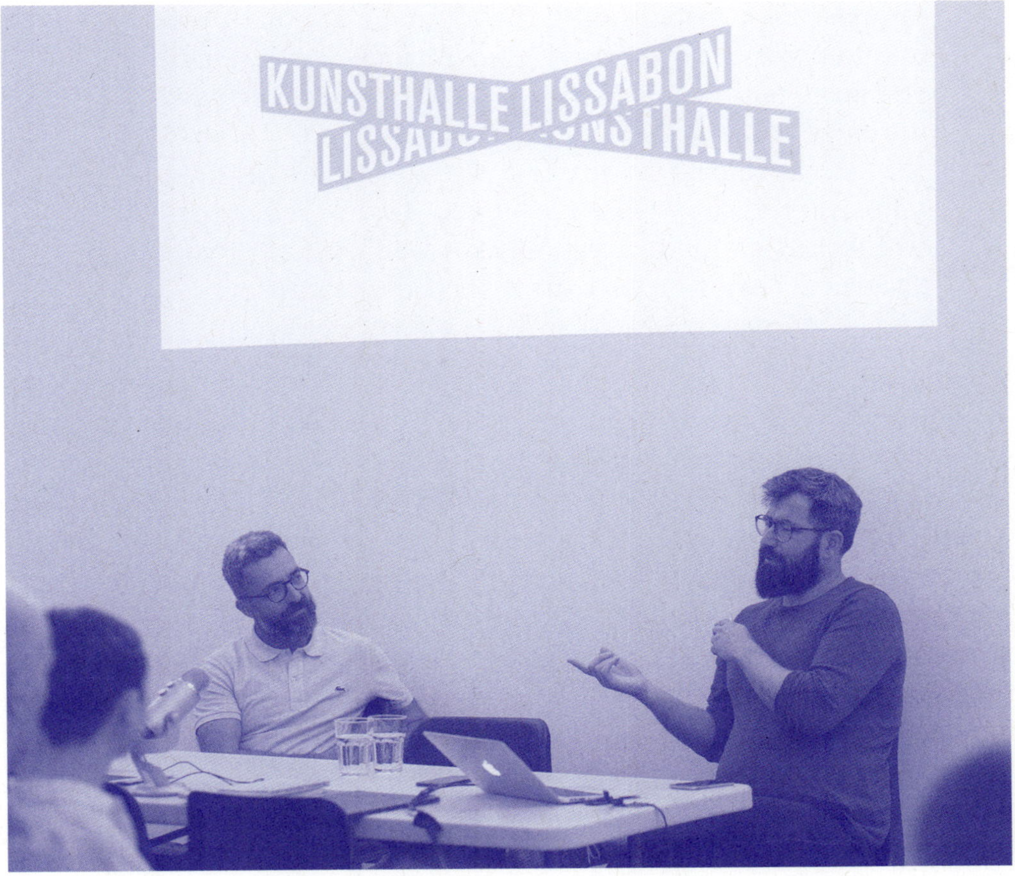

top: Kunsthalle Lissabon, a tentative model for institutional activities. Courtesy Kunsthalle Lissabon
bottom: Kunsthalle Lissabon (Luís Silva and João Mourão) in conversation, Freelands Artist Programme Symposium 2019, Site Gallery. Photo: Mark Howe

KL Looking closely at the diagram on the previous page, it comes as no surprise that Kunsthalle Lissabon understands dialogue as a very productive force. Collaborations are very important to us, as they represent dialogues made visible and, more importantly, made public. We collaborate mostly with similar institutions, with like-minded platforms and people who are committed to thinking critically about the world and about the place contemporary art has in it.

When we celebrated our tenth anniversary in 2019, the way we chose to mark this was to disappear and have four other institutions open up pop-up versions of themselves in our place. We had Pivô (São Paulo), CURA. (Rome) and its Basement Roma project, SALTS (Birsfelden, Basel) and ICA Philadelphia taking over our installations, our production infrastructure and our online presence in order to think about how institutions operate and relate to specific contexts other than the ones in which they are embedded by default.

At the same time we wanted to investigate withdrawal and temporary disappearance as a modality for reflecting on the cultural infrastructure of a city like Lisbon, the city in which we have been operating for more than a decade now.

EB This year of withdrawal is now concluded – what did you discover from the experience?

KL The main consequence of a year-long sabbatical is the amount of learning we did, both personally and institutionally. On a personal level we have learned that we love (and missed) curating. Engaging with the artists and developing new projects, producing them and presenting them to the world, as envisioned by the artists, is something we find very special. It took a year of not doing this to realise how important it is for our professional happiness. From an institutional point of view we realised that the Lisbon that was conducive to the emergence of projects like our own no longer existed. Ten years of gentrification, *coolification* and *touristification* have made it impossible for projects like Kunsthalle Lissabon to develop. We also learned that despite such massive changes, Kunsthalle Lissabon remains a relevant place within the cultural ecosystem of the city. One of the possibilities on the table, after the sabbatical, was to end the project. Relocation was another option, but we were told time and again throughout the sabbatical year that if we truly disappeared or relocated elsewhere, a big hole would be left in the city, since no one else was doing what we are doing: offering criticality and reflection on one hand, and commissioning solo projects from relevant international and local artists on the other.

As a response, we decided to continue. We reopened on 20 February 2020 with a solo show by Laure Prouvost, a beautiful new installation, but three weeks afterwards we had to shut down again due to the COVID-19 pandemic. It was frustrating and disheartening to be put once again on hold, this time round due to external factors. As we write this Q&A, we are preparing to reopen once again, but the situation is still very uncertain about what the future holds and how to mediate contemporary art under these new and strange circumstances.

EB In the immediate wake of COVID-19 lockdowns, many institutions rushed to put out online content, from artist film screenings to digital walk throughs of exhibitions. With some notable exceptions this felt like a poor simulacrum, or a 'performance of busyness', as g39 termed it. You are currently publishing a series of online recipes from your community of artists and curators – how consciously in opposition to this kind of online presence is the recipe idea?

KL The recipe idea was a conscious and explicit refusal to engage in that performance of busyness, while simultaneously staying in touch with and caring for our community. It was our way of making sure that all the relationships that define Kunsthalle Lissabon remained active and well. The ease with which some institutions abandoned any sort of criticality and started doing online exhibitions in which scrolling through photographs on a screen was hierarchically equivalent to engaging with objects in a physical space seemed reckless, to say the least. The institutional dismissal of the body and of physicality felt very problematic and politically dangerous in a time of lockdown. But also the Instagram live and Zoom conference madness were overwhelming and seemed to testify a refusal to engage with the more serious issues: how to move forward under these circumstances? What is the role of institutions, art and public space under such an unexpected and possibly long-lasting situation?

These questions weren't being addressed and people just kept doing what they did before. That felt very disappointing: the world changes, or appears to be changing, and you ignore the changes and refuse to deal with them. Our recipe hiatus was on one hand our acknowledging that sometimes art doesn't have a solution to every problem the word faces and on the other our commitment to pausing our activities. Stopping to reflect and think things through. Instead we just shared recipes we all had been cooking during the lockdown. Cooking as care if you will, but completely detached from any reference to the art world. Even the illustrations were as distant from contemporary art as possible, as a way of signalling that.

EB Will this pandemic truly force or engender change in terms of how institutions institute?

KL We honestly don't know. Institutions produce the world in which we live, but they also reflect it. If the world changes in a lasting manner due to the pandemic, then institutions will have to change as well, and in that process institute differently. What we've witnessed so far is that institutions have migrated all content online and engaged in an even more extreme form of overproduction. That to us doesn't seem like a change, just more of the same. But only time, and the virus, will tell.

6 May 2020 and 27 August 2020

Site Gallery

Sheffield, England

Alison J Carr

Yuen Fong Ling

Zoyander Street

Lucy Vann

Siân Williams

Site Gallery: An Introduction

Site Gallery is South Yorkshire's leading contemporary art space, specialising in new media, moving image and performance. The gallery was founded in 1978 as an independent photography gallery and was previously known as Untitled. The organisation is currently led by Co-directors Judith Harry and Sharna Jackson, and pioneers emerging art practices and ideas, working in partnership with local, regional and international collaborators to nurture artistic talent and support the development of contemporary art.

Site Gallery connects people to artists and to art, and inspires new thinking and debate through exhibitions, talks, events and other public activity. It partners with early-career to established artists to commission new work, produce solo and group shows, deliver residencies, performances, events and community programmes. Through its diverse programming, Site Gallery reveals the process of making art and invites audiences and participants to engage, explore and connect.

The two-year artist programme at Site Gallery is titled Platform, and is delivered with a consortium of local institutions: Bloc Projects, S1 Artspace, Yorkshire Art Space and Museums Sheffield. In year one, the residents work towards a cross-site, work-in-progress exhibition taking place in the summer months, which provides artists with professional installation shots and commissioned texts on their work; the second year is focused on the individual needs of each artist and addresses subsequent questions that arise from the show in year one. The cohort also has the opportunity to participate in a group trip.

Site Gallery provides support, access to networks, physical space and programme activity every month for our resident artists, alternating between studio visits and planned group sessions. To date these sessions have included a Summer School with S1 Artspace, an opportunity to delve into the collections at Museums Sheffield and access to alternative funding workshops with the crowdfunding platform Kickstarter.

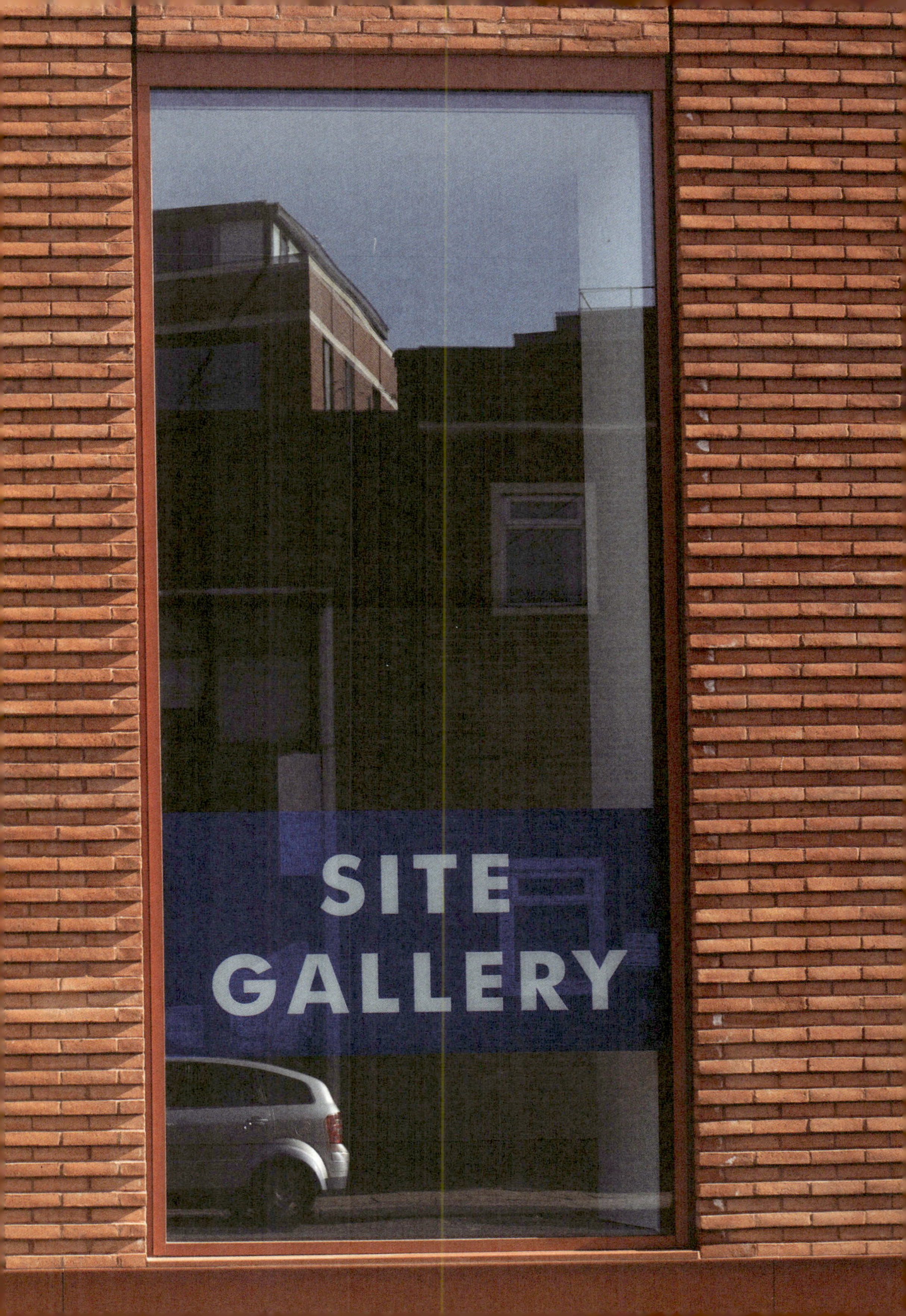
SITE
GALLERY

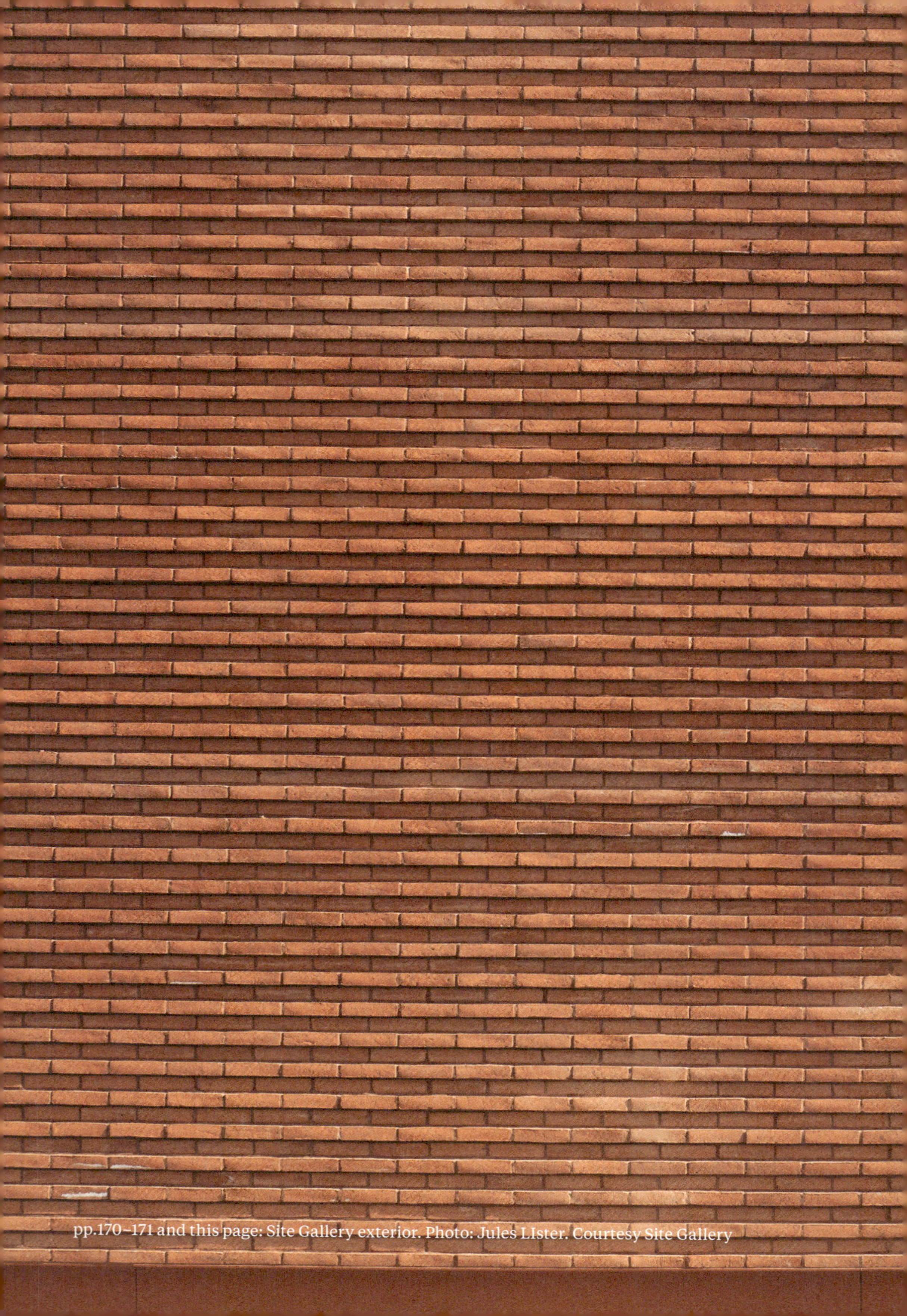

pp.170–171 and this page: Site Gallery exterior. Photo: Jules LIster. Courtesy Site Gallery

Sharna Jackson, Artistic Director; Angelica Sule, Curator;
Robyn Haddon, Producer

Site Gallery is delighted and honoured to be part of the Freelands Artist Programme – the benefit the partnership has brought to the artistic community in our city has been immeasurable. The programme has allowed us to dedicate time and resources directly to artists, which is at the core of our practice as a gallery.

The Platform artist programme enables us to reveal the process of making art and to invite audiences and participants to engage, explore and connect. This is most explicit in the interim exhibition we produce with the artists and partner spaces. The exhibition allows the artists to explore new ideas in a public and professional art space, testing new thinking with engaged audiences. The first iteration of this exhibition was a galvanising moment in Sheffield, bringing together artistic communities from around the city and creating a space to platform emerging talent.

We have watched the artists grow, artistically and personally, and their presence and practice has become embedded in much of what we do. During more recent times when physical meetings have been impossible, we have extended the programme to offer bi-weekly online conversations and monthly one-to-one sessions. The group conversations have meandered from discussing care and well-being to conversations about critical texts and artist videos that are watched collectively. These have provided a sense of togetherness at a point when isolation has been hard on everyone, and also offers a well-needed distraction for the artists and the team at Site Gallery during the challenges of the COVID-19 pandemic.

The Platform programme in Sheffield is a partnership with several organisations around the city, to build and maintain networks for artists and the partners alike, and we are grateful for everything they have brought to the programme.

Alison J Carr

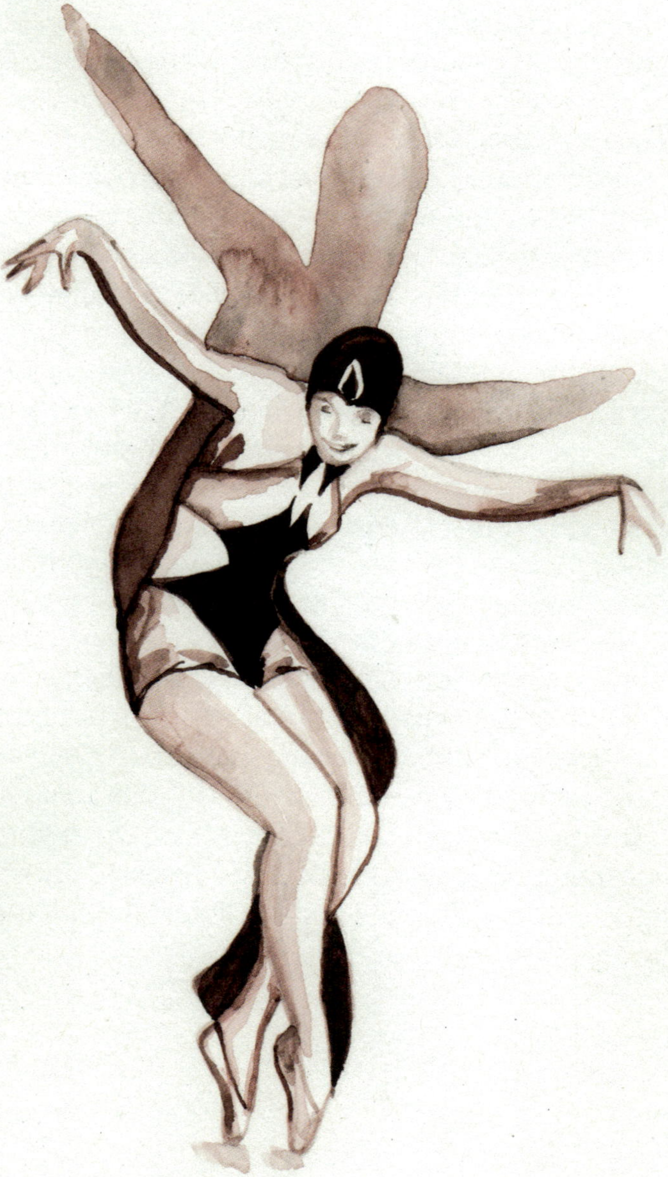

Counter Pose

Don't be fooled by these images, seemingly of the past. Alison J Carr's engagement with archival images and historical bodies is firmly rooted in the present, foregrounding sidelined subjectivities in the context of today. Bodies that have been othered, misunderstood, shamed, demeaned are empathetically recontextualised. 'What ifs' here are not nostalgic, but energetic with proposition: what if society had made room for this person in their own time; what if it were different? In turn, what could be different today?

The watercolours you see here on these pages are new, made specifically for the context of this book. In her series 'Pose and Shadow' (2020–), Carr begins with an archival image and isolates the figure from its background, tracing her exactness before bringing the image into soft colour. This process is an act of homage, delicately rendered by Carr's own hand. This one-step remove from the original introduces an element of fantasy, detaching the figure from the specificity of the original context, freeing it into something more universal. There is an ethics to this, on two counts. Firstly, in refusing to take the image as a totality, a concern which also sees Carr frequently employ collage, as there is an implicit refusal of just one reading, just one frame. Secondly, there is no way to obtain consent from the person to use their image in its original likeness, so Carr introduces this new, gently detached, context. Each of these figures strikes a pose – dancing, performing, on stage, on camera. Carr homes in on these fluid and free body lexicons. 'You aren't holding me down', the joyful and elegant subjects articulate in that moment. There is pleasure and play in this recontextualisation, a sometimes-forgotten component within critique. But take a closer look. This intimate presentation also confronts us with the fullness and complexity of the personhood on the page. Shadows lurk – spectral reminders of what is at stake.

To simply engage with and enjoy these images from the past is not where Carr's work resides. Instead, it is at the moment of rupture, when her source material is sufficiently distanced from its original context, that allows it to be read as contemporary, and to be read critically. It would, as such, be a mistake to intone nostalgia in Carr's work – quite the opposite in fact. Carr's work is urgent. But that is not to disregard visual pleasure. Aesthetically and intellectually, the artist is drawn to the cleanness of vision of Modernism – its optimism and universality – but also to its unresolved relationship with gender, how it 'failed to make inclusions for women'.[1]

There is a similar visual precision to Carr's watercolours, but in working with such a style, she unpacks its attendant cultural context in light of today's own. Carr does not simply restate the utopian visions of societal well-being that Modernism proposed, rather she allows parallels to be drawn; what inclusions and exclusions do we live with in 2020? The artist's new, related, watercolour series 'Stairs and Shadow' (2020–) – also created for these pages – depicts figures within a suggestion of architectural, and therefore sociopolitical context. *Stairs and Shadow, The Tiller Girls* (2020) highlights a kick-line of women, their perfect unison metaphorically redolent of the remarkable sisterhood and collectivity that came to define the Tiller Girls dance troupe.[2] With this, Carr also foregrounds constructive historical moments, and in the case of the Tiller Girls, a feminism of inclusion.

Carr's own body appears in her work, both gesturally and at times physically; it is presented in solidarity with those historical subjectivities she engages with in the present. Hers is an embodiment as ethics and process: placing herself in similar contexts of being looked at, in order to ask: what does it mean to be a body on show? A central tenet of Carr's work is that in visual culture we are shamed for our bodies.[3] What modes of resistance are available? French theorist Michel Foucault articulated how, historically, bodies became 'texts on which to inscribe dominant ways of doing things'.[4] And while language contains emancipatory possibilities, so too it possesses the power to exclude. A feminist critique would hold that a person – a subject – is infinitely more than a 'docile body',[5] one existing and constituted only in relation to such regulatory powers. Carr's work swerves from this constricting linguistic realm, into embodiment and into body vocabularies unconfined by normative paradigms.

'Refusing body shame is my politics',[6] Carr has stated. Her artistic practice is one of revision and expansion. Carr empathetically works with people in history who were looking to the future, who were living outside of the societal norms and received knowledges of the time. This work with historical materials, and embodiment as process, seeks to invigorate our vocabularies of the present. As the philosopher and theorist Judith Butler stated only days ago:

> We depend on gender as a historical category, and that means we do not yet know all the ways it may come to signify, and we are open to new understandings of its social meanings.[7]

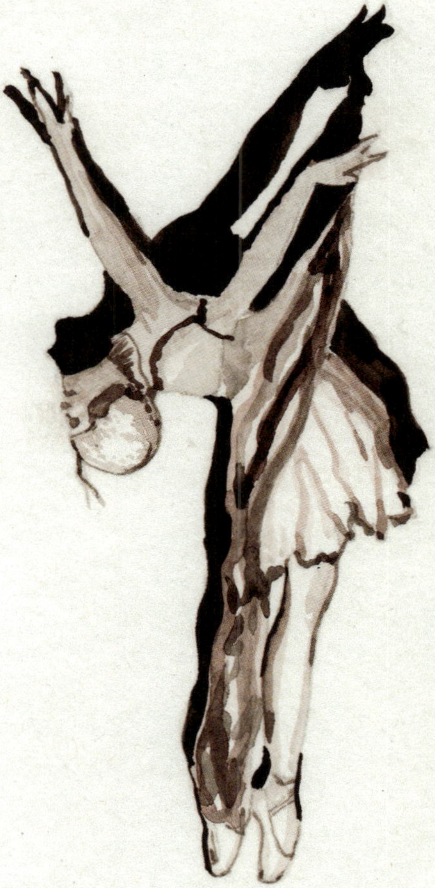

Carr's watercolours, and her work more broadly, are alive to such open significations, while deeply regardful of the ways in which bodies are shamed and marginalised today. The work continues. So, strike a pose – there's nothing to it.

25 September 2020

1 In conversation with the author, Tuesday 22 September 2020.
2 For further information, see: tillergirls.com. The Tiller Girls were formed in the 1890s, but became particularly well-known during the 1950s for their precise kick-lines. The troupes placed significant emphasis on close group ethics.
3 It is useful here to recall Kimberlé Crenshaw's 1989 proposition of intersectionality as a theoretical framework for understanding how aspects of a person's social and political identities (gender, sex, race, class, sexuality, religion, disability, physical appearance, height, etc.) combine to create unique modes of discrimination and privilege. See Kimberlé Crenshaw, 'Demarginalizing the Intersection of Race and Sex: A Black Feminist Critique of Antidiscrimination Doctrine, Feminist Theory and Antiracist Politics', *University of Chicago Legal Forum*, vol. 1989, issue 1 article 8, 1989, https://chicagounbound.uchicago.edu/uclf/vol1989/iss1/8/.
4 See Stacey Pigg, *Distracted by Digital Writing: Unruly Bodies and the Schooling of Literacy*, https://ccdigitalpress.org/book/strategic/chapters/pigg/problem.htm.
5 Foucault first articulated this in *Discipline and Punish* (1975). Scholars such as Nancy Fraser challenged such conceptions, in particular see Nancy Fraser, *Unruly Practices: Power, Discourse and Gender in Contemporary Social Theory*, Polity Press, 1989.
6 In conversation with the author, 23 September 2020.
7 Judith Butler Interview with Alona Ferber, *New Statesman*, 22 September 2020, https://www.newstatesman.com/international/2020/09/judith-butler-culture-wars-jk-rowling-and-living-anti-intellectual-times.

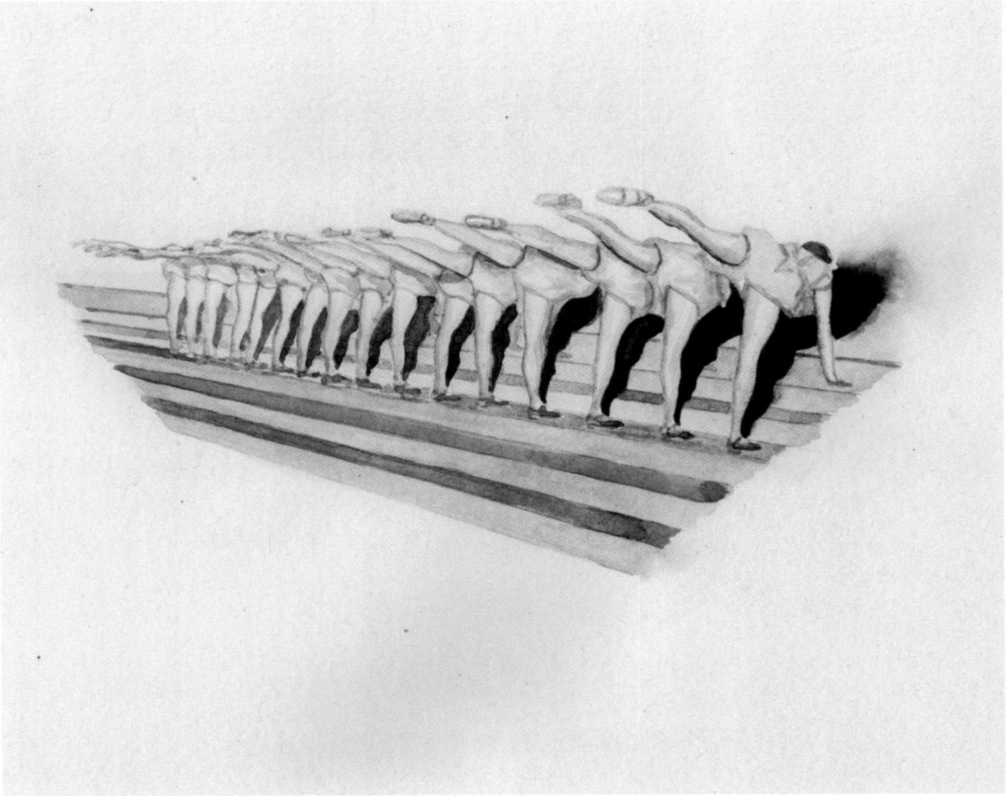

p.174: Alison J Carr, *Pose and Shadow, Dorissa Nelova*, 2020
p.177: Alison J Carr, *Pose and Shadow, Dorothy Dilley*, 2020
above: Alison J Carr, *Stairs and Shadow, The Tiller Girls*, 2020

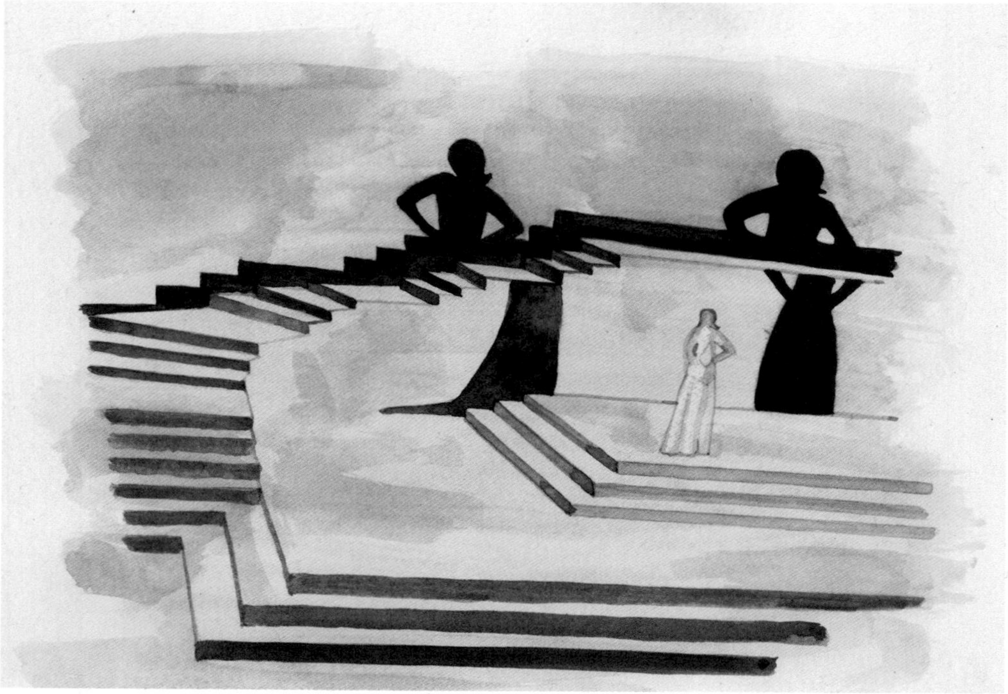

above: Alison J Carr, *Stairs and Shadow, Rosita Ritchie*, 2020
opposite: Alison J Carr, *Pose and Shadow, Tatiana Ryaboushinskaya*, 2020

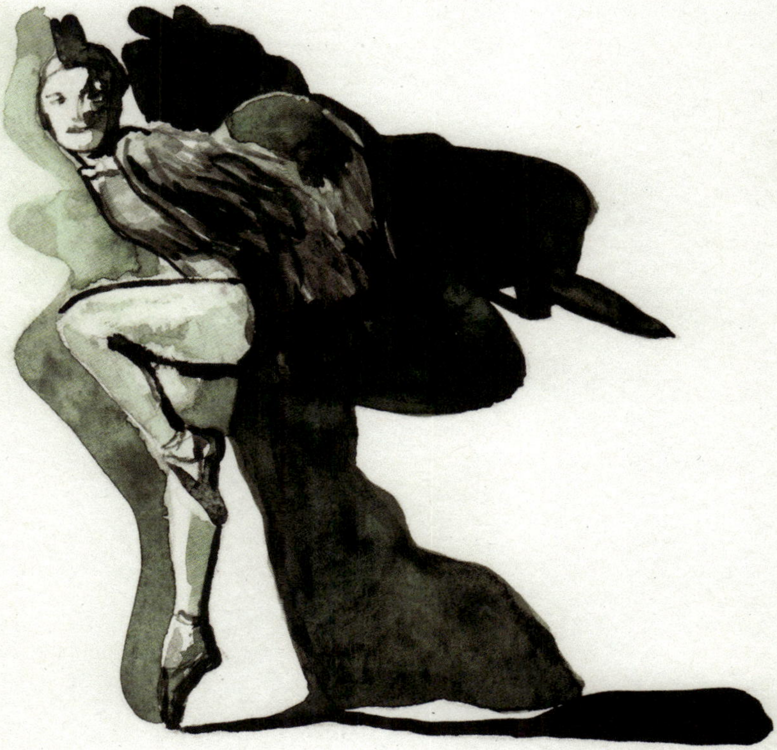

Yuen Fong Ling

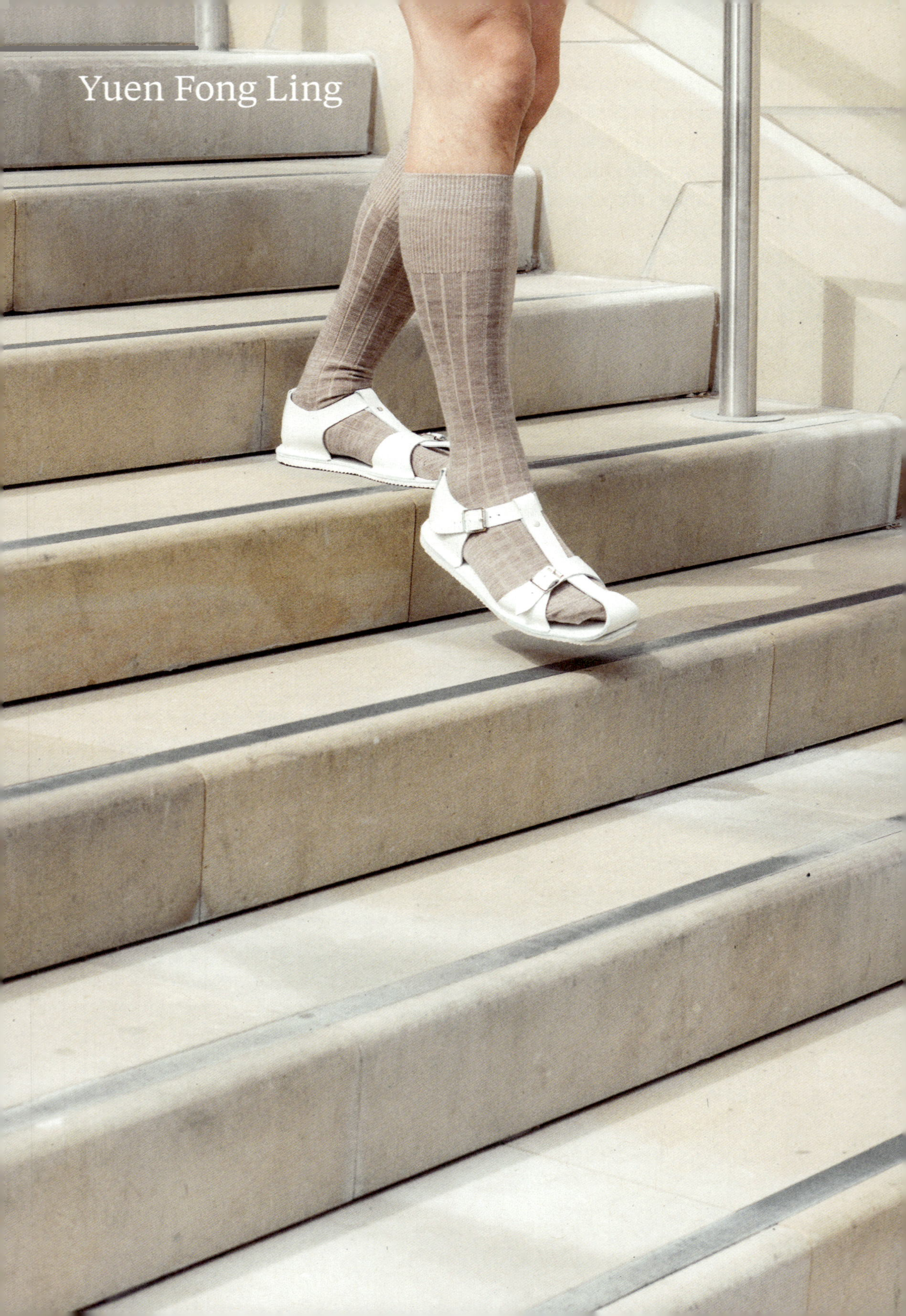

We Walk

It began in the Sheffield Archives, grew legs and started walking. Yuen Fong Ling's expansive project has become many things, yet at its base, it is a new, and ongoing, form of memorial-making to the socialist writer, poet and activist Edward Carpenter who lived in Sheffield, Ling's adopted city. The artist's generative project asks open questions as to how we might embody some of Carpenter's ideals, and how they might live out through us in the present. What is it to be queer now? How do we relate to the environment in a time of crisis? What other, sustainable lifestyles are out there?

Less well-known today, Carpenter was a pioneering supporter of many progressive causes we now take for granted, and his radical lifestyle became a symbol of liberation from the oppressive middle-class values of late-Victorian England. His writings were an important contribution to the development of the English socialist movement, and much later, to the gay liberation movement.[1] Carpenter also supported equal rights for women, and championed new understandings of queer relationships and identities at a time when homosexuality was illegal and while he was living openly with his lifelong partner George Merrill. This included a greater awareness of, and openness to, our physical and spiritual relationship with others and with the natural environment.

Carpenter designed and created his own sandals, which he saw as emancipating the foot from the working-class boot – part of his philosophical drive to imagine new relationships to class and a more spiritual connection to nature.[2] In the Sheffield Archives, Ling discovered examples of sandals Carpenter collected for reference, alongside original photographs of Carpenter wearing sandals. Further, he found paper foot patterns from Carpenter's customers, one of which was inscribed with 'Self 1892', a trace of Carpenter himself. Ling decided to materially interpret this pattern form, translating the source matter into a contemporary sandal design, and updating it to today's context. Ling also inbuilt a socialist principle into its creation, by working with a Sheffield craftsman to make the shoes, thus securing a source of income for a local trade;[3] and with every ten pairs of shoes made, one pair is gifted to a local activist, in so doing underscoring the ongoing importance of queer political action. The project memorialises through the creation of an object that can be worn, seen, given away and therefore disseminated – as object, as idea. The project unites too – creating a sense of belonging.

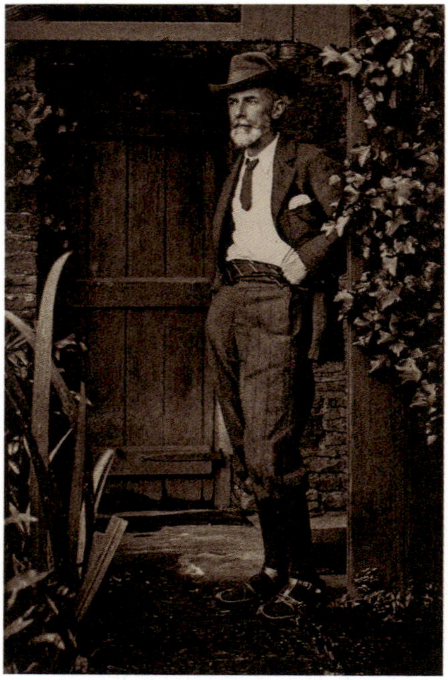

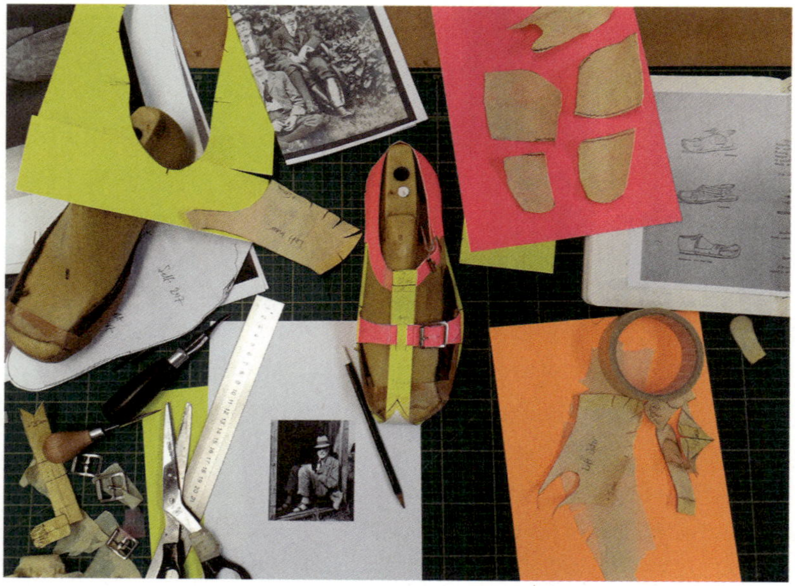

p.182: Yuen Fong Ling, *Towards Memorial: Photo Wall* (detail), 2019.
Photo: Mark Howe
top: *Edward Carpenter: Self on Porch*, 1905. Photo: Alf Mattison.
Courtesy Sheffield City Archives and Local Studies Library
bottom: Yuen Fong Ling, *Towards Memorial: Sandal Studio Production* (detail), 2016

In which places can Carpenter's legacy bring people together? An exhibition is only one such site. Ling's exhibition *Towards Memorial* as part of Site Gallery's *Platform 2019* played with the idea of the pop-up shop, where the artist designed displays for the shoes to emphasise their status as designed objects. Mirrors and TV screens were placed on the floor, emphasising the viewer's relation to the foot. The installation *Self 1892* was a brand and concept developed with designer Jon Cannon and drew from the sandal's paper patterns, alongside stylised product images by photographer Mark Howe. These images were shot in Sheffield, and the exhibition display played with the aestheticised forms of fashion spreads and billboard advertising. The work's vibrant rainbow colouration marked an unapologetic, celebratory form of queer visibility. The exhibition also presented a film documenting the making, gifting and wearing of the sandals, made with Picture Story Productions, reminding the audience that this design object is just one conduit of meaning for Carpenter's legacy.

Ling's project exists out there in the world, too, as an organically unfolding nexus of ideas and human connection. This happens through the artist's pivot from object to process – his gifting of the sandals opens up a space of conversation with the receiver, allowing for a socialised encounter with Edward Carpenter's life. Resonating with the Cuban American conceptual artist Félix González-Torres, Ling gifts his work away, literally and metaphorically. I am thinking particularly of González-Torres's work *Untitled (Loverboy)* (1990), a sculpture formed of single sheets of blue paper, stacked on top of one another to create a three-dimensional object. The pale blue colour of the paper evokes the oceans and skies that reminded the artist of his deceased lover Ross Laycock. The sheets could be taken away, in turn depleting the work piece by piece but taking those memories and scattering them to the wind, casting them out into an open future. For Ling, too, the point at which the work is complete is when the ideas carry on through someone else, aligning with Carpenter's interests in a kind of spirituality that exists beyond the body.

The poetics of the project rest in its mutability – the sandal is given away, worn, and activated, and can go anywhere. Wearing the sandal, you are placed in relation with that historical context. How can you free those histories from the social biases that held them from public view? Deciphering and interpreting the Carpenter archive has been a process of discovery and personal exploration of identity for Ling. As a queer British Chinese man, who has regrettably had to navigate cultural and racial othering in the UK,

Carpenter has become a source of unexpected connection, finding shared parallels such as the activities of teaching and lecturing. The work powerfully speaks to a broader genealogy of self-discovery, of how we might shape our own identities in relation to those we look up to, in some sense finding ourselves in relation to the past. For Ling, it has proved a kind of catching up with the self historically: 'I am telling stories about feelings I may have had 20 years ago',[4] he has stated. The inbuilt generosity of the project means that such discoveries are available to all.

Ultimately, this project transcends Edward Carpenter; distinct from a monument, this is memorial-making, a process-led, constant space of becoming. This distinction is crucial, and there is a timeliness to Ling's sensitive evocation. At a moment when statues of historical figures such as Edward Colston and Cecil Rhodes are falling or where their positioning is being contested,[5] Ling's memorialising of Carpenter is no such monument, instead it is an embodiment of certain ideals, passed down and open to change according to the context in which those ideals are encountered. Ling's work exists most potently as the gift of exchange – asking what we might learn from Carpenter, but crucially, what that process might teach us about ourselves. We walk together, side by side.

10 September 2020

1 For further information on Edward Carpenter, see https://historicengland.org.uk/research/inclusive-heritage/lgbtq-heritage-project/homes-and-domestic-spaces/millthorpe-and-edward-carpenter/.
2 The wearing of sandals was a truly radical proposition at a time when Edward Carpenter was advocating for a more democratic and free society.
3 Yuen Fong Ling worked with Sheffield-based shoemakers Noble & Wylie.
4 In conversation with the author Friday 21 August 2020.
5 Following widespread support for the Black Lives Matter movement, a statue memorialising politician and slave trader Edward Colston was pulled down during an anti-racism protest in Bristol (7 June 2020); the statue of Cecil Rhodes, mining magnate and politician, situated outside Oriel College, Oxford has seen increased calls for its removal, due to Rhodes's part in the ownership of land rights and voting in South Africa in the late 1800s.

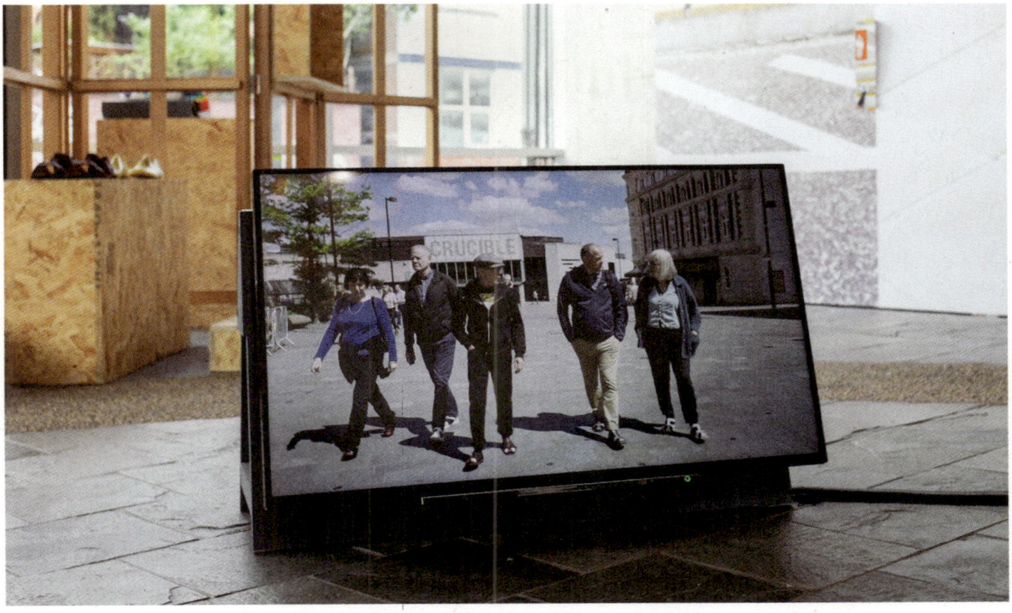

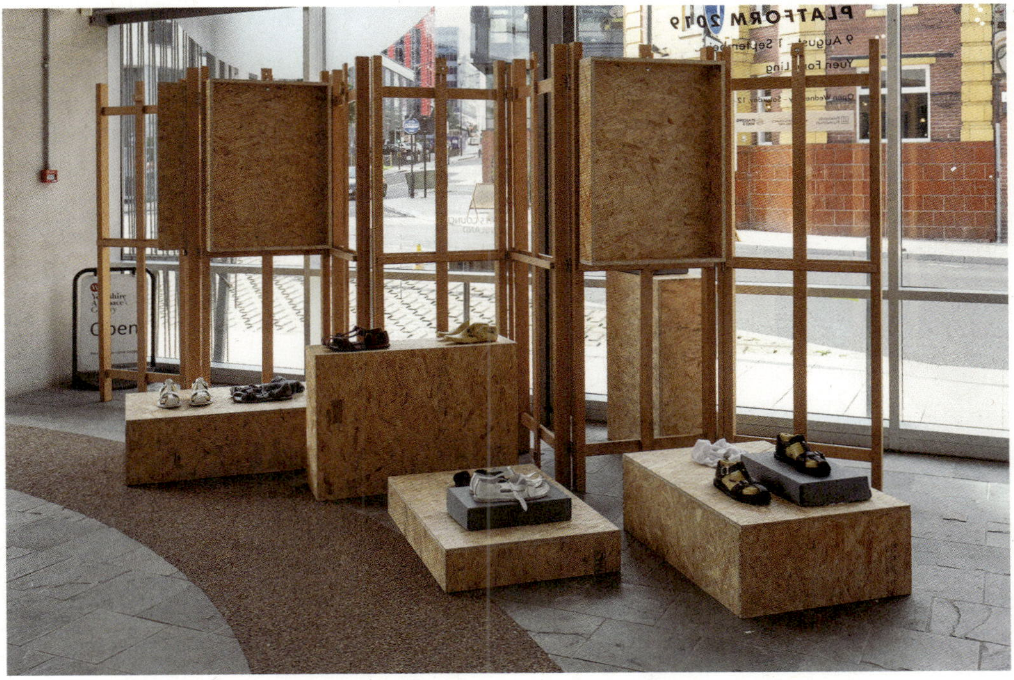

top: Yuen Fong Ling, *Towards Memorial: 3-channel film*, installation view, Persistence Works, Sheffield, *Platform 2019*, 2019. Photo: Jules Lister
bottom: Yuen Fong Ling, *Towards Memorial: Sandal Display*, installation view, Persistence Works, Sheffield, *Platform 2019*, 2019. Photo: Jules Lister

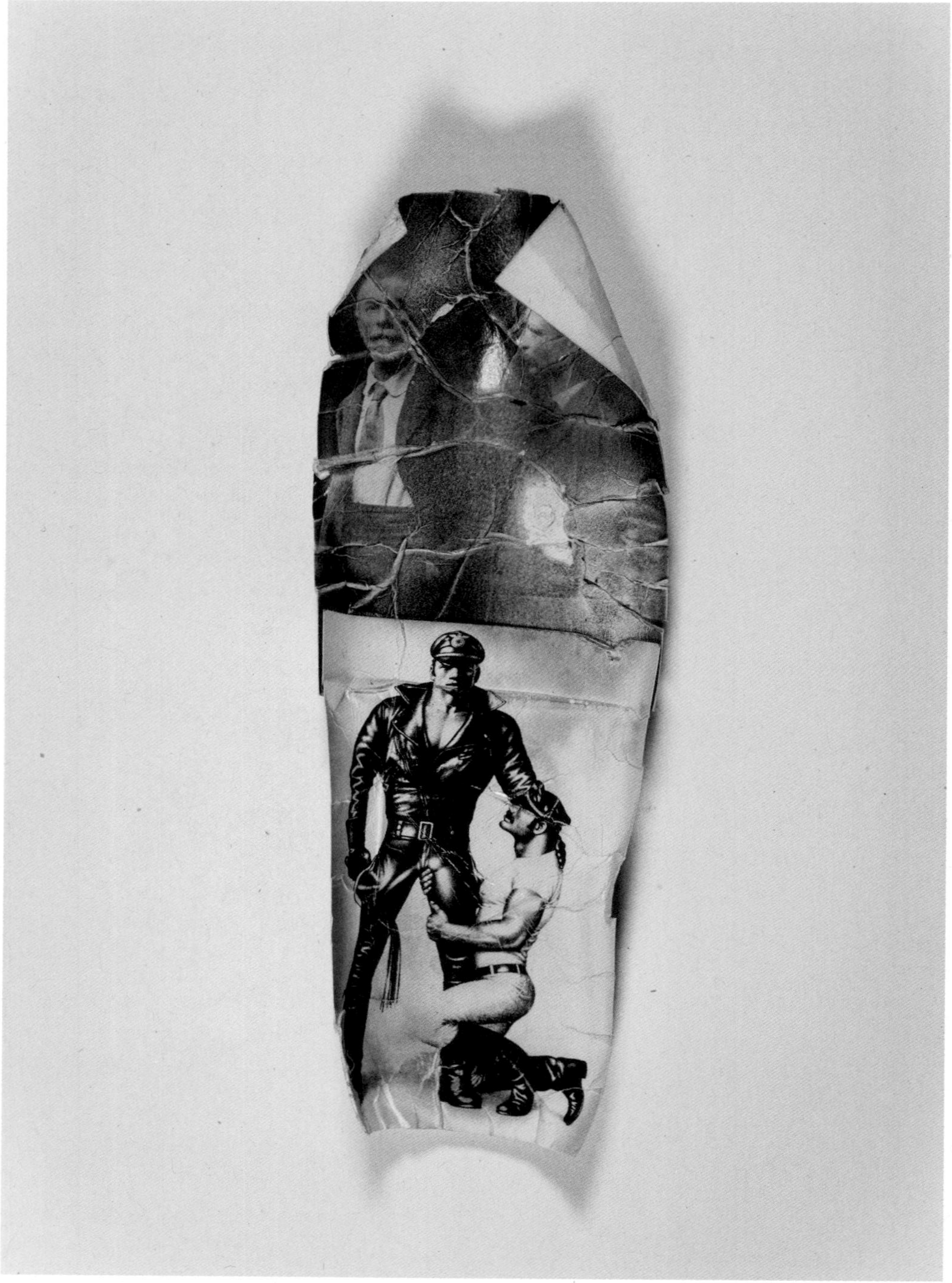

above: Yuen Fong Ling, *My Days with Edward Carpenter*, 2016.
Photo: Marcus Sarko
opposite: Yuen Fong Ling, *Towards Memorial: Photo Wall* (detail), 2019.
Photo: Mark Howe

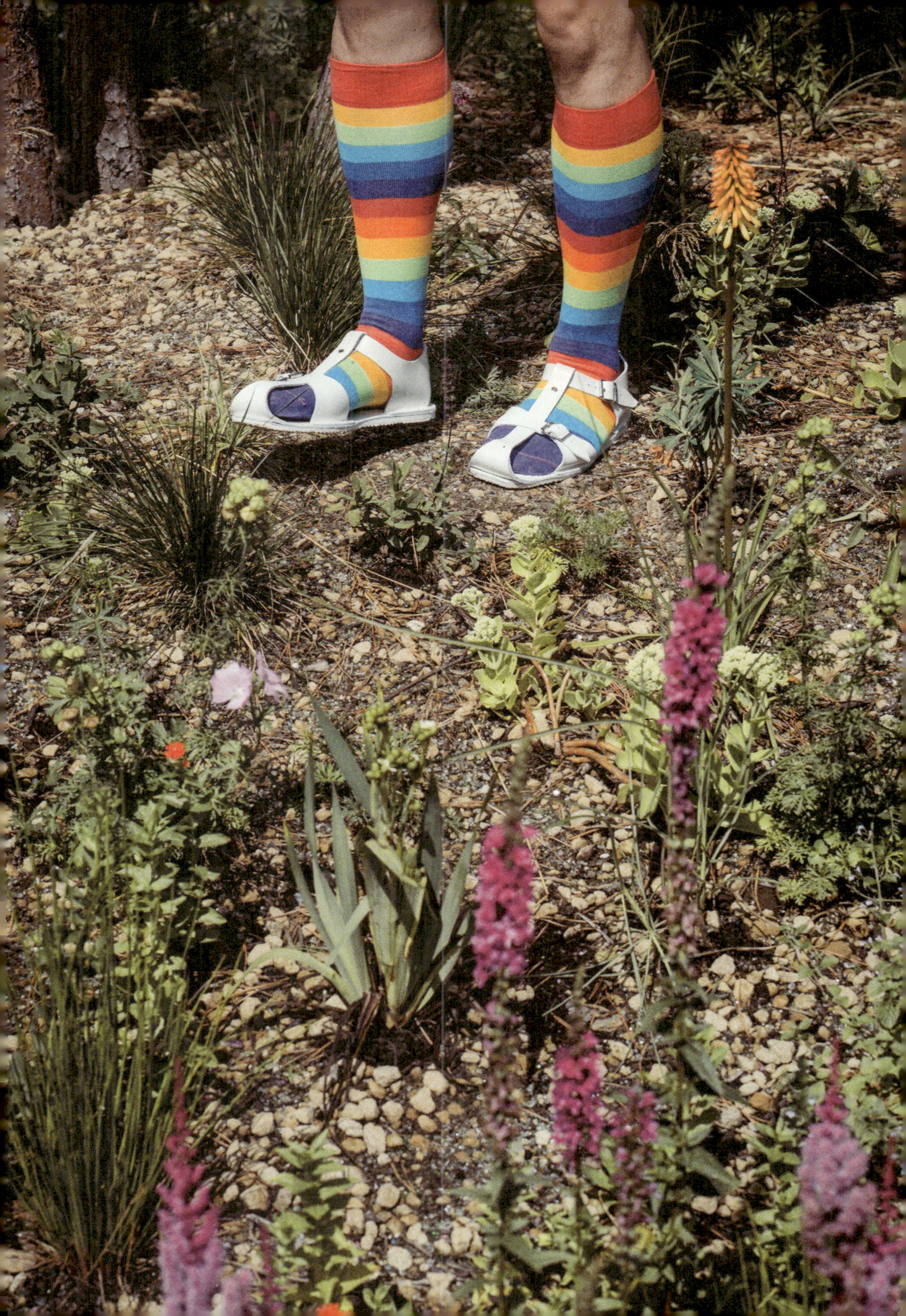

Zoyander Street

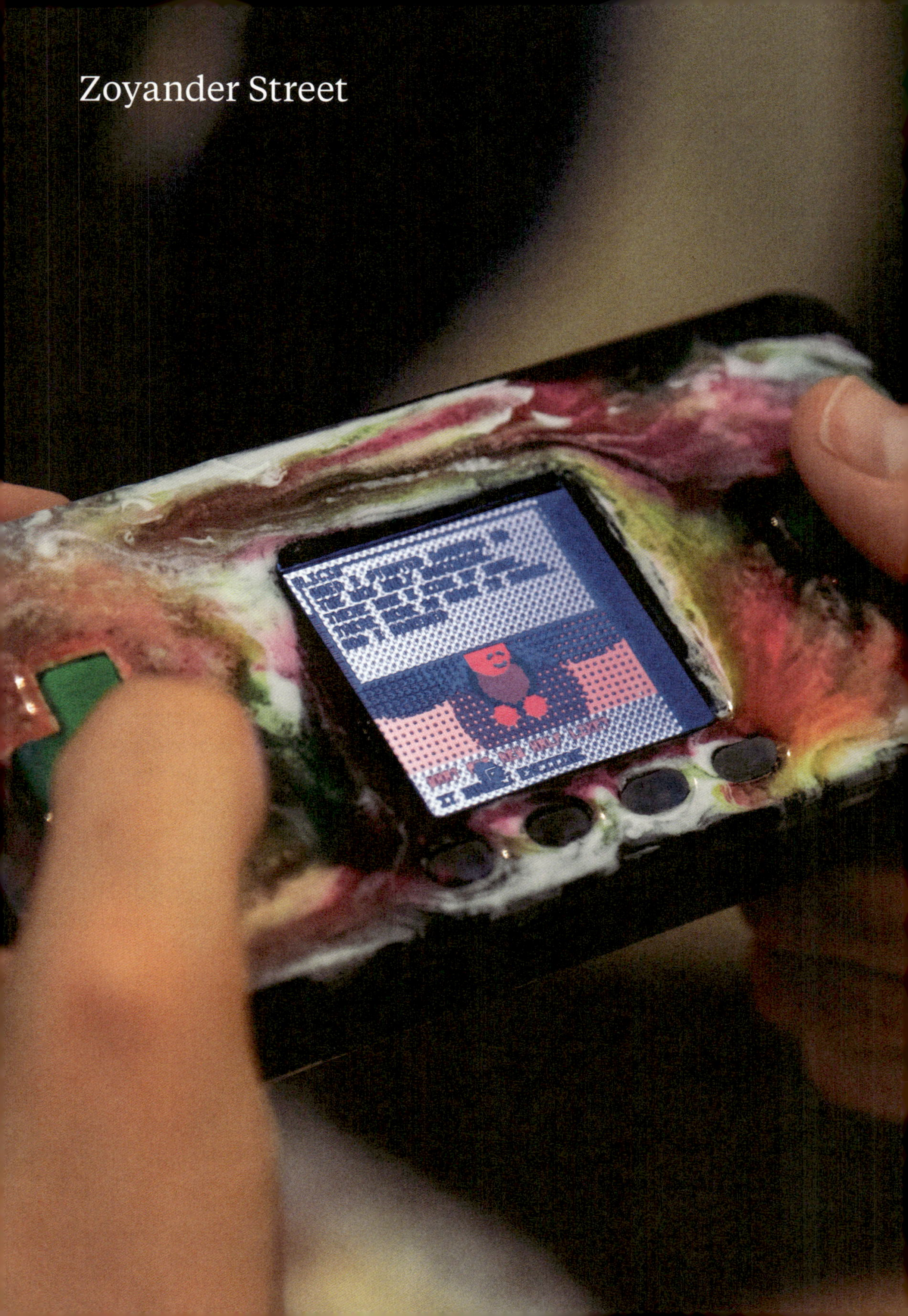

With Patience, Suspense

Enter into this vibrant world, charmingly alive in low resolution. Zoyander Street's *Cis Penance* (2020–) draws on game patterns that place us in intimate dialogues with transgender and non-binary individuals from around the UK. These interactive portraits, as Street terms them, are drawn from the artist's own interviews, and allow for a depth and complexity of experience to unfold the further in we go.

We begin at the threshold, and a long line of people are waiting to speak with us, evoking 'the Sisyphean bureaucratic processes imposed on transgender people in a country growing increasingly hostile to trans civil rights'.[1] Waiting and deferral come to predominate – both as metaphor and in the game's affective experience. Street has heighted this sense of suspense[2] in two ways: editorially, in foregrounding interview content relating to temporality; and visually, as intriguing motifs circle through – pyramids, single eyes, non-Christian angels – advancing an aesthetic of non-dual mysticism.[3] The ambient otherworldliness of the game gradually envelops us as we move through four different sections.

At the start of our journey, we meet individuals and their experiences of transitioning. The person introduces themselves and we are supplied with two pre-written responses, choosing one that resonates to keep the conversation flowing. As such, we become participants in the conversation by selecting words that are not our own. This additional aspect of participation moves the work out of documentary form or research study, into time-based media, creating a sense of active involvement in the game, even if this roadmap is a preordained one. We come to feel responsible for our choices, hoping not to make a mistake, or say the wrong thing. Street's work plays with our assumptions here – although we might fear such consequences, we're actually only here to listen. Some of the first interview accounts we come across concern the problems, blocks and delays experienced by those transitioning within the UK healthcare system. Already, we come to realise, whole worlds of lived experience reside in this humble interface.

Soon, we encounter people who are actively figuring out the arduous processes they must follow in order to get what they need from the existing provision. We also meet those with ambivalent feelings towards private healthcare, reluctantly paying for treatment to get what they urgently require much faster, despite their ethical concerns around privatisation. But the interactions *Cis Penance* presents us with challenges possible assumptions, and any suggestion of a linear progression through these stories, we begin to appreciate, is illusory. Metaphors open out, increasing in frequency and scope. A transgender woman talks about a static rowing machine, an exercise regime designed as part of her rehabilitation and recovery – stasis, exertion and not going anywhere hover in the air, despite us observing her own evident progress. Another person uses the analogy of the hunt saboteur, a form of protest in which hunts are interrupted, as a metaphor for intervening with a cruel system.

These metaphorical resonances prefigure an increasingly metaphysical dimension to the game. Things get weirder, by the artist's own delighted admission.[4] Here we begin to encounter time differently, perhaps not even existing at all, or at least suggesting a sense of something that is infinitely beyond our perception. We meet different experiences of subjectivity, and possibilities and freedoms to understand oneself outside of normative constructions. Metaphors of nature proliferate, and the problematics of the term 'natural' quickly come to the fore. A whimsical, yet serious, phenomenological conception of mushrooms unfolds a queer relationship to nature. The rhizomatic structures of mushrooms, and how they reproduce in ways we still do not understand, offer up new possibilities. This connects in a more expansive sense to the experience of building a queer life. We arrive, now, at world building, and how to build a better future, a better community for each other.

The path we have taken through this game, deeper into the pyramid with each personal encounter, draws some influence from the Tibetan Buddhist tradition of *Namtar*[5] – sometimes spelled *namthar* – a spiritual biography or hagiography, which literally means 'complete liberation'. In this tradition, 'establishing a mythical ideal and the communication of the sacred teachings takes precedence over providing a narrative portrait or "likeness" of the subject as a personality'.[6] Street's work employs a similar approach in its narrative structure, and, in so doing, accommodates different levels of truth and experience – which are not found in likeness alone. Realms of experience don't always fall within realms of perception.

Biography and portrait speak to the depiction of individual experience, yet across the game, a vivid sense of collective solidarity emerges. The visible and systemic harm to trans people in the UK affects an entire community: the one and the many. Street's work makes such problems visible to those with the power to make a difference. However, it must be stressed that although some of the people we meet have built happy lives for themselves, this is not to demonstrate that the system is working. *Cis Penance* is not an immersion in the experiential sense, instead it is a cultural one – simulating the immersion of an ethnographic study, with the attendant idea that you are changed by your encounters. The work does not borrow one person's perspective and ask us to walk in their shoes, instead we encounter polyphony, and emerge with a different understanding.[7]

2 October 2020

1 The artist's statement on the work can be read on their website: https://zoy.itch.io/cispenance where a preview of the game can also be played.

2 The work's title *Cis Penance* draws from an essay by trans writer Patience Newbury, and also half-rhymes with 'suspense', further evoking the sensation of endless deferment that trans people experience within the UK medical system when transitioning.

3 In conversation with the author, Street has spoken of their enjoyment of the game *Earthtongue* by June Hornby, who is working with the artist to develop the visuals for *Cis Penance*. You can read more about *Earthtongue* here: see Catherine Brinegar, 'Ants on a Rock: e-Biology & Human Intrusion', *Re:Bind*, 17 April 2019, https://www.rebind.10/ants-on-a-rock-e-biology-human-intrusion-1574.

4 In conversation with the author, Thursday 24 September 2020.

5 *Ibid.*

6 Tsultrim Allione, *Women of Wisdom*, Arkana, 2005.

7 For further reading see Jack Halberstam, *In a Queer Time and Place: Transgender Bodies, Subcultural Lives*, New York University, 2005, which is the first full-length study of transgender representations in art, fiction film, video and music.

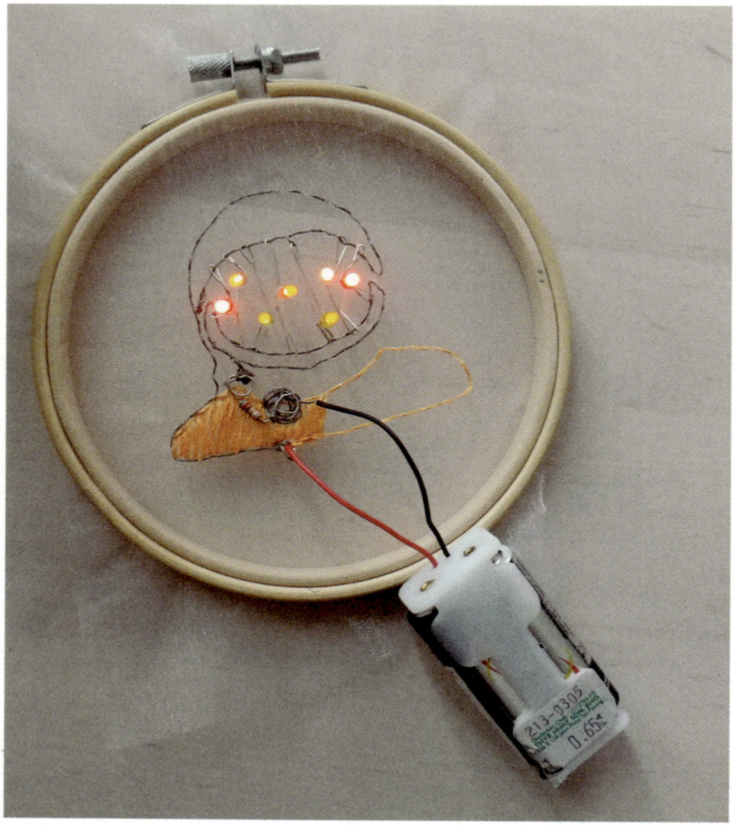

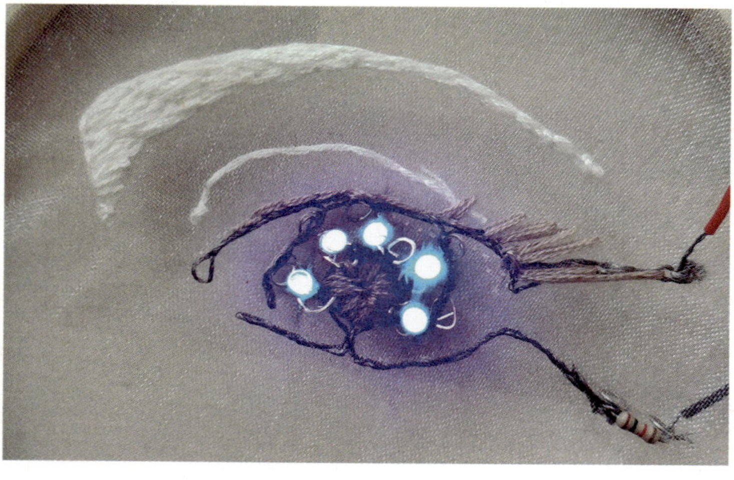

p.190: Zoyander Street, handmade, handheld console for *Interactive Portrait Cushions*, installation view, Site Gallery, Sheffield, *Platform 2019*. Photo Jules Lister
above: Zoyander Street, tests of soft-circuit embroidery techniques for planned installation of *Cis Penance*

Untidy Edges
Zoyander Street

When you interview someone, you're really just having a conversation. It's an everyday, human thing. Nothing special or new is being done in this kind of research – there is no cutting-edge apparatus revealing something previously invisible to human senses, no insight into the hidden machinations of life, no universal law being discovered. Just two people talking. But interviews feel to me like a window on to something inconceivably vast. I give someone a discursive space to fill, and whether they feel confident taking up that space or are unsure of themselves, the person always puts something into that space that inspires a little bit of awe in me.

Bringing a large number of interviews together into a collection of small vignettes leads to a decentralised kind of storytelling. A dropping of the 'hero's journey' in favour of what media scholar Hiroki Azuma has called 'database narratives'. Normal documentaries tend to have one protagonist, or perhaps a small handful of key players – often outsiders who we get to identify with for a while. You watch them, connect with them, and perhaps see them grow in some way. You cry with them, feel for them – their story feels like part of your story. But not everybody can be part of our story; and we shouldn't have to be persuaded to see the Other as like ourselves in order to stand in solidarity. I think all of us know that something remarkable happens when we see ourselves as a small, limited part of something much bigger.

Instead of identifying with someone else for a while, I try to get people to put themselves into relationship with others. Being in dialogue means that you don't have to see things the way others do, but you do have to decide how you adapt when you step into an unfamiliar context. Eventually, I want to make interactive worlds as a kind of cultural immersion in alternative spaces, where some of the most basic cultural assumptions that we rely upon have been stripped away. I want to put other people in that position of not knowing, because the thing I love most about the work I've been doing is putting myself in that position, and adapting conceptually to the multiple realities experienced and described by the people I interview.

I first became interested in interactive media because I wanted to be able to talk about history and ethnography without tidying things up and making them linear. I wanted to preserve the mess. Normal research and writing practices require a process of tidying up that puts one idea in front of the other, but ideas never appear in the world all lined up in a neat queue. They collide into each other, break off from one another, and move around the world getting more and more tangled up with one another. Unpicking the tangle can be a valuable way of approaching research, but the tangle itself also has value. Normally, an interview-based research project takes the twists and turns of conversation and organises it into a tidy analysis. Turning interviews into non-linear texts allows for more mess to unfold.

There are plenty of role models to look to for this non-linear, decentralised thinking. Gilles Deleuze and Félix Guattari's rhizome, Jean-François Lyotard's Moebian band, and Donna Haraway's SF (speculative fabulation, speculative feminism, science fact, science fantasy) all challenge the idea of an inside and an outside, instead figuring a world that folds and unfolds actively in the process of becoming. A great deal of fertile material can be found through anthropologist Anna Tsing's notion of the 'arts of noticing' at the 'unruly edges' of arrangements that seem tidy and neat. Eve Kosofsky Sedgwick, the writer and critical theorist, when exploring the 1960s cybernetic affect theory of Silvan Tomkins, makes a case for 'weak' theories. Weak theories make sense of what happens in a specific context, whereas strong theories are universally applicable. Since they are universal, strong theories are predictive, but weak theories leave room for surprises, since they do not assume knowledge outside of their own specificity, and do not position their specificity at the centre of the whole.

A world with no inside doesn't have insiders. From the perspective of a large number of non-linear, open-ended interviews with people who are marginalised, you never see the inside of society. The centre is out of reach, and the periphery is everything. The outside becomes incomprehensibly large, and the inside becomes a tiny speck, so small that no one person could fit inside of it. What you see isn't a world of 'mostly normal' with some outliers who don't fit in, but a galaxy of diversity, with a focal point that many of us feel compelled to orient ourselves around. The closer you are to the focal point, the more you feel pulled into it, like a black hole of normativity at the centre of the world.

Some of us are orbiting the black hole. From just outside of it, looking in, it looks like almost everybody else is inside. But they're all just getting pulled towards something that cannot contain them. Some of us are so far outside of it that it has no hold on us at all. The further out you travel, the more freedom there can be. But freedom comes in spaces where we can thrive, not where we are left alone in the dark. Marginalisation and inequality make that black hole look far preferable to the wide open periphery. But nobody wants to be crushed.

The first big discursive space that I invite interviewees to fill is the question, 'How do you see yourself?' Many people start out saying how normal and happy they are, and then quickly end up talking about the ways in which they are outside of the norm, and the ways they are in tension with the world around them. Both are true, and in the messy tangling of those contradictions, we all get joined together.

Lucy Vann

I don't know what made me say that

Heartbreak Songs for a Monday

Now and again Lucy and I send each other sad songs to listen to, enjoying the bedroom angst, the glibness of the refrains; 2020 has had it all, and it is a way of coping, I suppose. Lucy loves the plaintive expression of the heartbreak song, its performance of feeling and economy of phrase. If I think about Lucy's work, it's always been about the emotion just beneath the surface, and the different ways emotion arrives or drifts away on a melody.

The sun comes up, I think about you
The coffee cup, I think about you[1]

Small moments can seem so big, and big moments so small. The world speeds up, time stands still – all in a rhyming couplet. Lucy's work isn't heart on your sleeve, but it's in conversation with the form, working out where sincerity and authenticity overlap. Take the way Neil Tennant from Pet Shop Boys sings sometimes, as if he's reading aloud from a shopping list. Or the band's early Top of the Pops performances, studiedly standing there, unsmiling and stiff – charismatic in their awkwardness. But it's deadpan with a wink, solemn in inverted commas. It's performing and not performing, and artlessness can belie much more besides. Look at me but don't look at me – I think we all have a bit of that.

A pop song is compressed emotion – three, maybe five minutes at most. Lucy wants the moment to carry over sometimes, drawing it out in sweet melancholy. At Site Gallery's *Platform 2019* opening night, Lucy changed the emotive temperature of the room, performing an acapella version of the Dory Previn song 'The Lady with the Braid' (1971). The evening's chatter became whisper, became hushed tones, became still. We hung on her every word, as the silence between the lyrics filled the air like cloud. A few minutes of intimacy, connecting with us one-on-one yet all at the same moment. But there was something else too – and that's the thing Lucy is trying to reach.

What else might emerge when you pare everything back? I think Lucy is as interested in what isn't said, what is implied, the space around things. That's why her performances sometimes strip things back to the bone. In her acapella performance, she was just a woman standing in a gallery, singing us a sad song. It wasn't, you sense, so much about the song or the lyrics themselves, but the act of performing them. Yet there was ripple of humour in her delivery, a twinge of bitterness for comedic effect, just enough for us to hear the words a little differently.

The performing of an emotion can be a guise, trying something on to see if it sticks. It can also be something to hide behind. This is the central and seductive tension in Lucy's work – so often she is caught between wanting to and not wanting to. This is no cat-and-mouse with us, the audience, but with herself. The urge to withdraw, to hide behind cliché, meets the urge to walk into a crowded room and belt out a ballad. I wonder if Lucy's work is about making herself vulnerable; that she is working out what she wants to happen through being in that moment. Her performances rest on the inherent tension of not just performing, but arriving at that point in the first place.

I don't wanna go out
I don't wanna go dancing[2]

Ambivalence is a state of mixed feelings, and Lucy's work often holds space for opposing forces. There's laughter and there's sadness and there's seriousness too, and they frequently coexist. Despite the economy of her expression – a borrowed phrase, a knowing look, casually delivered – she lets us in on the joke, hinting at a realm beyond face value. I think there's some freedom in this. Lucy's work might seem confessional: the heartrending lyric, the performed authenticity. But ask yourself, how much of the 'real' Lucy we ever get to see?

2 October 2020

1 I am thinking of Liza Minnelli's 1989 version of Stephen Sondheim's 'Losing My Mind' (1971), which was produced by Pet Shop Boys and Julian Mendelsohn.
2 Pet Shop Boys, 'I don't wanna', 2020.

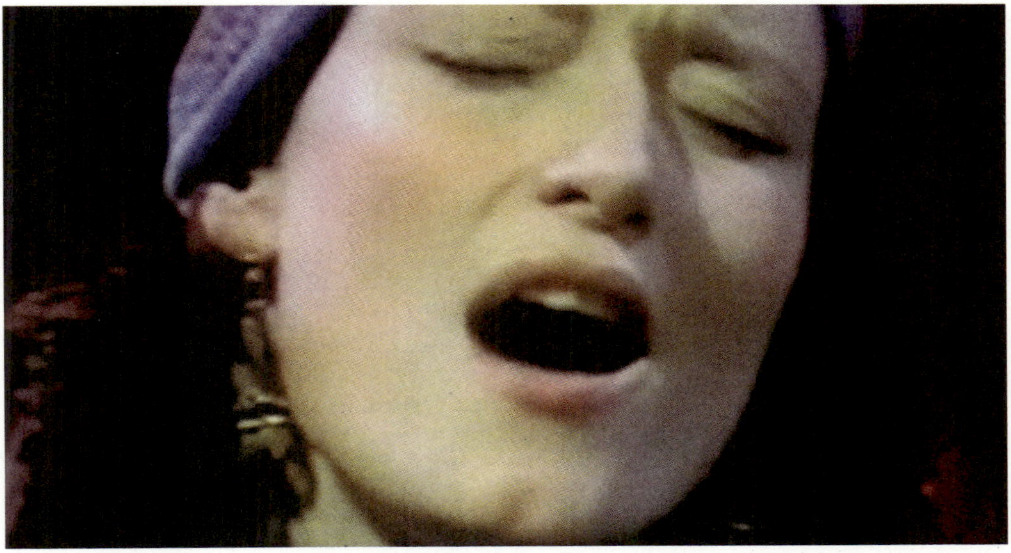

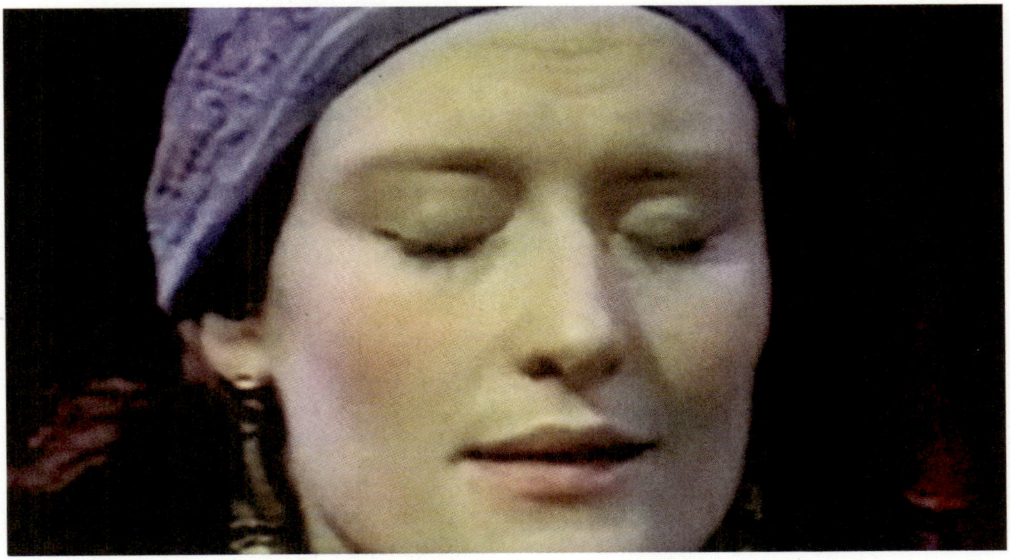

p.198: Lucy Vann, *The Lady with the Braid*, video installation, Site Gallery, Sheffield, *Platform 2019*. Photo: Jules Lister
above: Lucy Vann, *A Heart Needs a Home*, video (stills), 2020

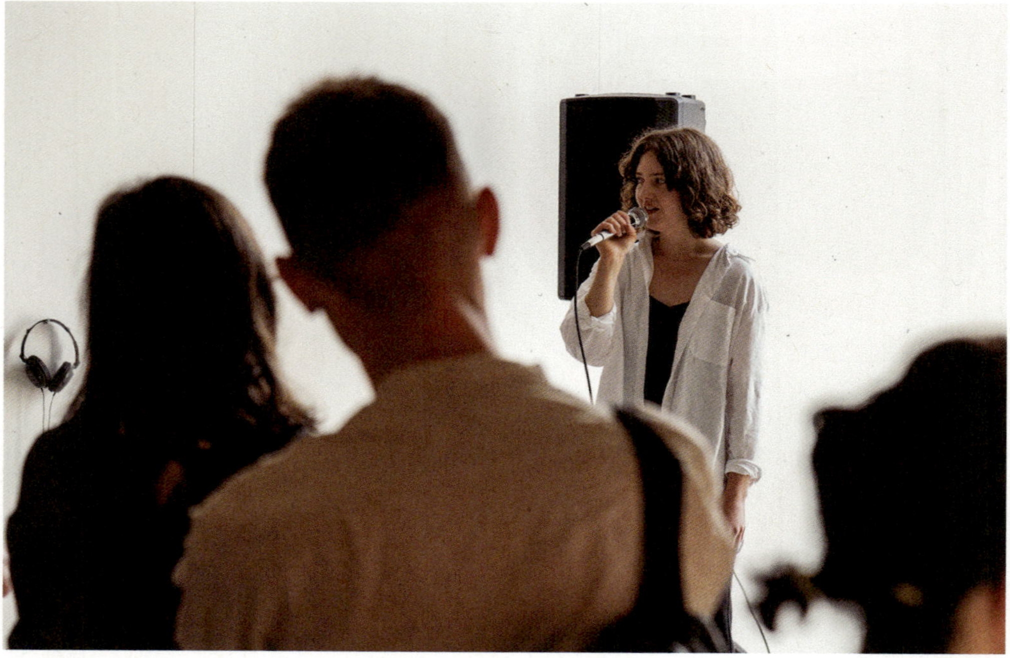

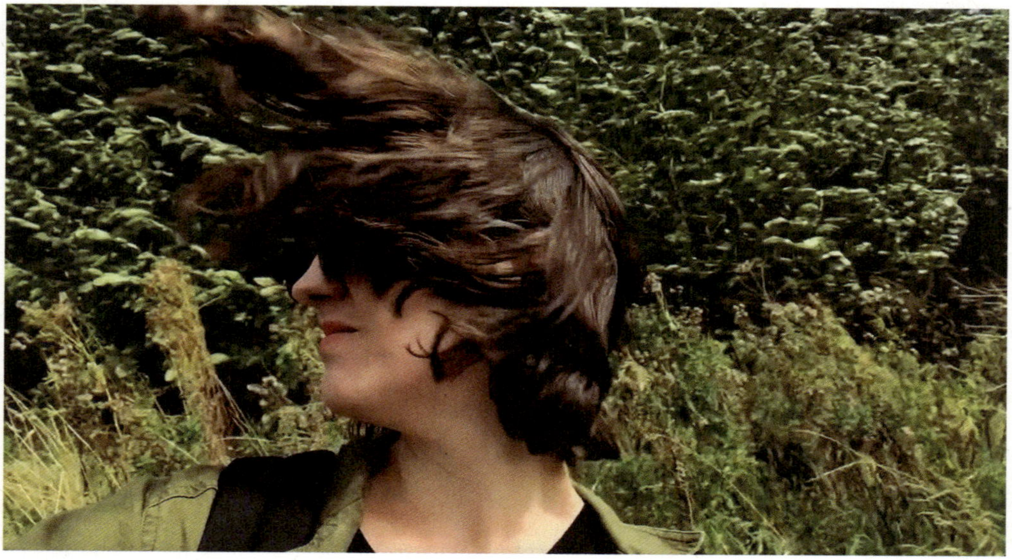

top: Lucy Vann, *The Lady with the Braid (karaoke attempt)*,
performance, Site Gallery, Sheffield, *Platform 2019*. Photo: Jules Lister
bottom: Lucy Vann, *I Still Haven't Found What I'm Looking For*,
digital film shot on iPhone (still), 2019

And Often

Lucy Vann

And often, Ricky Martin songs are in my head
And often, System of a Down are in my head
And sometimes I am sitting in my room
And often I am sitting in my room
And sometimes I want to take a long walk off a short cliff
Today I am going to take a long walk off a short cliff
Sometimes I joke about it but it doesn't feel like a joke ha ha
I feel really sad and soft
I want to be lovely and soft together
I have a dream about something impossible to do / resolve
Big rooms. Open plan. But not quite right
'Went out for a sad walk and took Pandora's horse
        two pounds of cooking apples'
Lately I have just wanted to bite into some bath sponges!
I'm singing 'Promise Me' by Beverly Craven
I'm doing the low parts
It's so beautiful I'm almost tearful
I am scared. I go away. I am in a room
Two rooms together
I'm supposed to be prepping for work
I'm switching stuff about and moving items
I'm full of trepidation but also thrilled
Bending forward straight legs
wide legged
twist from side to side
Close the back door slowly
slide big toe along floor lift big toe off floor for ten seconds
        bring knee back in
I should listen
I'll burn this book one day
I don't know any more
What to do tomorrow?
A dream of kissing on a sofa
Oooh sometimes

I hope I leave a big hole
A slow motion handstand
someone is holding me
A plastic bottle floating in the air
I'm trying to film it on my phone
I'm lying next to my phone
pink deep dark blue evening light
remorseful I did it in the first place
'video pen pals'
I take the bin out every day
I have a bath sometimes
I'm going for a walk now
I'm looking at a view
I'm sitting on the floor
And once it went on until 6 o'clock in the morning
And they're having an argument again
And no I don't have a TV
I had a dream about it and woke up and it was playing on the radio
'Are you still making silly videos?'
I see spiders everywhere and I can't do it
They are on me. I was terrified!
I want to recreate something I've seen
Three pages is a bit excessive
Is it pointless to keep going on?
Saying the same things
maybe we can talk about it
It's 4 o'clock in the morning and it's starting to get light
I'm OTT
I'm over the top
I'm on the outside of something I was on the inside of
I have something in the oven
There's flames and heat and gas, I can't move it
I think – I'm really in trouble now!
Climbing up
There are so many obstacles in the way
full of fear of falling
He was looking down on me from a swivelly office chair
And I was below in the dark like some creature on the sofa

Oh it was so wonderful and I'll never forget it
Maybe someone reading this will think otherwise
I need to write things down all the time
I was ready to kill him!
Not really, I was just thinking, 'Good God when will this end?'
Of course I would never say this
Who wants to hear it anyway
One day I will dedicate some time to listen to all the
    iPhone voice messages
Read all the iPhone notes
The vanity of small differences
The ball is in my court
No one has ever suggested that before but I wonder if they've thought it
I don't feel like a 'friend'
:-/
I think I'll risk it
I've said enough now
They are at the airport
They are getting a salad bowl
It was all very heavy
I am on a train
I was in a shopping centre
And suddenly I'm thinking, what have we done? Dear God
I will never be allowed to have my cake and eat it
I want to do a slowed down version
I want it to be really funny and really sad
The advice was somewhat shit and perhaps made things worse
You can't let that happen again
It can be one of those songs where the lyrics has nothing
    to do with the title
People don't want to hear about it
People must think this is an over-the-top response!
That it isn't real
That I'm being clingy
Meanwhile in the flat...
listening to 'Drive' by The Cars for the fourth time this morning
You call this connection?

Siân Williams

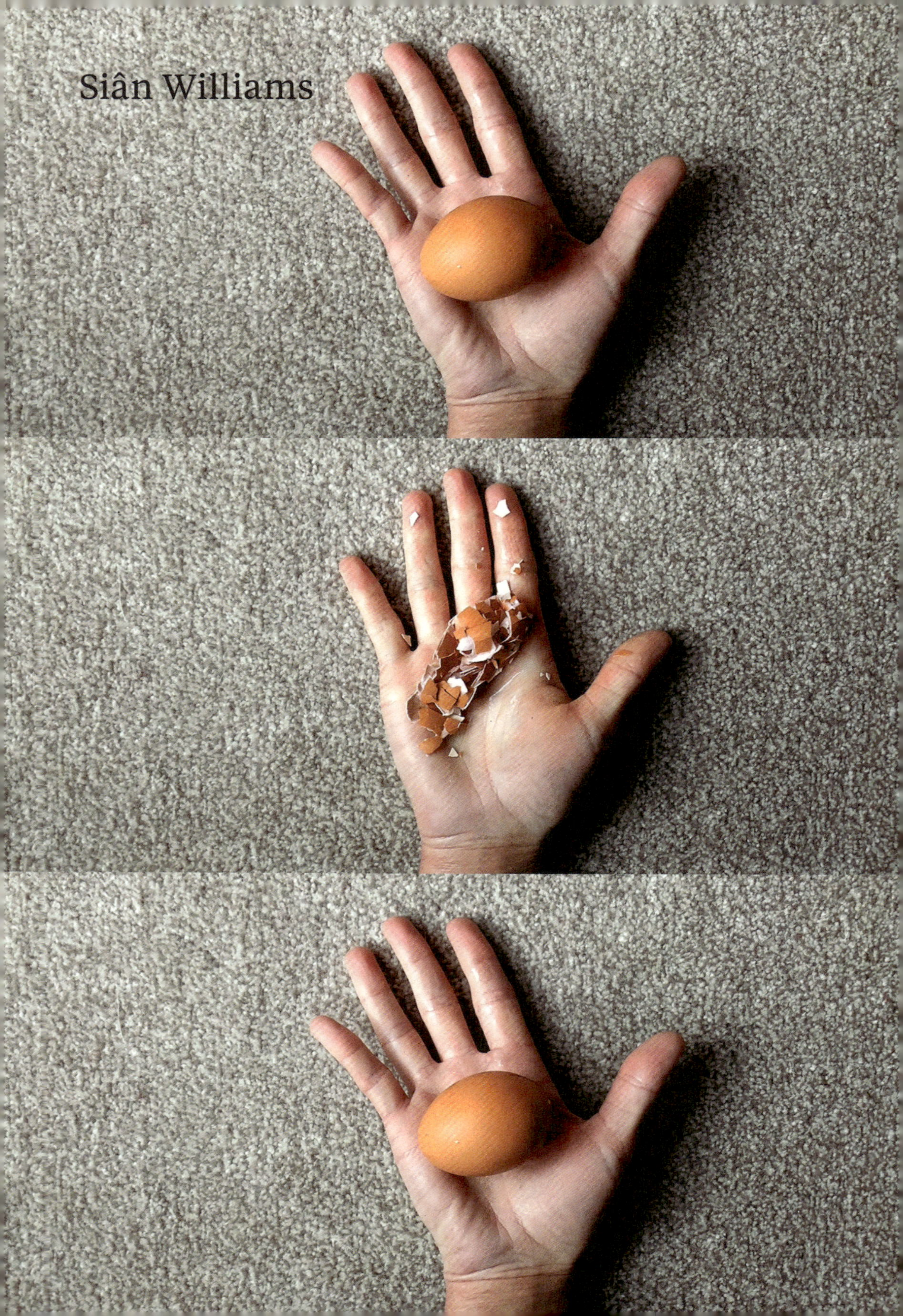

The Sensual World

The peal of church bells, sharp in the sky. Their crystal clarity led my mind outside, in search of the vividness of April birdsong. It's a cool September morning and the season begins its slow, maudlin retreat.

Siân and I have often talked about Kate Bush, and I'm reminded today of Molly Bloom in Bush's *The Sensual World*, stepping out of the page and into the technicolour of the real world, overawed by the sensuality of everything. The song opens with bells ringing in the distance, their sonic texture passing through like cloud. Bush intended originally to recite Bloom's breathless soliloquy at the close of James Joyce's *Ulysses*, but his estate wouldn't allow it. Instead, Bush wrote her own version, pastiching the original, keeping the sounds and rhythms.

So too a season was displaced and rewritten, aspirations stunted and refashioned. Siân's practice is its own sensual world, one of tactility, intimacy and connection. Each are qualities we have had to reshape, collectively experiencing the odd embodiedness of being indoors as the world blooms. I asked Siân last week what her home sounds like, and after a brief pause she said 'softer'. We spoke about the studio, how it became off limits; how the home became the studio, how the sensory pleasure of the hum of others working dropped away. Siân has been listening closely to this new domestic, interior idiom, drawing those perhaps familiar rhythms into sharper relief.

A right hand, palm facing up and fingers together, rests on the textured cream carpet. An egg sits atop. Siân's fingers seem to twitch, before enclosing the egg, gradually applying pressure until the – sudden – rupture. You attune to the straining muscles in her hand, before the shell cracks, crunching like glass in her fingers; more crystalline than before, now all else is taken away. Siân's fingers clutch at these shards, holding them tight and tenderly, for a few seconds longer than you anticipated. Her hand opens again, revealing the imprints of her skin, and the shape left by the palm. It's an act of wanting to know the material, a kind of hunger. The act ends in waste, a ruptured form. Or seems to, but keep watching. The process rewinds itself, undoing, back to the beginning, closing with wholeness. A seeming act of violence journeys through catharsis; from what could have been, back to where we began, but changed. I left the film to play, enjoying the crackle of the shell.

Siân's work has always liked to begin with what is at hand – whether in humble materials and techniques or drawing from her immediate environment. In whichever media, Siân's work takes place right here, at this moment. Lately necessarily domestic in scope, her filmic vignettes of interior spaces and objects, I notice, gaze only inwardly; never through the window and out into the world, but on to what is inside the walls. Siân is influenced by the American composer Pauline Oliveros, who coined the term 'deep listening' to articulate a practice of radical attentiveness. Such profound attention is, of course, political. Siân's sensory explorations of her interior and its sensations both gesture to interior states of mind and also speak to how we might become more aware of the world generally through our immediate environment; how it gives shape to experience.

The outside world has taken on a new somatic register, one of trepidation and possible danger. Single-use plastics cover our faces like second skins, a new piece of sensory vocabulary that, alongside the cool dry sting of hand sanitiser, form barriers between us. This new everyday lexicon of sensations is affecting social reconfigurations in ways we might not yet be conscious of. What is a practice of intimacy in the time of distancing?

Writing is of increasing importance to Siân's practice as a modality of connection; reaching out and touching. Collaboration is one such way – take her call-and-response writing with Kelly Best elsewhere in these pages. As it happens, a pamphlet of writing including Siân and Kelly has just been delivered to my door. This warm circulation continues – as I am writing Siân is writing too, for her contributions to her pages overleaf. We agreed to write side by side this week, only sharing the results come Friday afternoon. I wonder what overlaps we will find, and whether it might in some way be a conversation? Siân is always finding ways to share space with others, which points me towards a practice of solidarity. While Siân's reflections in her writing often depart from the sensorial, they open out like an outstretched palm, seeking out the sense of things, and then making sense of them. Her writing has an engaging slowness to it. It doesn't rush, instead it focuses on the moment. There is softness and small detail, but there is deep engagement with the world at hand. This slowness – less an ellipsis, more a comma – is a practice of taking stock, of careful thought rooted in the present. Could this be a kind of ethics? A thinking though of what you put into the world, how and when, not least when the world is changed.

I reflect back on Siân's work *Breath Circle* at Site Gallery's *Platform 2019* – a hanging pair of curtains, woven tightly from long strips of tin foil in an interlocking grid, like hands clasped together. A visceral, looping breath-piece reverberated through the human-sized space between them.

I remember how they shivered in the draft, how their unwoven tendrils touched the floor. There was delicacy still, despite the scale. I wonder how Siân feels about the work at this moment, and the contrasts of scale from then to now? Do we return to what is old and re-vision it, or start again?

The sensual is political.

4 September 2020

p.206: Siân Williams, *Resurrection*, video, 2020

But What Now?
Siân Williams

I walked past my swimming pool the other day. A small Victorian building housing a small Victorian pool. We swim in 25 yards here, not 25 metres. A community space where the regulars nod and wave to each other, where strangers sit almost thigh to thigh in the tiny sauna, and where I have regularly found myself passing the time of day, completely naked, with women in the communal changing room with the same level of ease as if we'd bumped into each other on the street.

My pool is still closed. Open only to the mysterious 'private hire' (which is so private I can't find out anything about it). My guess is that it's too small to open to the public with effective social distancing. The big shiny Olympic-sized pool in the city centre is not opening at all because it is not 'financially viable'. The cost of opening such a large venue to such a small amount of people is not one the local authority can reasonably meet. So despite the government's posters, which decorate the city encouraging us to get active and be fitter, the places where we might do this remain closed to us.

Standing on the street outside looking up at the facade, I am reminded of another pool that I swam in last year in Belfast. Equally small and equally Victorian, a swim here costs only £2. There were no lanes in that pool, just a wide expanse of water; but everyone was very careful and swam up and down in neat straight lines as if some unspoken agreement said: 'we all need to share, so this is how it works'. I went there so often during my week in the city that someone remarked, 'you're a local now'. I wonder what has happened to that pool? I wonder if it's reopened or if, like mine, it lies dormant, closed because of space or money (perhaps two sides of the same coin), the regulars going about their lives waterless and swimless.

The first time I went swimming since lockdown, on the 24 June, was in a mill pond about an hour's walk from where I live. The pond is shallow, maybe five feet at the deepest part, and on a hot morning there would be surprise pockets of warm water, where the sunbeams touch the surface, which are a delight to swim into. With no bath at home, I hadn't been immersed in water since the beginning of March, maybe even the end of February (if I had known what was to happen I would have marked the date). I didn't realise how important being able to submerge myself was. I didn't realise how much being in water was like being held in a very gentle hug, one that reaches round and touches the whole of your body all at once.

There is a kind of intimacy attached to swimming with strangers. The most immediate intimacy is that of being semi-naked; there's not a lot of protection when you're just wearing a swimming costume. I can't imagine going to the supermarket in only a leotard, but somehow it seems perfectly reasonable to be in close proximity to several bodies all wearing next to nothing when those bodies are in water. The vulnerability of being exposed. But there is also the intimacy of sharing the water. We share the air around us all the time of course, but the tiny vibrations and changes that happen with each person's movement aren't as obvious in the air as they are in water. As my friend swims out into the pond I see the ever-increasing ripples caused by her movement, movement that is mostly hidden to me because it happens underwater. Those ripples touch me, even when she's far away. After we get out the surface returns to its relative stillness, but underneath our presence can still be felt in the mixed-up silt and mud at the places where our feet touched the bottom.

I keep thinking to myself, 'what now?' What now when my swimming pool is still closed and winter approaches, making the mill pond less appealing? What now when we're encouraged to forget, but the wreckage of everything that's passed lies around us, not always visible but there somewhere? Once, in my studio, I listened to a biblical scholar explain the apocalypse doesn't have to be the end of everything, that destruction brings the chance for new beginnings. I'm not religious and I've never read the Bible, but what if we thought this way instead of trying to get back to the old way? Even now, sitting here writing this, knowing that you're there writing that, 150 miles away, these words are different, nudged around by the invisible tension between us. What if the air was like the water and we could see the waves and ripples that connect us all? What if we start a different story?

4 September 2020

Continued from page 35

↓

That the sound felt solid was about as close as it was possible to get to it physically before it was gone. I'd never thought of sound as weight before. A physical object. Perhaps more a thing, thing being vaguer than object. Off topic, I wish more things came submerged in vagueness so we could pull them out and redefine them using our own criteria and in our own time. On topic, if it *is* physical then it *must* have weight to it. Just because we can't see it doesn't mean it is without form or doesn't occupy space. In a spoken context, sound is ejected out of the mouth, momentarily propelled forward, it is flying not falling. Falling, falling, falling and hits the ground. Sometimes it stays there, unable to penetrate the surface. Usually it disappears as quickly as it's expelled. Gone, but not before passing through a membrane of memory where, if lucky it might be registered, catalogued and remain. And wait. And wait, at least until a newer version replaces it or it falls down the back of the shelf. August 2019

aboutaboutaboutaboutaboutaboutaboutaboutaboutaboutaboutaboutabout

I've been thinking about intimacy again, about proximity, and about shared space. I've been thinking about the shape of someone else's body next to mine and how sometimes, even if we are not touching, I can still feel them in some way. I've been thinking about our awareness of each other, and about the subtle shifts and changes when someone enters or exits a room. I've been thinking about how some people hold presence whilst others blend into the background. I've been thinking about what it means when those things are taken away and we no longer have proximity and we no longer have shared space. I've been thinking about what might come to fill that void. April 2020

↓

The journey towards the organ on the far side of this room is slower than before. Everything about this scene, the barren walls, a lack of anything soft or forgiving; the steadfast teak floor is primed for the amplified CLOMP that will come when my boots make contact with the wood. But my journey continues in perfect silence as if the two surfaces never touch. These muted connections continue even with a heavy measured drag of the stool. I take my seat, positioning myself appropriately and with respect. Spreading my fingers above the organ I'm suddenly aware of the scale of the possible connections. Touching the surface, my digits depress. Silence continues. Every single point of pressure should carry a train of signals, a runaway pulse at an undetectable speed, generating a specific action. Only stillness awaits at the platform. I try a different sequence, but the organ does not respond. The wires of communication are severed, forcibly redundant and unable to deliver their messages. Are we prepared for this level of betrayal? Motor learning is now extinct and the organ no longer has control over my movement. Matter triumphs over mind, and fingers, unable to detach themselves, fuse with the external layer of the organ. April 2020

aboutaboutaboutaboutaboutaboutaboutaboutaboutaboutaboutaboutabout

I've been thinking about listening; how we listen not just with our ears but with our bodies. I've been thinking about listening happening across time and through generations. I've been thinking about listening as memory and memory as collective, as gathering, interpreting, transforming and as active not passive. I've been thinking about listening as both intimacy and solidarity. July 2020

↓

When I lay down, that's when it happens. It's not always immediate but it is guaranteed to happen then. In fact, it only happens then. But it gets even more specific. If I turn left there is no reaction. Nothing. *Nada. Niente. Rien*! But if I turn right, well, it's only a matter of time. I used to think it was a natural occurrence. A bodily function of sorts, triggered directly by the act of rotating my body. But since speaking to you I started suspecting it was more inexplicable than that, a phenomenon closer to the supernatural than scientific. A sound only I can hear, communication just for me. A sound produced from within the very device that exists to hear it. Thoughts are soundless words. But this noise is not thought. This noise is just noise. A noise that is intimately mine. July 2020

M62

Andrew McMillan

how many times has it been crossed
this styx   that's really just a stitch
of heathered land   or a tunnel
or a bluemetal waymaker
names of places   distance called
like birthdays as the road dips east

and how did it feel   that first time
heading west   your young life boxed up
the empty theatre
of the service station   the scone
you split with your parents   the bowl
that slipped from its crate and shattered

on the floor of the shared kitchen
its dust   like blown dandelions
gathering in corners   and even now
couldn't there be a tiny freckle
of porcelain still on your lungs
that hums each time you reach the border

is that the sharpness you always
thought was just cold air   is that why sometimes
it's difficult to breathe   a thing
got broken and is inside you
like a tiny flint of arrowhead
your body pointing who knows where

Talbot Rice Gallery

Edinburgh, Scotland

Aideen Doran

Stephanie Mann

Rosie O'Grady

Tako Taal

Talbot Rice Gallery: An Introduction

Talbot Rice is the public art gallery of the University of Edinburgh. It was founded in 1969 and opened in its current form in 1975. With a nineteenth century former natural history museum and a contemporary white cube to fuel its engine, Talbot Rice is dedicated to exploring how the University can contribute to contemporary art production today and into the future. Solo exhibitions provide international artists with access to University research and collections, while conceptual group exhibitions foreground key political and social issues.

Past exhibitions have explored frontiers in the age of Brexit; raised the volume on female self-empowerment; and considered the cognitive theory of the 'extended mind' in relation to contemporary art. Talbot Rice Gallery positions itself at the forefront of research and creative practice in the visual arts.

Talbot Rice Residents programme provides time, support and nurturing for a group of early-career artists based in Scotland to work within the unique context of Talbot Rice Gallery, Edinburgh College of Art and the University of Edinburgh. Residents are provided with ongoing curatorial and technical support from the Talbot Rice team, as well as studio and office space and access to workshops, libraries, collections and contact with the vast academic community within the University of Edinburgh. The Residents are brought together for a week every two months for a programme of masterclasses, workshops and social events. The end of the first year of a two-year programme is marked with a European research trip, and a commissioned text on each artist's practice.

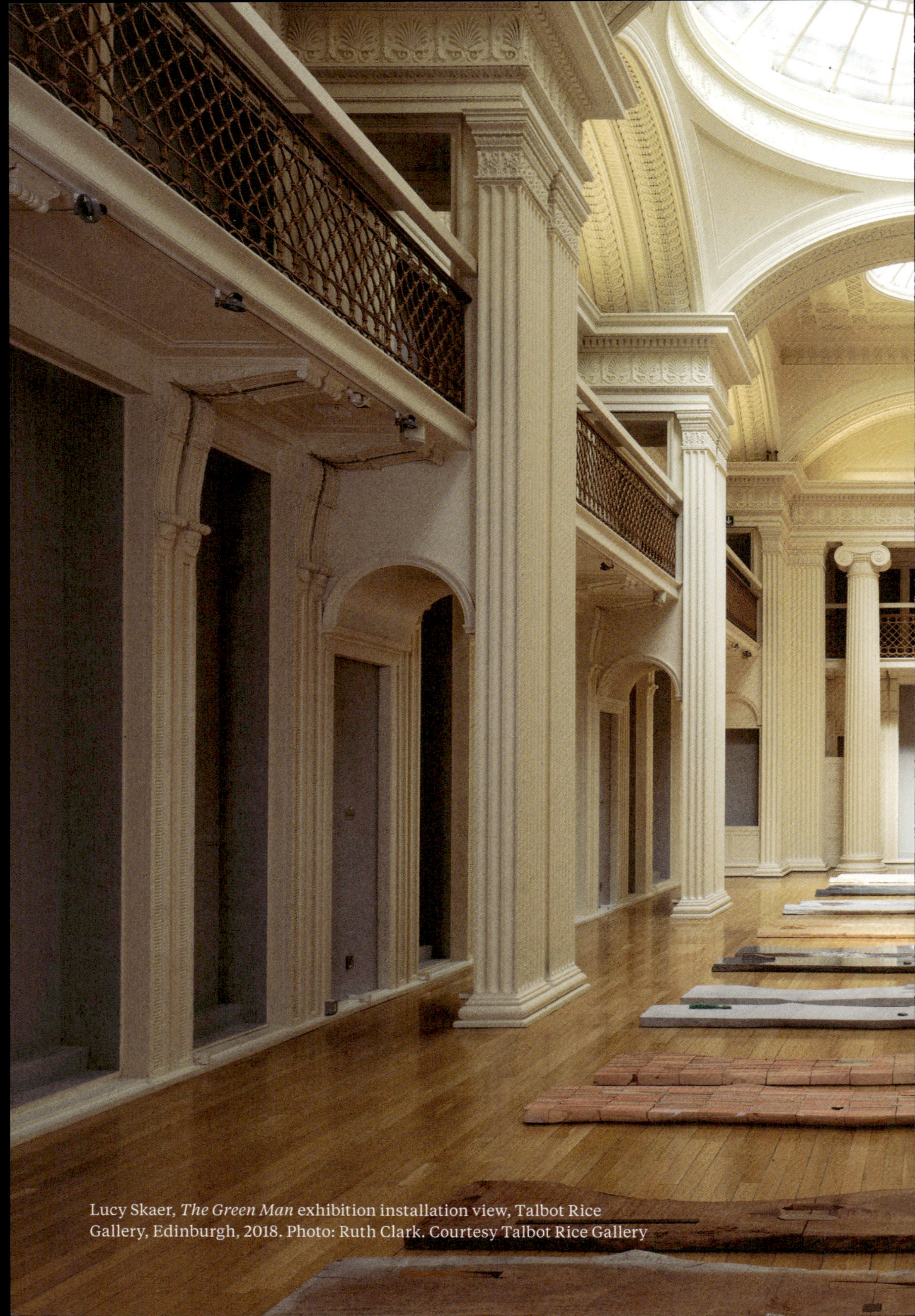

Lucy Skaer, *The Green Man* exhibition installation view, Talbot Rice Gallery, Edinburgh, 2018. Photo: Ruth Clark. Courtesy Talbot Rice Gallery

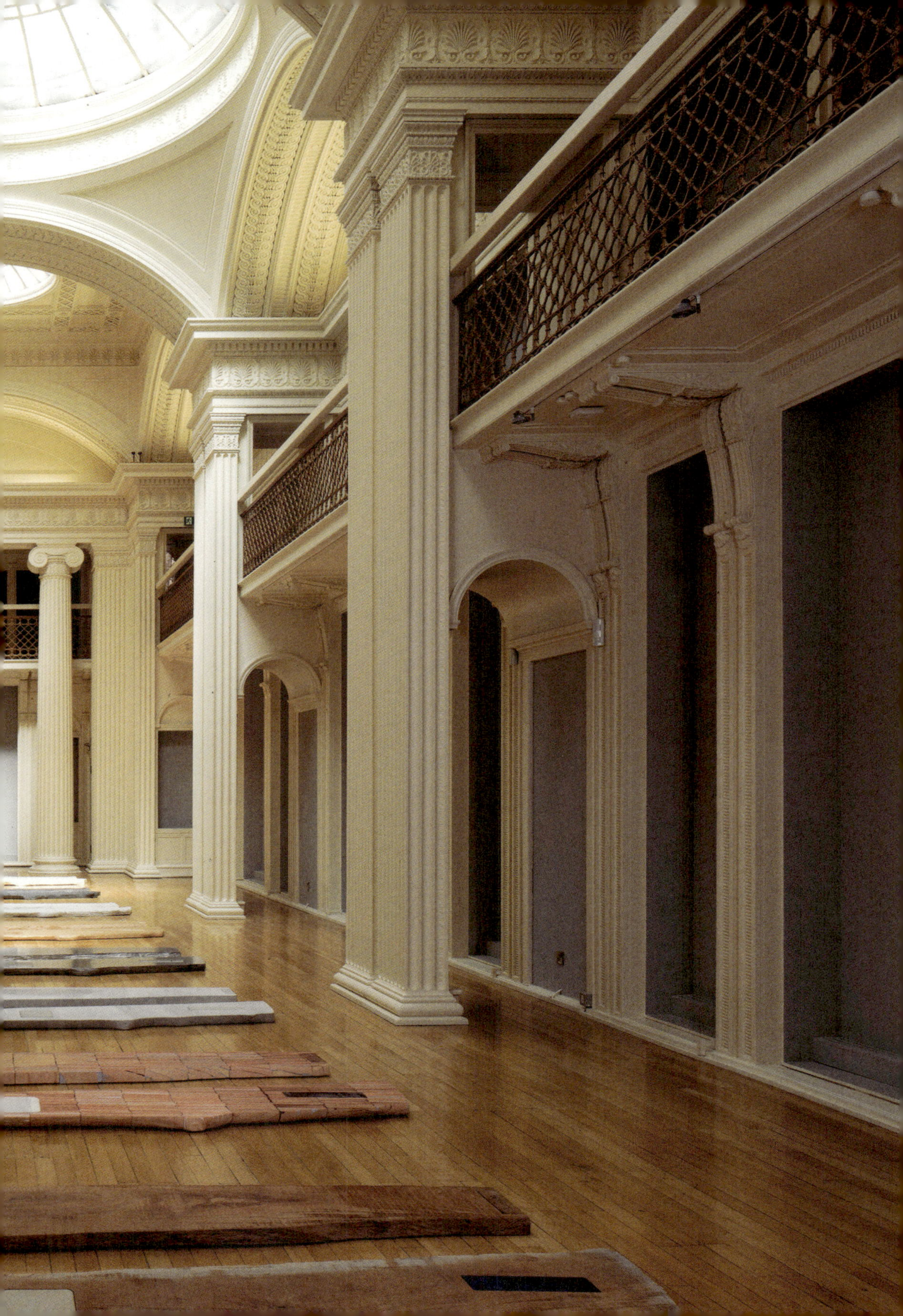

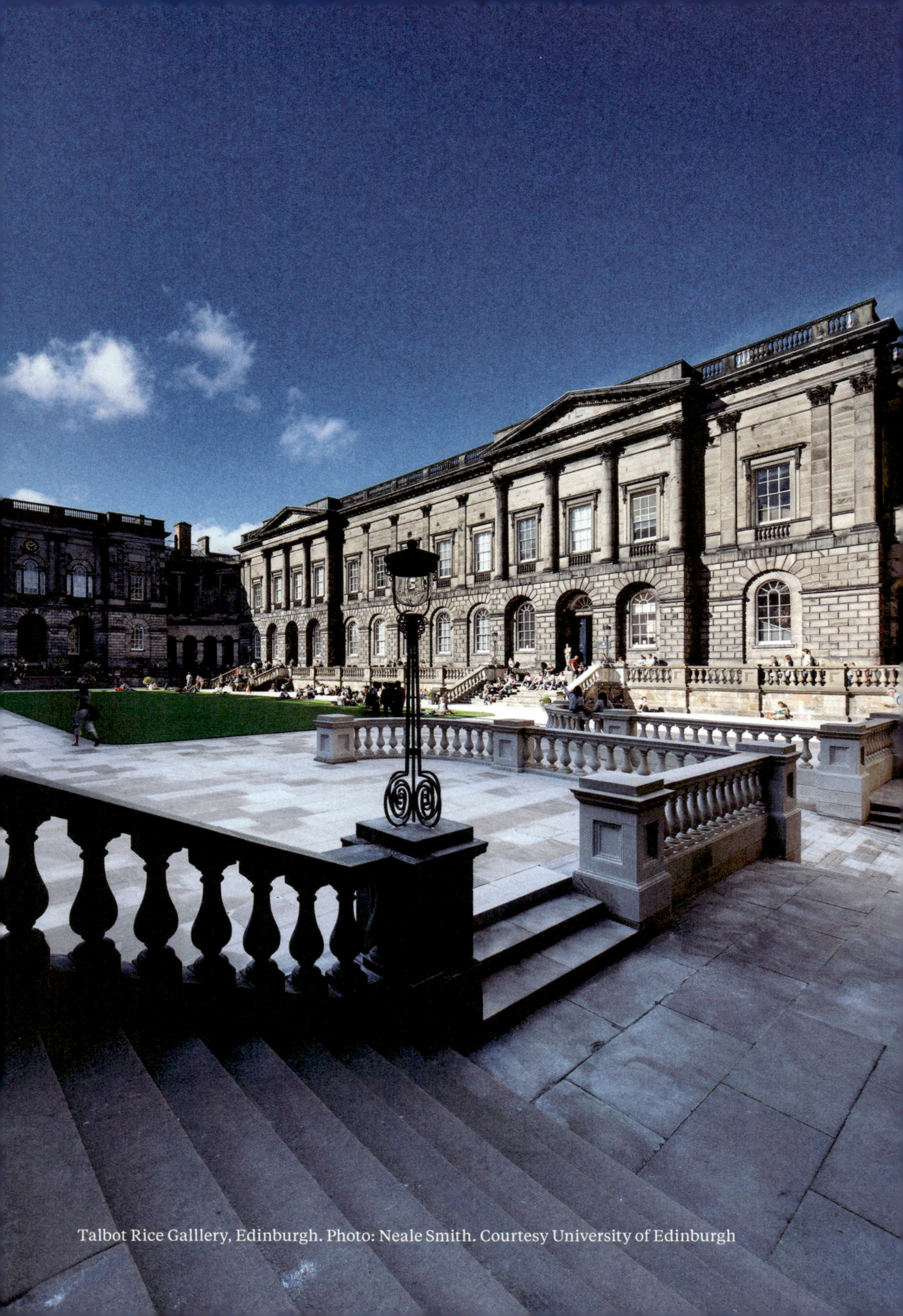

Talbot Rice Gallery, Edinburgh. Photo: Neale Smith. Courtesy University of Edinburgh

Talbot Rice Gallery Team

At root the word 'reside' means to *sit, again* – evoking a moment to pause and reflect upon progress. For Talbot Rice Gallery, a residency is about artists having the space to really inhabit their practice. With the Freelands Foundation, we've been able to design a programme that feeds artists' curiosity and helps them push the boundaries of their work. To 'reside' is also to remain or be present in a place for a significant period of time, and the time our Residents spend embedded in our community allows them to deconstruct, rebuild and consolidate their practices. There is time to be consumed by research or esoteric study; time to build new networks, communities and lasting connections; and time to critique and reconsider the very structures that we all work within. It's our job to build a secure scaffold around them, to become attuned and remain responsive to their specific needs, and to create the right kind of space for them to develop – to create an environment where innovative ideas and practices can incubate, ready to resound in the world beyond and outlive the bounds of the programme.

Run with an awareness of broader social, cultural and economic issues, the programme also aims to be responsive, adaptive and relevant. The challenges presented by COVID-19 are huge and unprecedented, making people working in the creative industries and those of low income and precarious employment status especially vulnerable. Like never before, a robust and supportive infrastructure for artists is paramount. Concomitantly, the global environmental crisis must drive thinking around the facilitation and production of artistic practices; just as the Black Lives Matter movement must compel new forms of learning and enquiry. For the Residents programme, this means an emphasis on working locally, working deeper rather than wider, using resources that are close to hand and supporting Scotland's creative ecosystem. It means promoting an understanding of ecological issues and other cultures, as well as a promotion of diversity in all its forms. As we work to establish a new 'normal' we will double down on the vital work the programme allows us to do, further progressing alternative modes of maintaining togetherness, and building the shared resilience necessary if we are to emerge on the other side: stronger, closer and fundamentally changed for the better.

(1)

A

BILL

INTITULED

An Act for explaining an Act made in *Ireland* in the Twenty-ſeventh Year of the Reign of His preſent Majeſty, intituled *An Act to prevent tumultuous Riſings and Aſſemblies; and for the more effectual Puniſhment of Perſons guilty of Outrage, Riot, and illegal Combinations, and of adminiſtering and taking unlawful Oaths.*

WHEREAS an Act was made in the Parliament of *Ireland* in the Twenty-ninth Year of the Reign of His preſent Majeſty, intituled *An Act to prevent tumultuous Riſings and Aſſemblies, and for the more effectual Puniſhment of Perſons guilty of Outrage, Riot, and illegal Combinations, and of adminiſtering and taking unlawful Oaths*: And whereas it is in and by the ſaid recited Act enacted, that every Perſon who ſhould voluntarily enter any unlawful Combination or Confederacy to defraud any Clergyman of the Church of *Ireland* or Lay Impropriator of any Tythes or Dues to which he is legally entitled, or of any Part thereof, or to obſtruct him in the collecting thereof, or ſhall by Force, Threats, or other unlawful Means, prevent any ſuch Clergyman or Lay Impropriator, or any Perſon or Perſons employed by him, from viewing, valuing, ſetting, or ſelling any Tythes to which he is entitled, or having heretofore

(40.) entered

Closed Doors, Broken Windows

The Overton window is a political theory that refers to the range of policies a given public will accept. This window shifts, and previously unpalatable or unthinkable ideas can become normalised, naturalised – dare I say it, institutionalised. Within this metaphorical framework of social order, of governance, things come to seem inevitable. And yet, and yet. If, as the political theorist Chantal Mouffe has elegantly shown, every order 'is the temporary and precarious articulation of contingent practices',[1] what happens when – as 2020 has so desperately revealed – systems stop working, or when those systems work only for some? Established orders can be crises in themselves, but what appears fully formed can be approached, and subverted, from many different directions.

Aideen Doran's practice doesn't crack the pane but pivots around it, engaging new, other ways of seeing. She takes things that are in the world – archival images, found footage – and flips them on their back, revealing the visual codes and hidden ideological structures that have made them that way. Her approach is not to distort the object of inquiry, but to upend the readings around it – the ways it comes into the world. Doran is drawn to subtle acts of insubordination: in literature, in poetry, in the margins and footnotes of historical narration. What might such acts of power from below reveal? The artist's engagement with archives and historical materials is a way to think through today's problems, and seeming inevitabilities at a distance.

A new work is forming, originating at the point where an act of protest escalates and becomes riot. Riot is a kind of carnivalesque in its temporary upending of order; both public disobedience at the injustices of the status quo and the attendant justification of violence by those in power, clamping down on insurrection. A historical telling of a riot, as such, diverges in who speaks it, and Doran's work attends to these disjunctures. The artist is drawing together historical materials in connection to two such moments of rupture in Ulster, where the artist grew up: a late-Victorian-era trial in her hometown of Lurgan, and a rent strike in the 1970s. The rent and rates strike was a campaign of civil disobedience, principally against the reintroduction of internment in 1971, and more broadly an expression of the Catholic population's alienation from the government.[2]

Riot is justified – made inevitable – in one account of a trial Doran is currently researching. This pertains to the murder of a young boy, John

Furfey, by a Captain Redmond in 1879, after an incident in the town. Doran's materials – the coroner's report, the Parliamentary account, and the boy's gravestone – each vary in register, detail and bias. Witness descriptions conflict in the coroner's inquiry. The Parliamentary account provides only a narrative statement, and concludes that Redmond's use of force was lawful and proportionate, as the 'rioters' were breaking the law by damaging property. On his gravestone, John is named alongside another man killed by Redmond – which is the only place that this death is recorded. These details alone highlight the power of those entrusted with recording history to omit, obscure and tailor the narrative. What histories remain occluded here, what else must be brought to light? What 'incident' led to this tragedy?

Mistrustful of the voice of history, this ongoing research and work find connection with Doran's *The Acute Disaster* (2012) a moving image work in which a solemn, dramatic voiceover appears to be narrating what we see, until later we realise this is not quite the case. Found footage from the Trades Union archive, interspersed with shots of ruined buildings and groups gathering – a seeming riot – is accompanied by a voice preparing us for 'if, and when, disaster might strike'.[3] We later realise the voice is speaking from a handbook for archivists on disaster management rather than narrating a possible societal crisis, as we may have assumed.[4] Parts of the footage are grainy, damaged – what we see is fragile, metaphorically resonant of the frailty of historical, voiced authority. With this, Doran also highlights the malleability of the archive, which is made even more conditional by the subjectivities of its interpreter, its archivist. Doran's own slippery narration is a distancing device, making us more conscious of how we see and are made to see.

For this new work, Doran is again paying close attention to register and voice. In *Writing Degree Zero,* the theorist and philosopher Roland Barthes advanced the impossibility of neutrality in written expression.[5] The implication of this in Doran's work is that pretence to neutrality can conceal motivations. Perversely, too, an unreliable narrator can be productive, if, as hoped, this fickle account encourages the audience to question what they encounter. As part of her research Doran is currently exploring the practice of 'Verbatim Theatre', in which plays are constructed based on the precise words spoken by those interviewed about a specific topic. Holding a mirror to life and giving it space. Yet even that which is presented verbatim is still the product of unknowable and imperceptible subjectivities. Doran's approach in relation to this conundrum is two-fold: treating her source

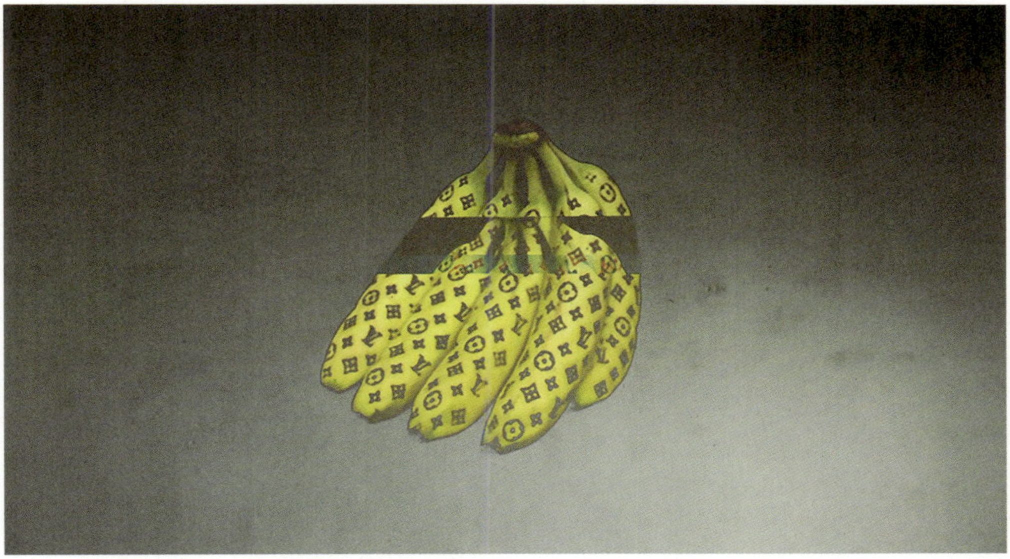

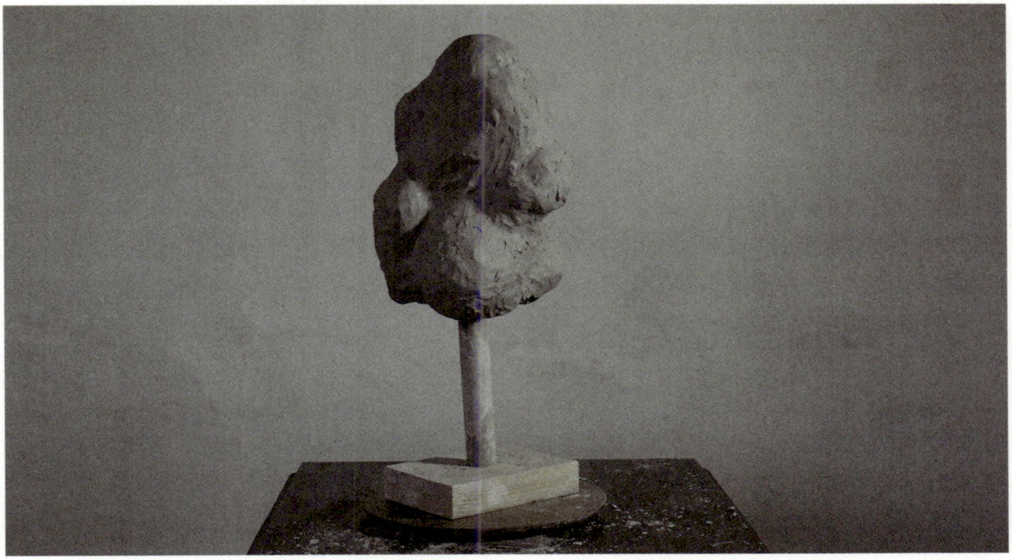

p.230: Inverted copy of Tumultuous Assemblies (Ireland) Bill, 1816.
Image from ProQuest's *House of Commons Parliamentary Papers*
displayed with permission of ProQuest LLC
above: Aideen Doran, *The Mechanical Child*, video (stills), 2017

materials antagonistically, scratching below their thin veneer for less varnished accounts, while simultaneously aestheticising a viewing mode of critical distance. Across Doran's practice,[6] she resists the idea of making things too smooth, refusing to wash over things, encouraging us, in turn, to become productive sceptics.

Doran dismantles the reception of upheld histories, siding herself, and us, against inevitability. This disassembling is highly generative as a practice, as its goal is to uncover alternate histories – those less patriarchal, less authoritarian – and accounts that jar with enlightenment narratives of progress. How do you denature such systems of power? Uncovering suppressed accounts is one such step. Doran's work highlights the power of the act of insubordination, however minor. Small subversions, acts from below, can debilitate structures of power from within, it might just not seem that way. Doran's own artistic acts of antagonism weaken dominant narratives, revealing those windows on to the world for what they are – lenses from which subjective accounts are formed.

26 August 2020

1 Chantal Mouffe, 'Artistic Activism and Agonistic Spaces', *Art & Research*, vol.1, no.2, summer 2007, p.2, http://www.artandresearch.org.uk/v1n2/pdfs/mouffe.pdf.
2 For further reading, see Rosa Gilbert, 'No Rent, No Rates: Civil Disobedience Against Internment in Northern Ireland, 1971–1974', *Studi Irlandesi, A Journal of Irish Studies*, no.7, 2017, https://core.ac.uk/download/pdf/228564651.pdf. Internment was a government policy introduced in Northern Ireland during the Troubles, in which civilians were arrested and held without trial.
3 Aideen Doran, *The Acute Disaster*, 2012.
4 Script adapted by the artist from Claire England and Karen Evans, *Disaster Management for Libraries: Planning and Process*, Canadian Library Association, 1988.
5 Roland Barthes, *Writing Degree Zero* (1953), Hill and Wang, 1977.
6 See in particular Doran's *Oblomov's Dream* (2015), which takes place on a desktop setting intercut with a range of images from YouTube, narrating a protagonist who refuses to submit to the societal conditions assigned to him.

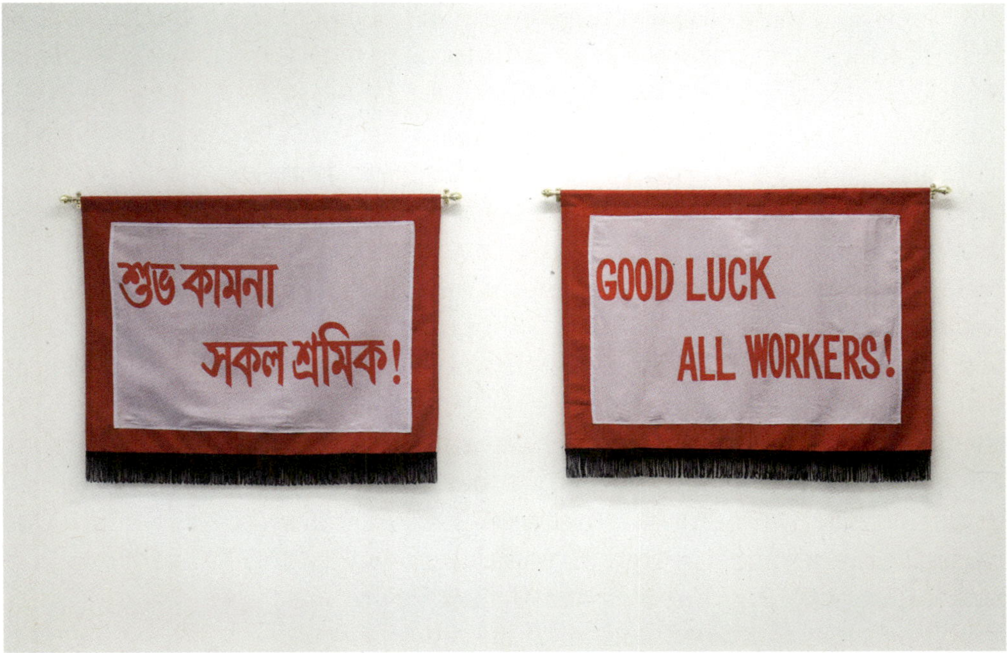

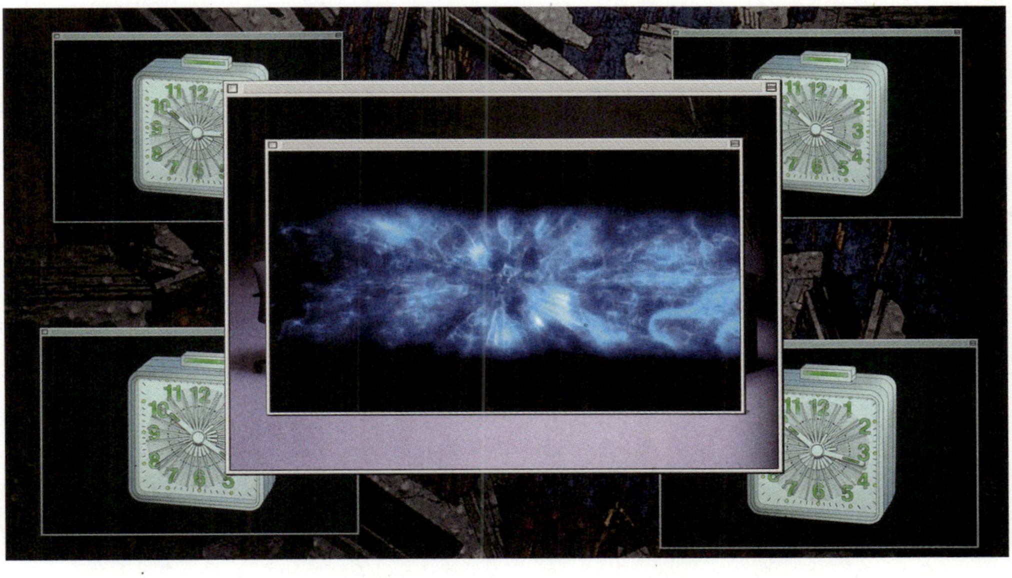

top: Aideen Doran, *Good Luck All Workers* (in English and Bengali), 2013
bottom: Aideen Doran, *Oblomov's Dream*, video (still), 2015

Extract from 'Woman Sitting at the Machine, Thinking'
Karen Brodine

she thinks about everything at once without making a mistake.
no one has figured out how to keep her from doing this thinking
while her hands and nerves also perform every delicate complex
function of the work. this is not automatic or deadening.
try it sometime. make your hands move quickly on the keys
fast as you can, while you are thinking about:

the layers, fossils. the idea that this machine she controls
is simply layers of human workhours frozen in steel, tangled
in tiny circuits, blinking out through lights like hot, red eyes.
the noise of the machine they all sometimes wig out to, giddy,
zinging through the shut-in space, blithering atoms;
everyone's hands paused mid-air above the keys
while Neil or Barbara solo, wrists telling every little thing,
feet blipping along, shoulders raggly.

she had always thought of money as solid, stopped.
but seeing it as moving labor, human hours, why that means
it comes back down to her hands on the keys, shoulder aching,
brain pushing words through fingers through keys, trooping
out crisp black ants on the galleys. work compressed into
instruments, slim computers, thin as mirrors, how could
numbers multiply or disappear, squeezed in sideways like that
but they could, they did, obedient and elegant, how amazing.
the woman whips out a compact, computes the cost,
her face shining back from the silver case
her fingers, sharp tacks, calling up the digits.

when she sits at the machine, rays from the cathode stream
directly into her chest. when she worked as a clerk, the rays
from the xerox angled upward, striking her under the chin.
when she waited tables the micro oven sat at stomach level.
when she typeset for Safeway, dipping her hands in processor
chemicals, her hands burned and peeled and her chest ached
from the fumes.

well we know who makes everything we use or can't use.
as the world piles itself up on the bones of the years,
so our labor gathers.

while we sell ourselves in fractions. they don't want us all
at once, but hour by hour, piece by piece. our hands mainly
and our backs. and chunks of our brains. and veiled expressions
on our faces, they buy. though they can't know what actual
thoughts stand behind our eyes.

then they toss the body out on the sidewalk at noon and at five.
then they spit the body out the door at sixty-five.

*Reproduced with kind permission of Red Letter Press,
Seattle, with thanks to Helen Gilbert*

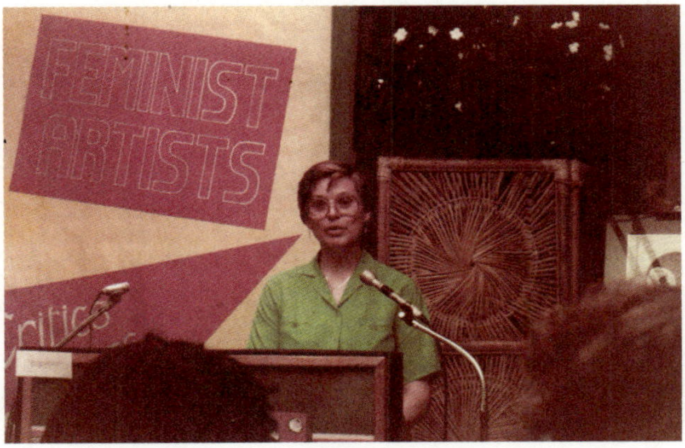

above: Karen Brodine conducting a reading at a programme on feminist artists in the 1980s. Courtesy Red Letter Press
pp.236–237: source material for Aideen Doran's sound piece *Women Sitting at the Machine, Thinking*, 2020

Stephanie Mann

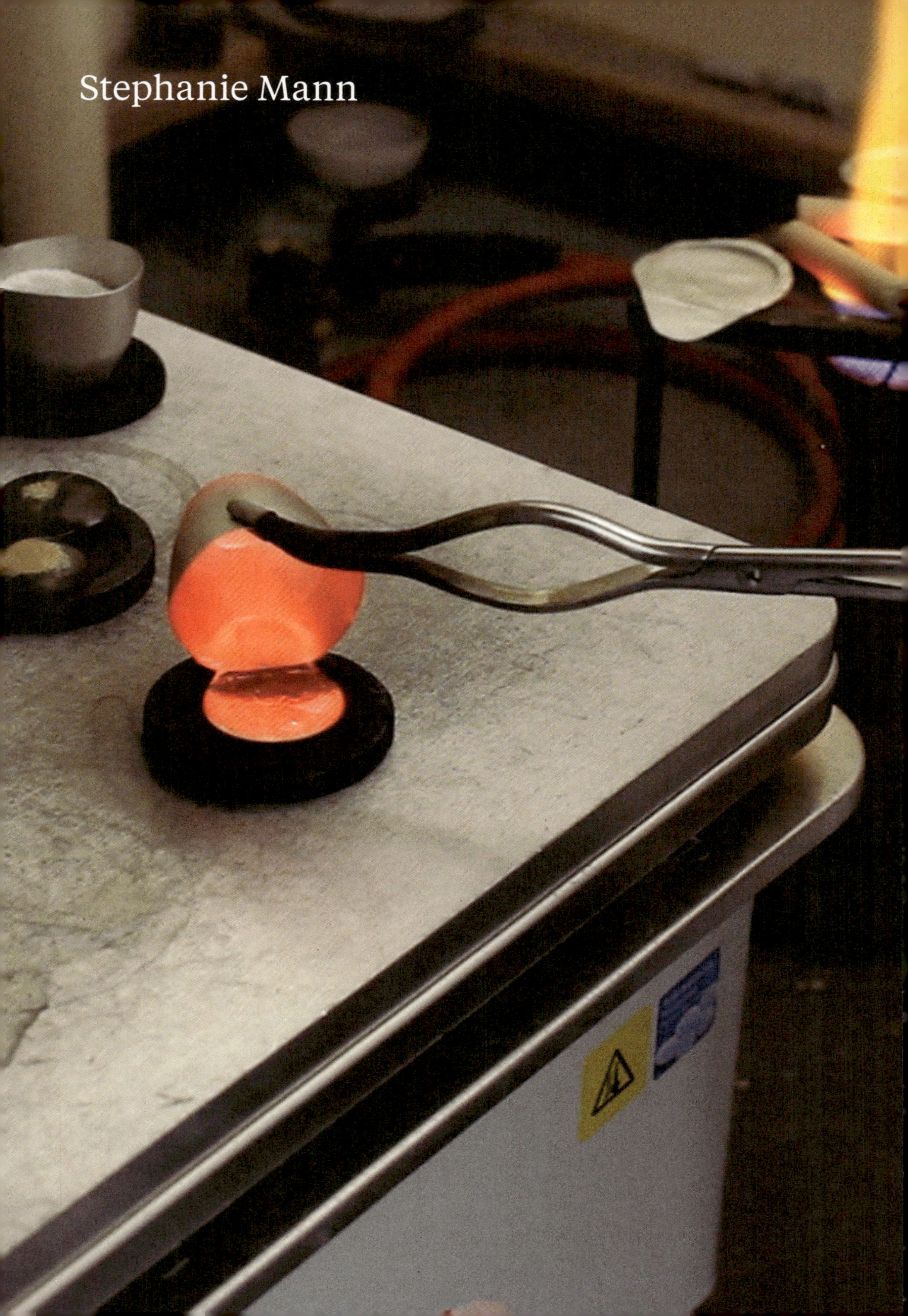

Gathering Dust

Any idea is a leap of faith, a question that begets another. Eighteen months ago, Stephanie Mann approached the University of Edinburgh's collection with the question: 'What is an object?' in mind.

Object-oriented ontology holds that objects exist independently of human perception. Take a rock: a rock is compressed time, an expanse beyond anthropogenic life. A rock can be collected, catalogued, quantified, dated; it is porous, and contains multitudes unknown and unknowable. Mann's work is not a pathway to knowledge. Instead, it is similarly permeable, and intrigued by the imperceptible.

The Geology, Anatomy and Art collections within the University of Edinburgh are sites from which Mann is exploring how objects are learned from and given value by human activities. What is collected? What is kept? When does something become valuable, or cease to be valuable? Very quickly these questions proliferate. How 'known' can such objects ever be? Drawn to outliers in the collection, Mann has worked with collection staff to identify objects that have fallen by the wayside. This occurrence could be for one of two broad reasons: either the object has ceased to be 'useful' as a teaching tool due to decay, erosion or change of state, or the object is unclassified, that is, little or nothing is known about it, and, deprived of context, is unteachable.

An object has many lives seen through this prism alone, moving through various states of (human) value. When an object formally joins a collection, a complex archival web is spun around it: of provenance documents, research reports, narratives and anecdotes. Yet Mann enters into this chain and destabilises further already fragile ontologies. For this work, four objects at the edge lands of the university collection are to be transformed. Mann will collaborate with staff in the Geosciences department to grind these four objects into dust – to the particle size of one micron.[1] Then, these dust particles will be absorbed into the porous cavities of found pieces of sandstone, transmuting material properties and object narratives alike. If these processes go as anticipated, Mann then intends to employ geoscientific imaging techniques to reveal the material composition of these 'new' objects; taking objects that are somewhat known and radically recontextualising them, removing their relatability by deaestheticising them and subsuming them into another form. Is an object simply a product of its material history? Does an object exist to us only because we think it?

Mann's project pivots elegantly from a research project rooted in the object-oriented ontological tradition to the anthropological – how we tell ourselves things about objects, but how, in turn, these same objects are things that tell us about ourselves. A collection, after all, is predicated upon the whims of the human. How does an object come to be part of a university teaching collection? Is that history a part of the materiality of the object, or simply context?

The material histories of the objects collected find connection with the process Mann plans to submit them to. The first item selected for transformation was for many years a teaching object in the Department of Geology. It is a piece of graptolite: a fossil from a species of an ocean dwelling, filtrating creature. When they died, these organisms would sink to the seabed, becoming progressively compressed by the pressure of the sediment forming on top of them, eventually becoming a carbonised impression, an imprint. Yet despite this millions-of-years-long process, a recent water ingress in the storage facility in which the fossil was housed has damaged it beyond repair, all but destroying its use value as a teaching object through corrosion. The resultant 'image' caused by compression is disappearing. Mann engages with this unanticipated occurrence and disappears the image further. At one point in its life cycle, this object, as part of its biological process, would have been a receptor for other molecules, and now it will be turned to dust and absorbed by another host.

In 1980, the Scottish artist Eduardo Paolozzi was commissioned to design a mural for Tottenham Court Road Underground station in Central London.[2] During recent station renovations, the mural was taken apart and relocated. According to Transport for London's website, 5% of the mural could no longer be housed and was donated to the University of Edinburgh by the Paolozzi Foundation. What is not divulged is why 5% no longer 'fitted' or had use value in the mural's updated context. These leftover scraps of mosaic, in some cases still attached to chunks of tunnel wall and London clay, now have new contexts of their own as teaching objects. Additionally, the Paolozzi Foundation has granted Mann permission to turn a piece of this mosaic into dust, in so doing contextualising anew once more. As Mann has noted, these glass mosaic tiles were originally sand.[3] Understood in this way, becoming dust is in a sense a process of return to that prior state, as is the case for the graptolite fossil. Yet these material transformations are only known to us because of the language that we use to narrate them. How 'readable' is any object or material? What would we encounter of the objects, if we knew nothing of the process which brought them to their current state? For this, we must trust in the facts of the imperceptible.

'What is an object?' can never be satisfactorily answered, but nor is this Mann's goal. Rather, hers is a poetics of transformation, relishing in contingency. Mann encourages us to appreciate the limitations of our languages and knowledges when it comes to making sense of the material world around us. If, as is hoped, Mann's objects are ground to dust, will the resultant sandstone objects enter the university collections, and be named, catalogued and narrated in turn? What might these objects teach us in the future? Moreover, what can they tell us right now? Human beings have a clearly defined life cycle, whereas objects have a life cycle only in the sense that we meet them from the parameters of our own making. Like the rocks of Mann's ontological study, knowledge is a porous body, ever open to influence.

14 August 2020

1 A micron is ten times smaller than a human white blood cell.
2 The mosaics were completed in 1986; for further information see https://art.tfl.gov.uk/projects/paolozzi-restoration-at-tottenham-court-road-station/.
3 In conversation with the author, Tuesday 11 August 2020.

p.238: Stephanie Mann, silica and flux melting in platinum crucible (research documentation), 2019

When you
unfasten an object
from its form,
function and
relations,
what remains?

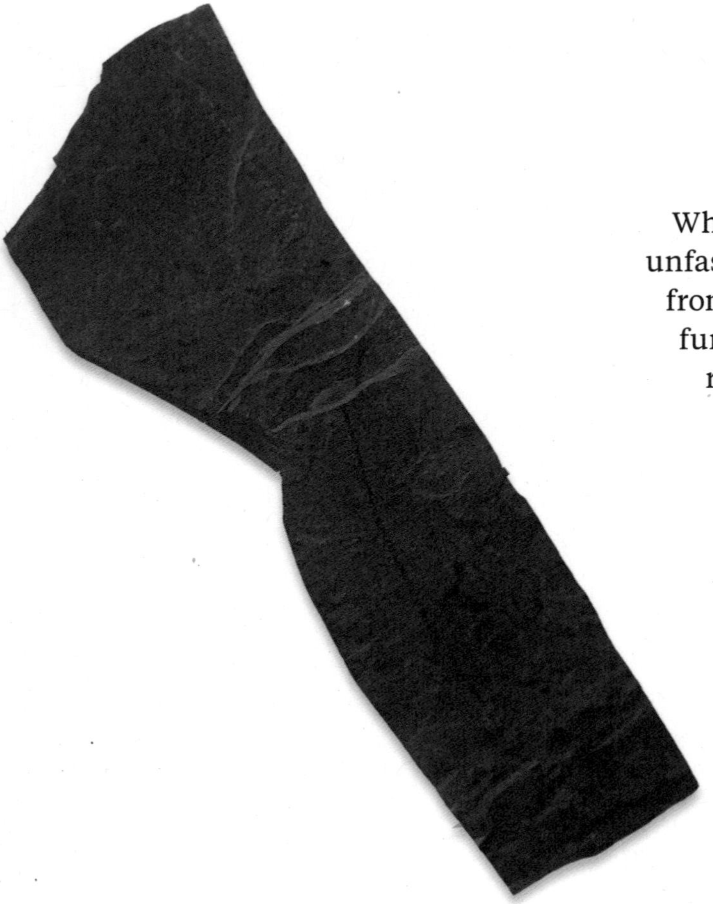

[1]

I break the physical
down
to its
smallest
possible
parts.

[...] reality itself is
not mechanical or linear
when it comes to causality.
Indeed, causality is a secretive affair,
yet out in the open – an open secret.
Causality is *mysterious*, in the original sense of Greek
mysteria, which means that
things are unspeakable or secret.
Mysteria is [...] derived from *muein*,
to close or shut. [...]
the realness of things [is]
bound up with a certain mystery,
in these multiple senses: unspeakability,
enclosure, withdrawl, secrecy. [2]

I look at the glass of water in front of me,
close my eyes and summon its visual
projection to mind. Did the object split in two?
Is the version existing in my perception
a separate, shifted copy?
Or is it tethered to the other?
The conjured and observed
connected by imperceivable
spider silk or string theory waves?
I imagine drinking the water
and in my mind the glass empties;
a premonition
which ushers an atomic action in the physical.
As I drink the water I sense its journey down my throat,
towards its eventual destination as it merges with my cells.
Is the object now me?
And what of its place in this text, fixed in ink in the book you hold?
Rising from words
forming an avatar
in you...

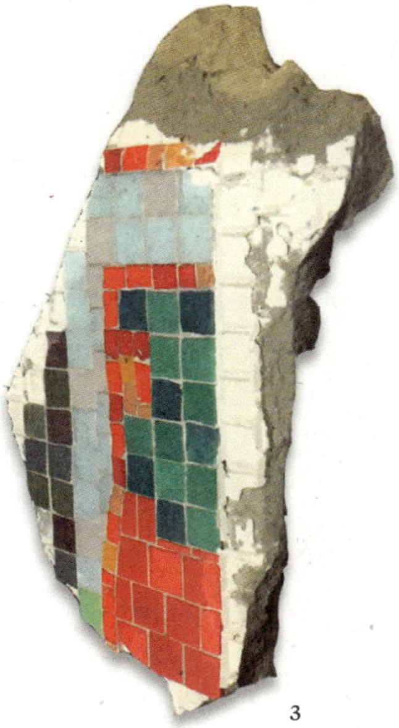
3

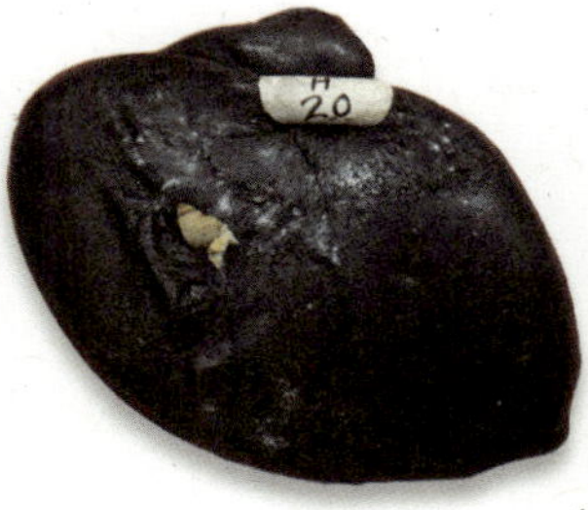

4

Ancient
filtering
creatures,
apartment-block
dwellers
metamorphosing
into their environment.

No person
ever steps in
the same river twice;
for it is not the same river
and they are
not the same person.[5]

Can a lost
object find
identity in
another?
Does it
need to be
known?

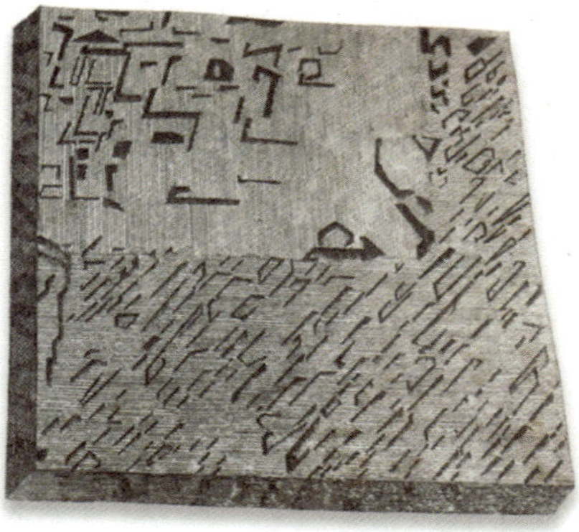

6

Does the chair remember who sat on it? Does it
differentiate the value
of buttocks?

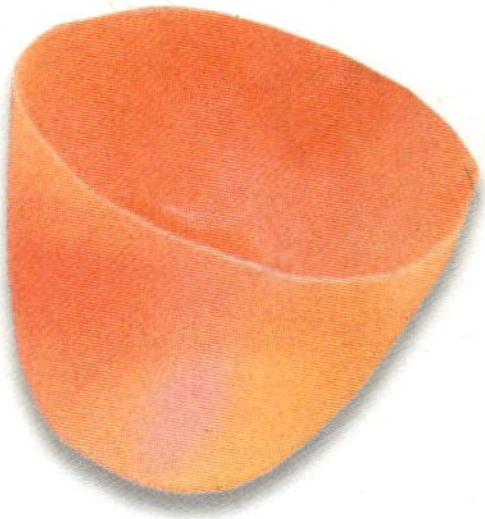

7

With every
choice to hold
is another to let
go. The things
we retain close
to us are a
refusal of
another.

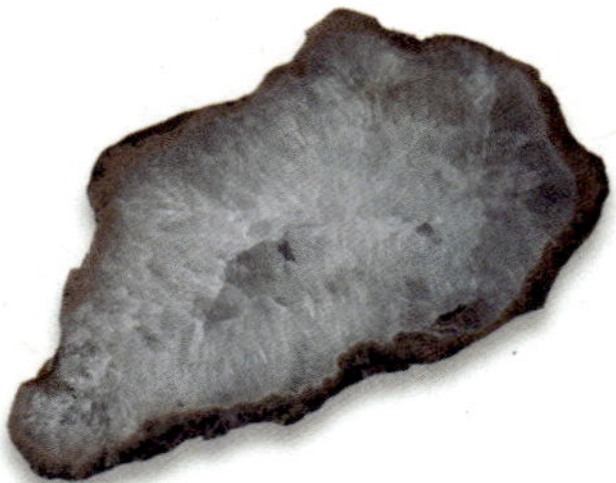

8

I rub lotion on my skin
to mend the damage from
the sanitiser. Overuse
of the protector has
disrupted a balance.
Lotion on skin,
a barrier on a barrier,
neither are impenetrable.
The balm is transposed,
to cloth,
to gate,
to other beings.
And the skin welcomes
the less-familiar,
as pores receive
and the salve matter is
hidden within the body.
I, absorbent vessel.

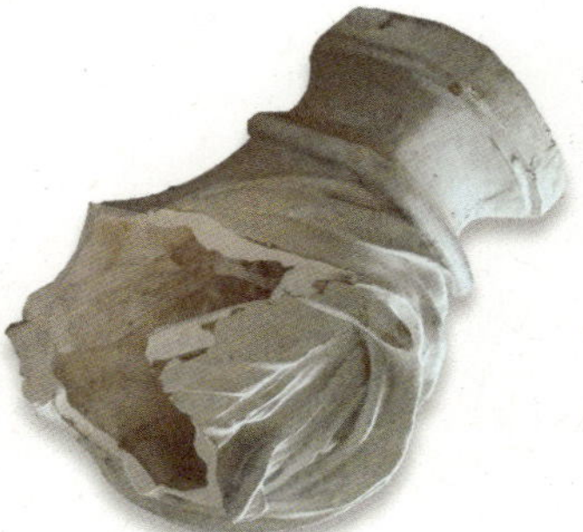
9

Where
do
you end
and I
begin?

We attempt to fix and
hold, to preserve an
instance and
prolong the
inevitable entropic
processes.

1. Graptolite fossil in shale, Canada. Graptolites were suspension feeders and strained the water for nourishment. They drifted with the ocean currents as a conglomerate of individual keratin-based life forms.

2. Timothy Morton, *Realist Magic: Objects, Ontology, Causality*, Open Humanities Press, 2013.

3. Eduardo Paolozzi, Mosaic fragment from an archway in Tottenham Court Road, London Underground Station. Removed and damaged, 33% of the work is part of the University of Edinburgh Art Collection.

4. Tar sample (c.1902), The Cockburn Museum, University of Edinburgh. An active substance, the object absorbs its original label.

5. Heraclitus (c.535 BC – 475 BC).

6. James Hutton, *Theory of the Earth*, vol.1, plate 1, fig. 3, Royal Society of Edinburgh, 1795. Hutton developed the theory that geological features were not static but underwent perpetual transformation over long periods of time.

7. Platinum crucible, containing a molten sample, The Grant Institute. This process plays a preparatory role in allowing us to experience the molecular and microscopic properties of objects, using instruments such as the Secondary Ion Mass Spectrometer and the X-ray Fluorescence Spectrometer.

8. Geode sample (collected c.1970). Formed from prolonged mineral ingress inside cavities of rock.

9. Plaster cast of unknown bust, fragment. Provenance unclear.

With thanks to: Julie-Ann Delaney, Anna Hawkins, Gillian McCay, Liv Laumenech & Nicolas Odling.

Rosie O’Grady

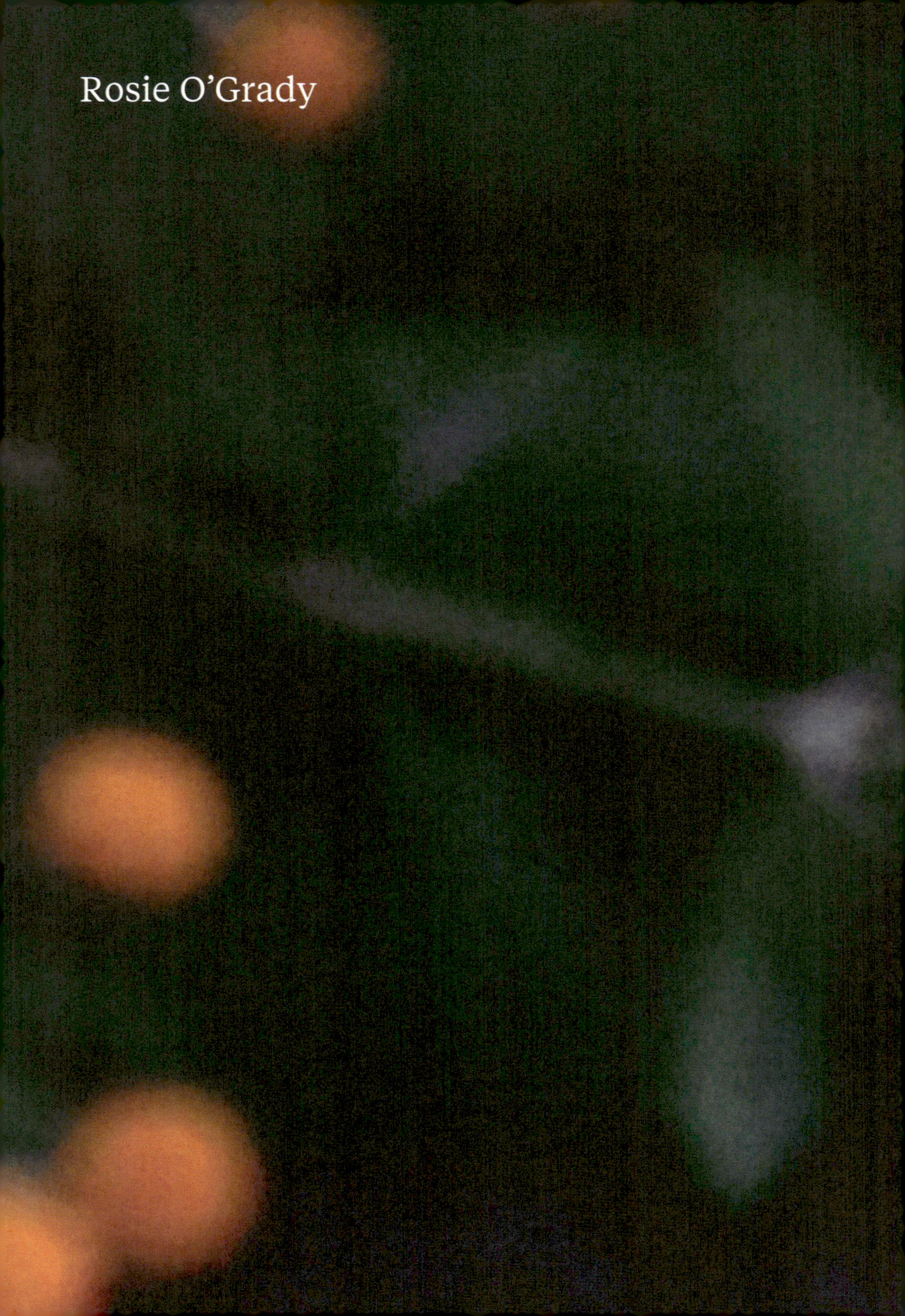

A Clock, Stopped

It's a passing sensation of disquiet. Something feels 'off', if only for a moment. But it's a seductive limbo, one of anticipation, hesitation. Moments when silence becomes loud and the air a little thicker, a little cooler. Such sensations abound in Rosie O'Grady's work, a serpentine and shifting tone that pivots through discomfort, levity and hyper-awareness.

A close-up of a flower, perhaps a zinnia, cropped and still. Then a crunching auditory intrusion – the shunting keys of an old typewriter, as the image shifts shifts shifts downwards, then right. 'How did you first find out that you had leukaemia?' a gentle voice enquires. The camera homes in on a man's left ear, greyscale, hovering and fuzzy, oddly tender.

In artist Nancy Holt's video work *Revolve* (1977) the artist, off-camera, interviews her friend the filmmaker Dennis Wheeler, who is dying of leukaemia. Oscillating from three fixed cameras – 'designed to give the illusion of infinity'[1] – the starkness of the filming counterposes the empathetic and philosophical depth of the conversation. Due to the age of the material, Wheeler's head in profile is disturbed by a hazy, flickering band running down the right-hand edge of the video. O'Grady enters into this material with attention, carefully cropping footage and inserting images of flowers. O'Grady's edit consists only of Wheeler's left side. This disturbance excises all other perspectives, yet in so doing, creates another. Such close looking is in effect to zoom in, so that we see Wheeler's head but not his face, which heightens our awareness of the act of listening, giving us a curious feeling that we might be eavesdropping, interlopers in a private moment.

Guided by tensions already in the work, O'Grady amplifies, gives more space to, in this instance Wheeler's florid, fluid metaphysical imagery in the face of the stark reality of death. The original image disturbance becomes an increasingly spectral presence, as it swells in metaphorical resonance, a balloon stretching its skin. Interposing Wheeler's ear with O'Grady's own photographs of flowers further affects this disjuncture, while also functioning as an aperture into a broader aesthetic and philosophical dimension on the imagery of death and dying. Certain flowers are inevitably associated with the funerary, yet O'Grady doesn't overdetermine their inclusion. Instead, she uses what is at hand – things that were already there – images from her phone camera roll. O'Grady's own edits and instinctive insertions introduce a new, softly whispered conversation with the material. Wheeler speaks frequently of control and uncertainty, particularly in relation to remission. O'Grady's approach channels the content of the interview itself, taking Wheeler's words and reflections on filmmaking as empathetic coordinates for her own process.

O'Grady's willingness to be guided in approach by the material at hand finds curious parallel with another of Holt's works: *Trail Markers* (1969), 20 photographs of orange spray circles on fenceposts and walking routes. These photographs were originally taken in 1969, while walking on Dartmoor with artist Robert Smithson, although Holt did not formalise this process, these images, into an artwork until 2012. Rosie O'Grady's footage of flowers was gathered on walks during lockdown, likewise finding their way into the work at a later date. The work, this seems to say, was already there. As art historian and writer Joy Sleeman notes, '*Trail Markers* was made in an era when walking had taken on new significance in art and culture. Artists such as Richard Long (b. 1945), a recent acquaintance with whom Holt and Smithson met up briefly on this trip, had made walking into art.'[2] A trail marker only provides a sense of direction, you must still connect the dots to find the way.

Regrettably, Holt's remarkable artistic output and legacy have been overshadowed by Smithson's. O'Grady's *May Day* (2018) similarly practises a careful process of homage, in this instance amplifying the work and life of Scottish artist Margaret MacDonald. O'Grady quite literally amplifies: upscaling MacDonald's work into an intervention in the landscape. To read this act as solely site-specific, however, is to miss the importance and ethics of O'Grady's approach. Glasgow's House for an Art Lover was built in 1990, constructed from an earlier speculative design proposal by Margaret MacDonald and her husband Charles Rennie Mackintosh, which was originally submitted as part of a competition in an architectural magazine. Yet the latter-day construction of the building, in its interpretation of the plans, foregrounded Mackintosh and muted and reduced MacDonald's presence and legacy. Over the years, MacDonald's gesso panel *The May Queen* (1900) was neglected and fell into disrepair, even being overpainted in 1970. Depicted in the work is a central figure being crowned the May queen by four female figures, two either side. Drawing a connection with another form of erasure, O'Grady linked this knowledge to two French educators and activists, one male, one female, who had realised a 400ft clitoris in a field in southern France, to protest about the absence of female sexual pleasure from the curriculum.[3] O'Grady and four female friends etched MacDonald's *The May Queen* large-scale in the landscape, intimating an artistic lineage for the crop circle as one of protest, as 'distress signal'.[4] O'Grady's approach was to distort perception – disorientating scale, and as such readability of the image – in relation to the warped historical perception of MacDonald's work. To be inside the crop circle is to have your vision of the whole restricted. The work also intervenes into the history of artistic intervention on the landscape. As such, *May Day* is also about potential, suggesting future pathways, not merely recontextualising in the present.

Developing in parallel to her work with Holt's *Revolve*, O'Grady is reflecting on the legacy of the Surrealist artist and photographer Eileen Agar. In 1936, Agar took a series of photographs of distinctive rock forms on the Brittany coastline in France. Agar later traced them in an intensive process of trying to attain a deep understanding of those forms. Magnifying the effect of Agar's original process, O'Grady is reproducing Agar's photographic series as flashes of light, creating the physiological phenomenon of an after-image. An after-image is literally that: temporarily produced in the eye of the onlooker, contingent on blinking. To 'see' the work is to first relinquish sight, destabilising your own body in order to perceive anew.

O'Grady shadowboxes with her material: tracing, cropping, mapping, excising, juxtaposing; each a process around missing information. Hers is a close looking at practices of close looking. Curvilinear lines in the earth, silhouettes, spray circles marking the way – a hazy and circular trail of relation with historical practices. A disquieting pause. What might we be absorbing without realising?

26 August 2020

1 Carrie Rickey, 'Nancy Holt: Whitney Museum of American Art, New York', *Arts Magazine*, no.52, November 1977.

2 Joy Sleeman, 'Nancy Holt "Trail Markers" (1969), or the walk from Wistman's Wood', Holt Smithson Foundation, December 2019, https://holtsmithsonfoundation.org/nancy-holt-trail-markers-1969-or-walk-wistmans-wood.

3 In 2016 Marie-Noëlle Lanuit and Jean-Claude Piquard created a clitoris-shape crop circle in a field in the village of Montferrier-sur-Lez, France.

4 The artist's own term.

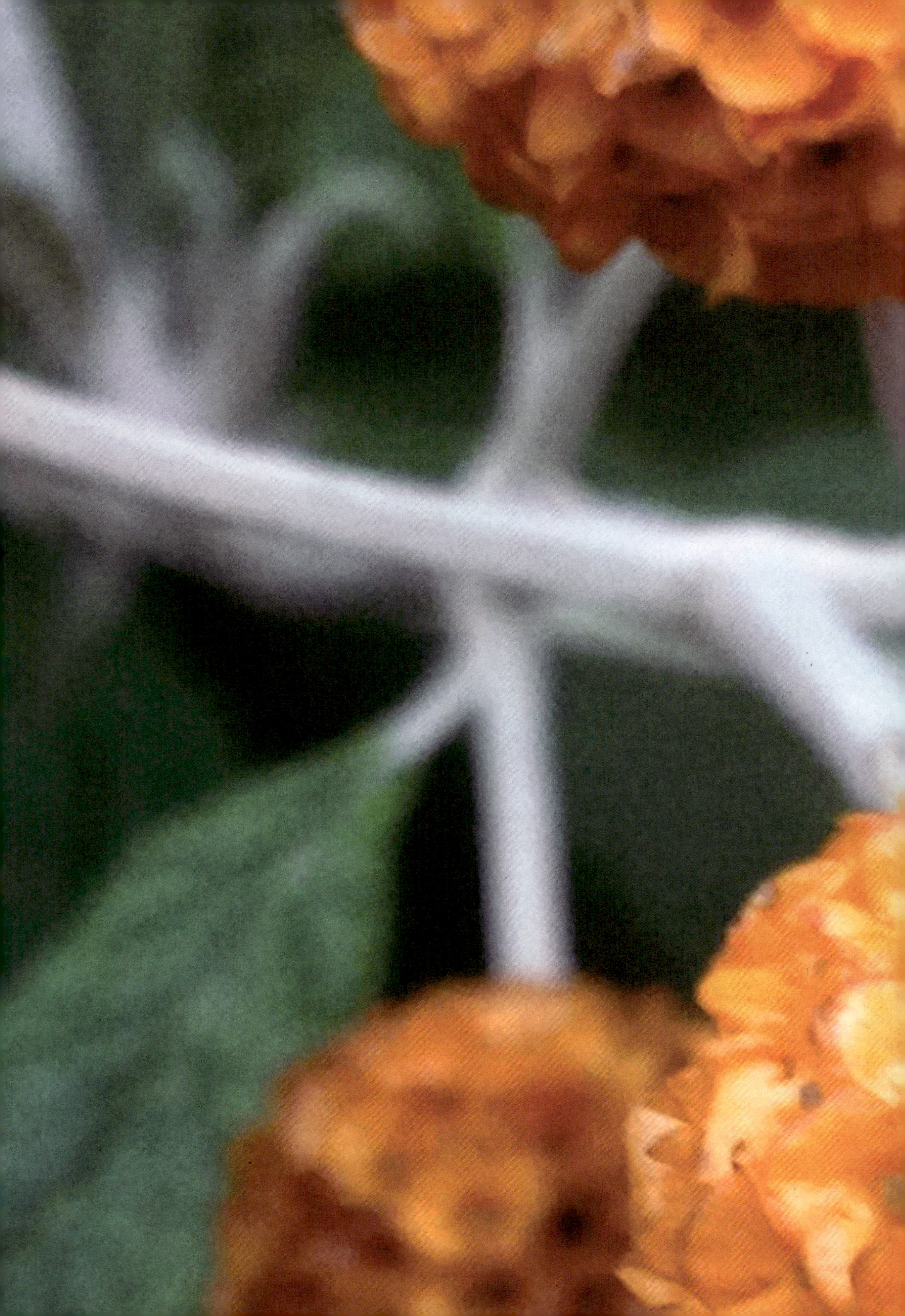

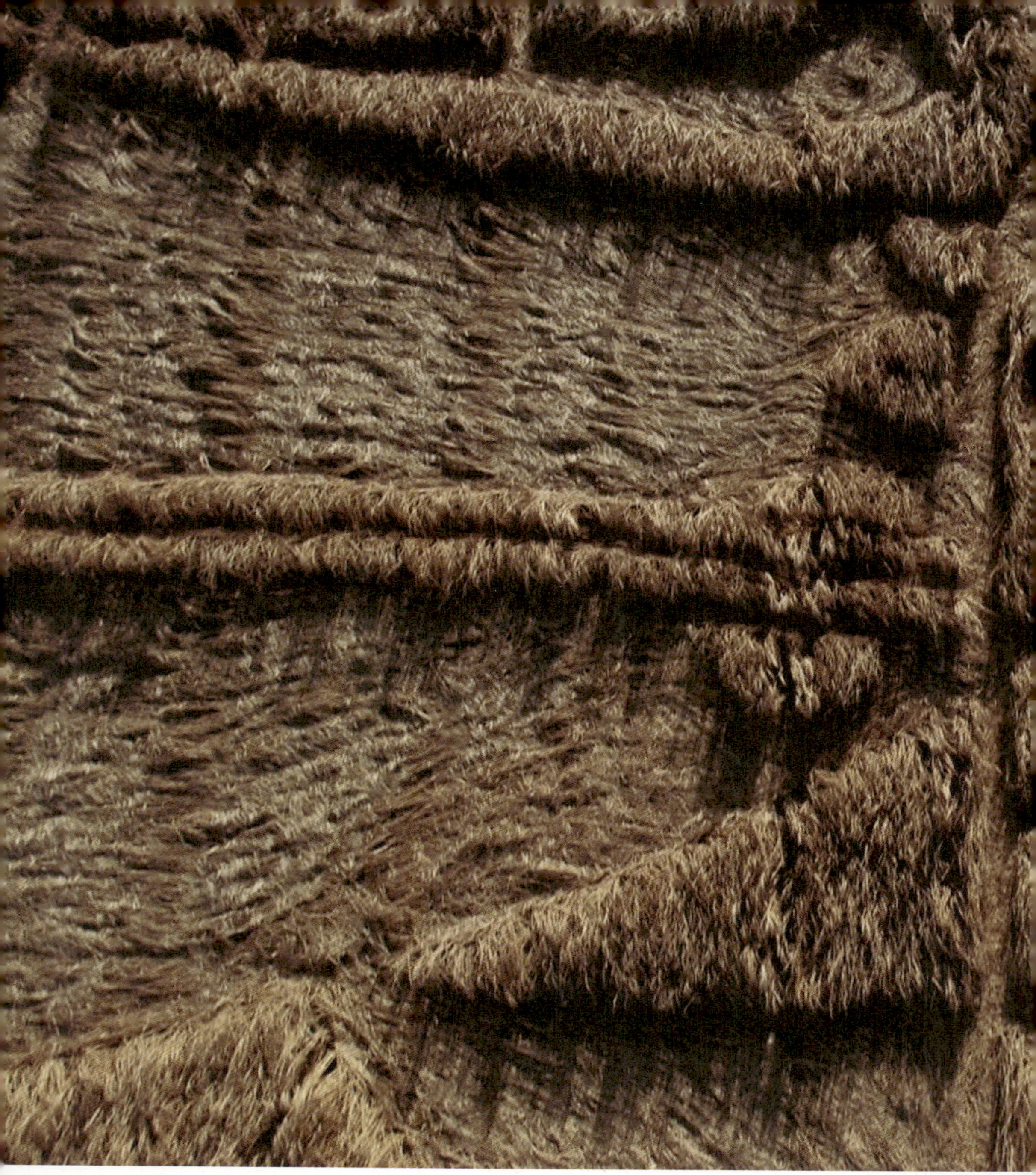

Rosie O’Grady, *May Day*, video (still), 2018

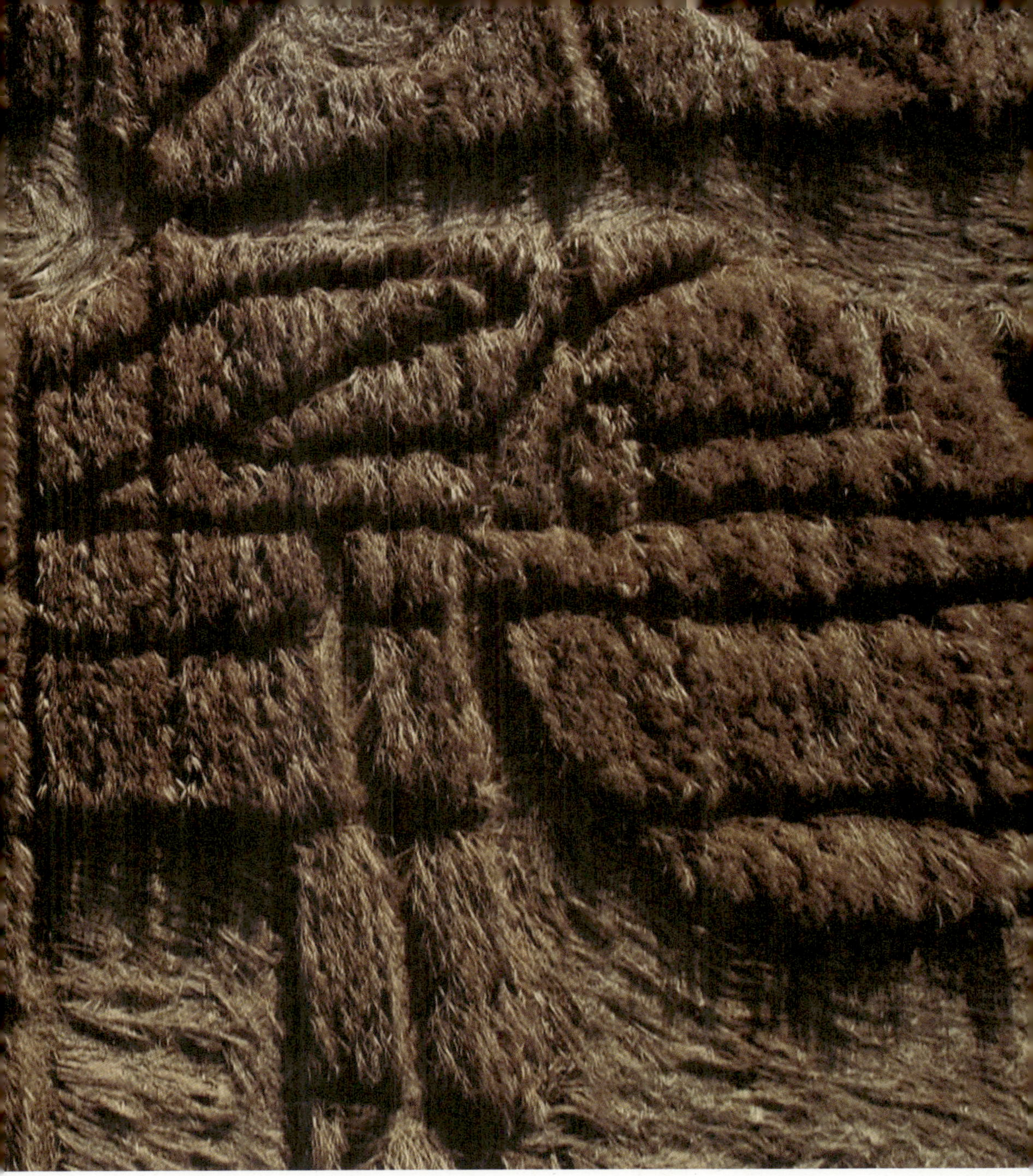

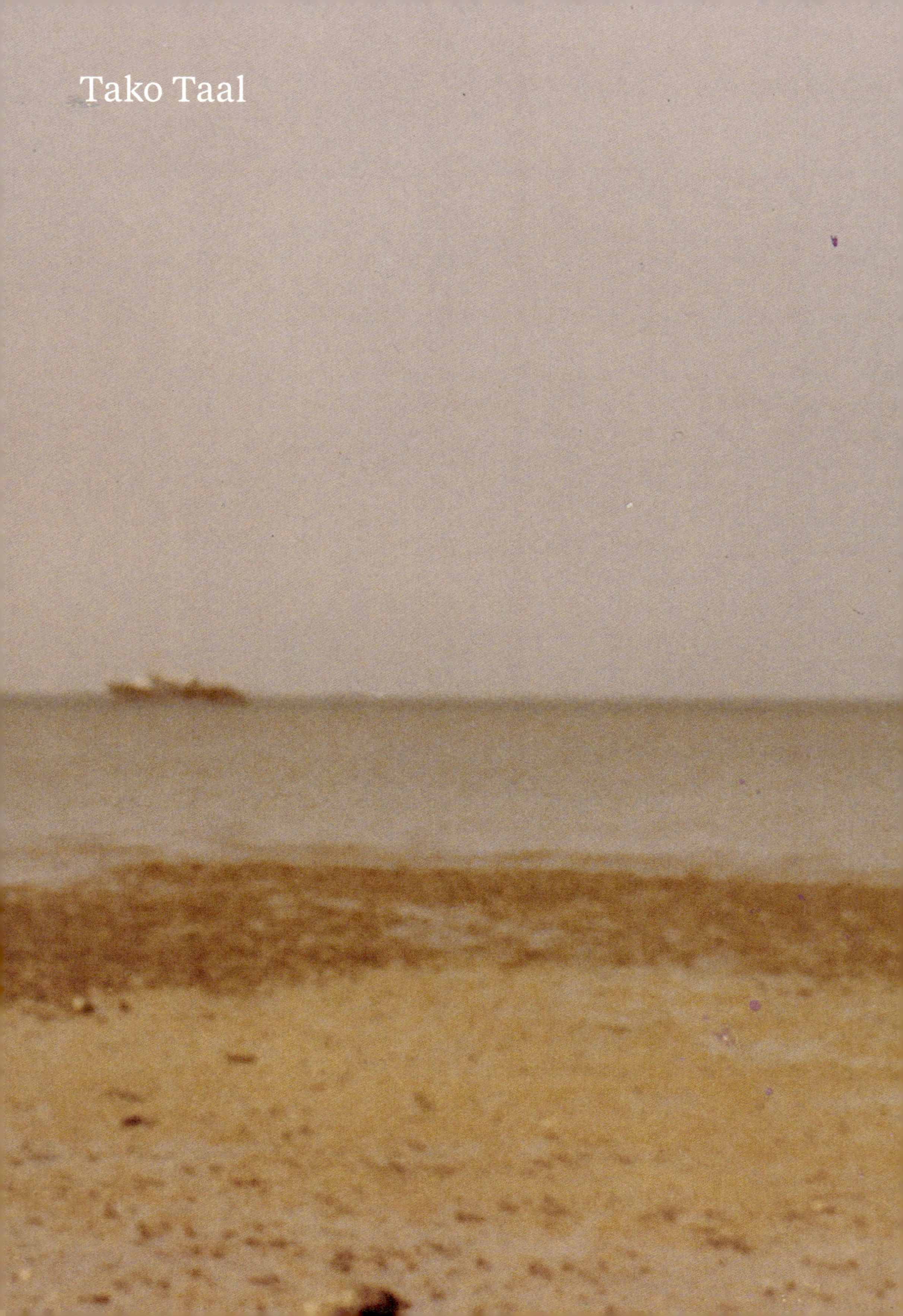

Tako Taal

At With To You

A preposition presupposes; direction, relation, position. It grafts. Can it undo? Can it be undone?

Grafting. To join the tissues of plants onto one another, and so together. A genetic act of influence: to shape the growth. Now growing as two but once as one. Now growing as one but once from two. Splicing the scion to make fit.

'The West onto which I have been so strangely grafted', so James Baldwin wrote, in a 'Stranger in the Village'.[1] Onto which; he had been acted upon. Fixing the act but not the subject. The subject who looks forwards and backwards and beyond and from and is not just of this moment.

Kunta Kinteh was captured in Juffureh, the Gambia, by slave traders and forced into enslavement in America. Kunta Kinteh Island was a fort during the slave trade. Because of. Uncle Lamin is speaking now, recounting the horrors inflicted upon enslaved peoples. It is tourist season. 'People are trapped in history and history is trapped in them.'[2] The journey there and back, there and back, paying for the present with pieces of the past.

'On the way back from Kunta Kinteh Island, formerly James Island, formerly Andrew Island, I held the camera steady for 46 seconds.'[3] Re-naming does not erase, nor does it undo. Instead it makes another.[4] A name is also an inheritance. *SAMT.* A root and a route.

The camera is moving with while leaving behind, yet the still image that forms an overlay is multivalent. Can an image ever control its arrival, the terms with which it meets another? Two cameras from different times meet at the same place. Two sets of eyes looking at the Island and into one another, and so across.

'Grief is a path to understanding entangled shared living and dying; human beings must grieve *with*, because we are in and of this fabric of undoing.'[5] Can a process of finding be a process of unfinding?

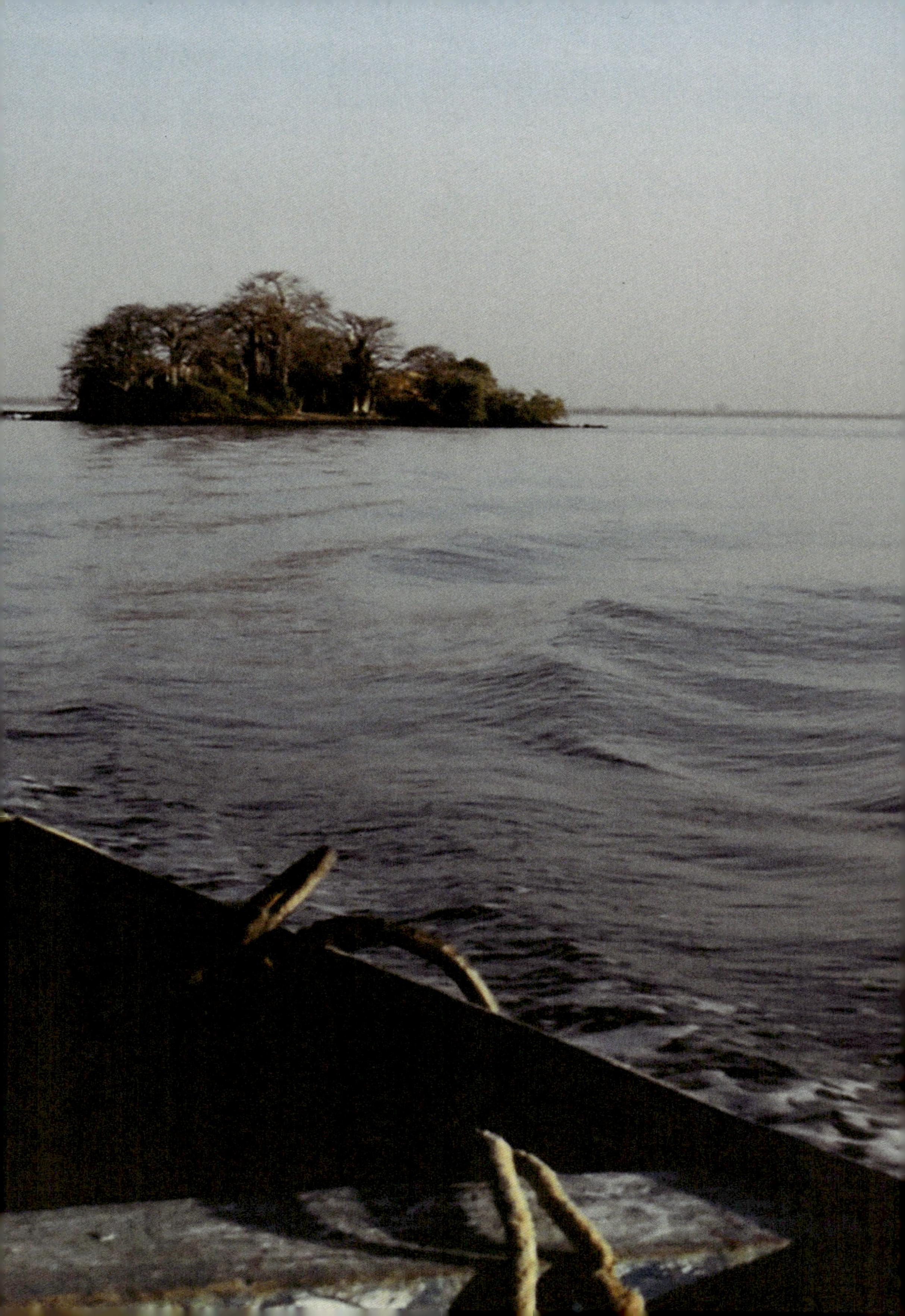

To mourn is to relate; with absence, with an archive of whispers, with what could have been. Yet absence is not the absence of matter. The space between two parallel lines is not a void but a magnetic field.

'Nothing exists for the sake of an always-having-existed [...] that commands the impression of stability from what is in fact a set of contingencies.'[6] A latent image is one that is not-yet; although not visible, it is pure potential. How do you journey towards that condition without naming it or shaping it but allowing it to come towards you?

Filmmaking as holding space, as sifting through and it sifting through you;[7] a material set of contingencies that are always under construction. Filmmaking as a practice of repair, which begins with undoing.

'A complex whole without order.'[8] Can you connect without presupposing, and in so doing undo? 'A political subject emerging [...] through a sentence without a (self-determined) subject.'[9] Unlearning old grammars, making new.

Looking right back. At with to you. She meets him in the material.[10]

14 August 2020

1 James Baldwin wrote of his experience in the all-white village of Leukerbad in Switzerland. His temporary stay there, away from his home, sharpened his view of America. James Baldwin, 'Stranger in the Village', *Notes of a Native Son* (1955), https://www.janvaneyck.nl/site/assets/files/2312/baldwin.pdf.

2 James Baldwin, *ibid.*

3 Tako Taal, 'A View From' research document, 16 January 2020; also to note that this essay retains the artist's spelling for names and places associated with her research for *SAMT*.

4 In colonial botany, a plant would be extracted from its original location and renamed in Latin, erasing its origins. Ros Gray and Shela Sheikh introduce the implication of plants and plantation in systems of extraction and violence in 'The Coloniality of Planting', https://www.botanicalmind.online/podcasts/the-coloniality-of-planting, 31 July 2020.

5 Donna Haraway, *Staying with the Trouble*, Duke University Press, 2016, p.25.

6 Ian White, 'What is Material?', *Here is Information. Mobilise*, Mike Sperlinger (ed.), LUX, 2016, p.280.

7 Alycia Pirmohamed, *You Know It But It Don't Know You. After Tako Taal*, a five-poem series, *MAP* #58, July 2020.

8 Denise Ferreira da Silva, 'On Difference Without Separability', *Incerteza Viva, 32 Bienal de São Paulo*, Fundacion Bienal de São Paulo, 2016, https://issuu.com/amilcarpacker/docs/denise_ferreira_da_silva.

9 Denise Ferreira da Silva activates the disruptive force of blackness, a force which breaks out of the enclosures of modern thought, undoing determinacy and grammatical causation. Denise Ferreira da Silva, '1 (life) ÷ 0 (blackness) = ∞ − ∞ or ∞ / ∞: On Matter Beyond the Equation of Value', *e-flux journal*, #79, February 2017, https://www.e-flux.com/journal/79/94686/1-life-0-blackness-or-on-matter-beyond-the-equation-of-value/.

10 The artist's own phrase.

p.254: Tako Taal, *A view to James Island? SAMT*, photograph, 1980s
pp.256–257: Tako Taal, *On the way back from Kunta Kinteh Island, formerly James Island, formerly Andrew Island. I held the camera steady for 46 seconds. 16.01.20*, video (still), 2020
overleaf: Tako Taal, *A cry, a havoc, 1500-1980-2020*, composite image, 2020

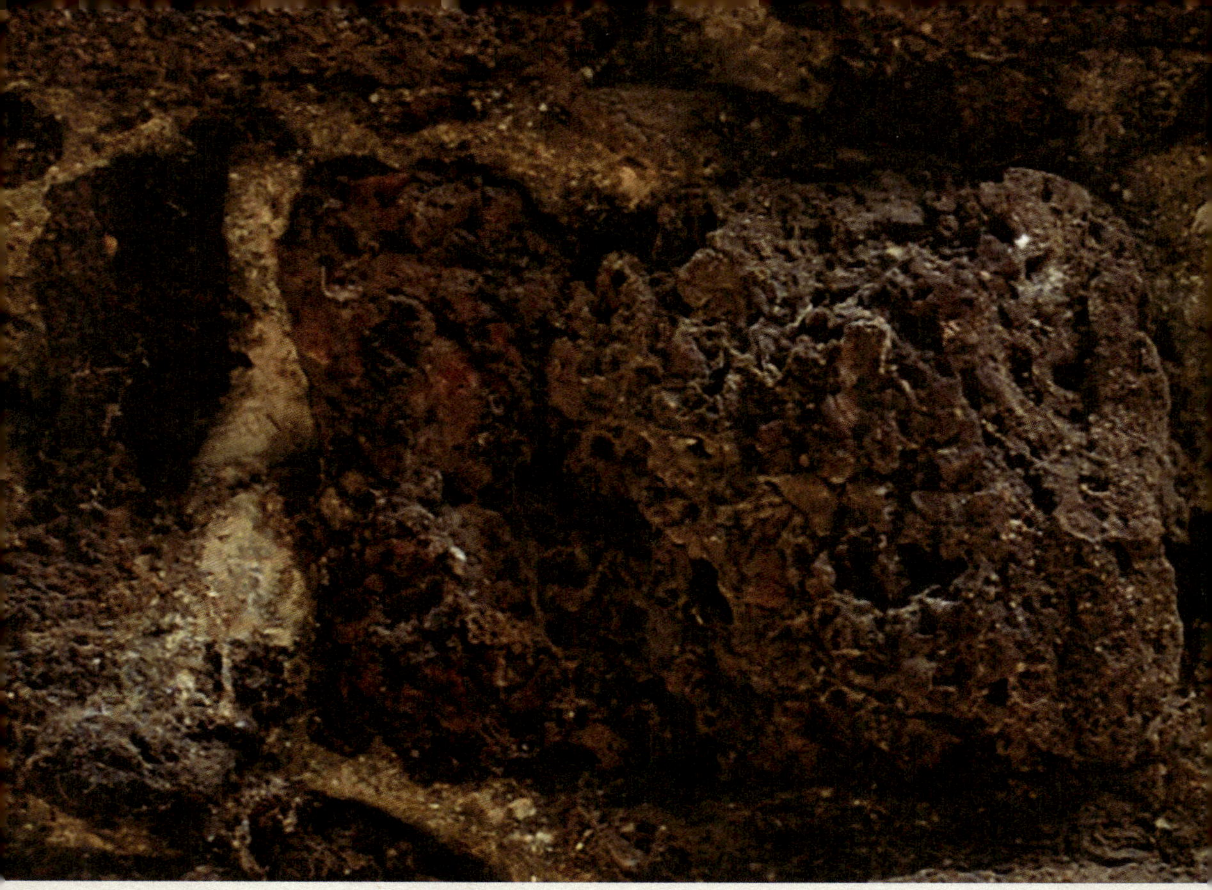

A cry, A havoc
Awaits your next generations.

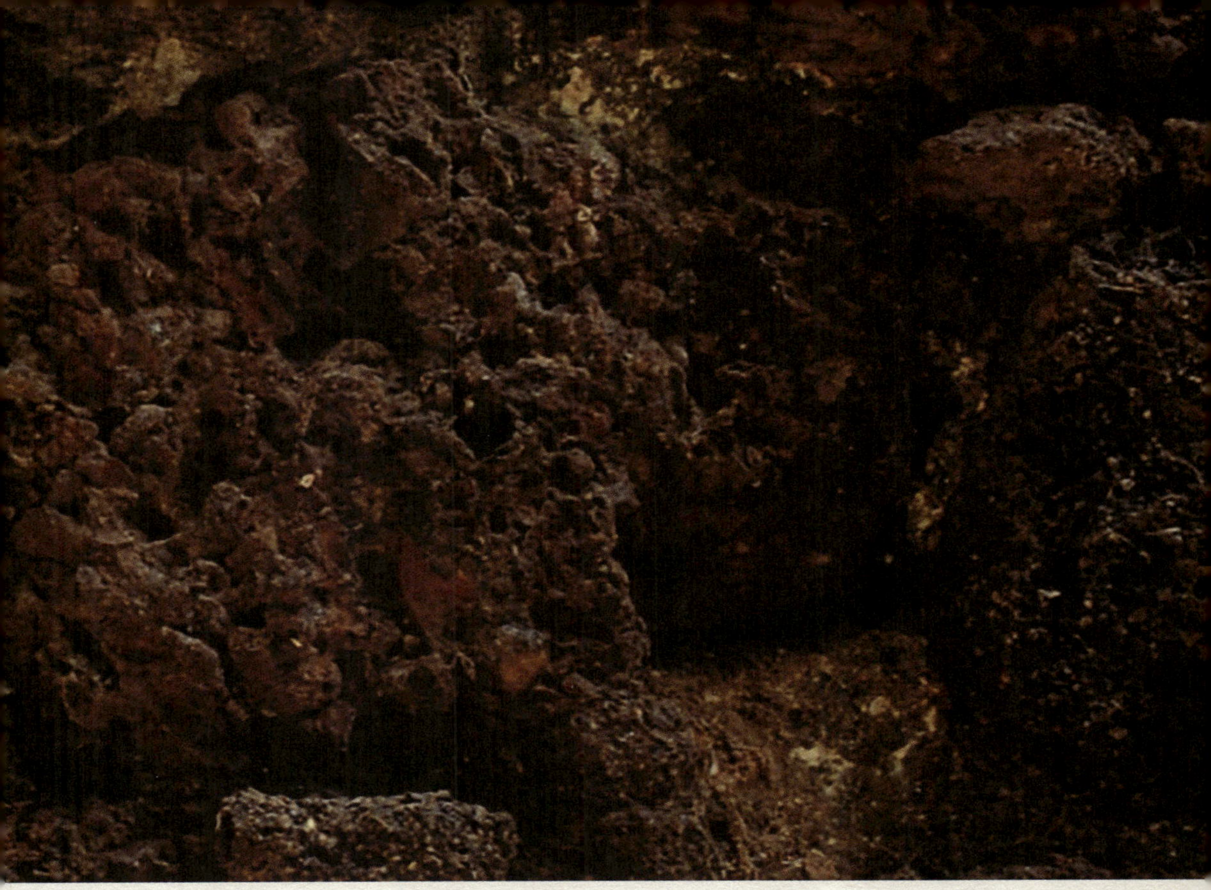

samt.

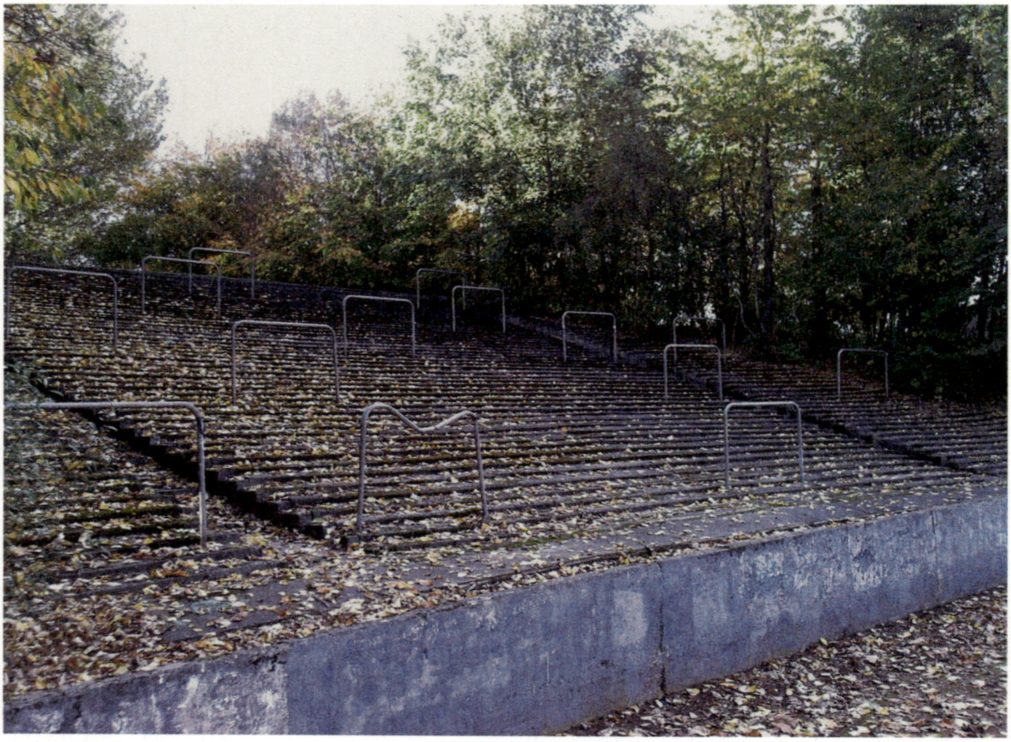

Adrien Hester

what did this to you? this is
a poem about the letter M

in a park near my house
is a pitch and a track
tiered concrete all mmm-ing in empty stadium
for standing or leaning on over or into

concrete which
becomes hard over time yes
I hear what you're saying a fact of concrete is
just that it is hard but by this I mean it has become hardened beyond
basic properties in the way that only things can be made
hard over time outside

where mosses form in damp
shady places for them perfect
concrete being porous meaning open to change
moss is non-vascular meaning
without roots and so
given the right conditions can grow
anywhere that is to say
in only specific places sewing itself
onto structures small threads

a biology meets a chemistry to make
a trendy new sofa velvety green cushions
you saw it here first in the park down the road

curve of shoulders and flatheadedness unremarkable uniformity
slim alloy legs set in ground
M bent in order to make language from wrought material
bent by the will of the meaning
before it has been forged and set in stone
and it shows
how one thing can be another
how one rigid thing can become m
where I [for example] only works in vertical lines

M is a letter for reclining on
it is also the symbol for the 8th astrological sign
deriving the scorpius constellation
M meaning water meaning moon meaning feminine meaningmasculine
but I bet it means everything else too
metal and cement both archetypal materials which are
open to change

one foot in the past and on in future
writing on next
letter to make language
M is the first letter of my brother's name
and there is not a single one in mine

now

the stadium we uncover   the skeleton of a word
illegible glyphs   scrawled on concrete
large M   small m   large m small m
M
        m
                M   m
                                                            they say it's called graffiti

letters are compound   and stars
are just big explosions   far off   anyway
which ultimately   one day
will be gone   tell a friend
tomorrow
                                        they won't believe me though

I can hear   the water or maybe
that is the sound   that metal makes when it resonates
the song it sings to   the ear
is the part of the body
most commonly   associated with listening
but the ear   makes a sound of its own
listening happens   elsewhere

Jan Carson is a writer and community arts facilitator based in Belfast, Northern Ireland. Her novels, short stories and micro-fiction include *Malcolm Orange Disappears* (2014), *Children's Children* (2016) and *Postcard Stories 1* and *2* (2017). She was shortlisted for the BBC National Short Story Award 2020 and her novel *The Fire Starters* won the EU Prize for Literature for Ireland 2019, and the Kitschies Award for speculative fiction 2020. She has two books forthcoming in 2021: *The Last Resort* and *No Promised Land*.

George Clark is an artist, writer and curator. His work explores the history of images and how they are governed by culture, technology and social political conditions. Recent projects have sought to build new models of assembly, exhibition-making and moving image production. His films have shown at festivals and museums internationally. He is co-founder of the West Java West Yorkshire Cooperative Movement with Ismal Muntaha, Bunga Siagian and Will Rose, a collaborative platform with Jatiwangi Art Factory and Pavilion. His curatorial projects focus on broadening the histories of film and video practice globally.

Adrien Hester is an artist and writer based in Glasgow. They work both independently and collaboratively across writing, sound, performance and moving image. Selected projects include: *12-Hour Non-State Parade*, Cooper Gallery, Dundee (2019), *To stumble and to slip | Slipping, stumbling | Things we both know | …*, Auto Italia, London (2019), *The Depth of Foundation is According to the Nature of Ground*, Talbot Rice Projects (2018), and *There is no visible route to the vanishing point*, Intermedia Gallery, Centre for Contemporary Art, Glasgow (2017).

Natalie Ann Holborow is an award-winning writer whose debut collection, *And Suddenly You Find Yourself* was launched at the international Kolkata Literary Festival in 2017. She is co-editor of the *Cheval* anthology, and her second poetry collection, *Small*, was released with Parthian in 2020. She won second place at the Anthony Cronin International Poetry Awards 2020 and was shortlisted for the Cursed Murphy Spoken Word Competition. She lives in Swansea and works as a copywriter in the learning and development industry.

Kunsthalle Lissabon was founded in 2009 by João Mourão and Luís Silva. Kunsthalle Lissabon presents an original and dynamic programme in Lisbon, according to: 1. an ideological proximity to institutional critique and to the later concept of new institutionalism; 2. a DIY ethics and aesthetics that allows for fluidity, agility and independence from a more commercial approach; and 3. a close collaboration with artists. It has presented projects by artists including Céline Condorelli, Bo Zheng, Jonathas de Andrade, Petrit Halilaj, Amalia Pica, Ad Minoliti and Laure Prouvost.

Andrew McMillan's two award-winning collections of poetry are *physical* and *playtime*, both published by Jonathan Cape. A third collection, *pandemonium*, will be published in 2021. He is Senior Lecturer at the Manchester Writing School at Manchester Metropolitan University.

Grace Ndiritu is a British-Kenyan artist whose artworks are connected with the transformation of our contemporary world through her films, photography, paintings and social practice projects with refugees, migrants and indigenous groups. Works such as *The Ark: Center for Interdisciplinary Experimentation*, *COVERSLUT©* and *Healing the Museum* have been shown across the world. Recent exhibitions include Bluecoat, Liverpool (2019), SMAK and MSK, Ghent, Belgium (2019), Eastside Projects, Birmingham (2018), Fundació Antoni Tàpies, Barcelona (2017), Museum of Modern Art, Warsaw (2014), Musée de la Chasse et de la Nature and Centre Pompidou, Paris (2013).

Helena Reckitt is a curator and researcher developing curatorial and critical research projects focusing on the overlapping realms of art, curating, feminism and sexual politics; affect & relationality; and curatorial education. Her research explores the undetonated potential of earlier moments of cultural and political radicalism, particularly those from the feminist and queer past. She is a Reader in the Art Department at Goldsmiths, University of London, and coordinates the Feminist Duration Reading Group (est. 2015), which considers under-known and under-valued feminisms.

Old Land New Waters

Published in 2021 by
Freelands Foundation
113 Regent's Park Road
London NW1 8UR
www.freelandsfoundation.co.uk

Edited by Edward Ball
Copy editing by Eileen Daly
Design by Daly & Lyon
Printed in Belgium by Graphius

All texts by Edward Ball, unless
otherwise stated

All website links last accessed
22 October 2020

ISBN: 978-1-8382572-0-0

Old Land New Waters marks two years of activity for the first cohort of artists who are part of the Freelands Artist Programme. This initiative aims to champion emerging talent and is designed to support relationships and collaborations between artists and arts organisations across the country. Our thanks to all the participants:

g39, Cardiff
Team
Anthony Shapland, Chris Mooney-Brown, Cinzia Mutigli, Sam Hasler, Ellie Young
Artists
Kelly Best, Jennifer Taylor, Neasa Terry, Fern Thomas, Ian Watson

PS², Belfast
Team
Peter Mutschler, Alissa Kleist
Artists
Janie Doherty, Michael Hanna, Julie Lovett, Jan McCullough, Emily McFarland

Site Gallery, Sheffield
Team
Sharna Jackson, Angelica Sule, Robyn Haddon
Artists
Alison J Carr, Yuen Fong Ling, Zoyander Street, Lucy Vann, Siân Williams

Talbot Rice Gallery, Edinburgh
Team
Tessa Giblin, Stuart Fallon, James Clegg, Melissa MacRobert, Corinne Orton
Artists
Aideen Doran, Stephanie Mann, Rosie O'Grady, Tako Taal

With thanks to:
Claire Lyon, Wayne Daly, Eileen Daly, Nicola Sim, Marie-Anne McQuay, Taylor Le Melle, Fatima Hellberg, Fi Churchman and all contributors and authors

Freelands Foundation

Freelands Artist Programme